The Municipal Money Chase:
The Politics of
Local Government Finance

Also of Interest

† *Of, By, and For the People: State and Local Governments and Politics,* Morris J. Levitt and Eleanor G. Feldbaum

† *Managing Local Government for Improved Performance: A Practical Approach,* Brian W. Rapp and Frank M. Patitucci

Reorganizing State Government: The Executive Branch, James L. Garnett

† *The President, the Budget, and Congress: Impoundment and the 1974 Budget Act,* James P. Pfiffner

The National Planning Idea in U.S. Public Policy: Five Alternative Approaches, David E. Wilson

Social Security: A Reciprocity System Under Pressure, Edward Wynne

† *Politics in the Rural States: People, Parties, and Processes,* Frank M. Bryan

† *Rural Society in the U.S.: Issues for the 1980s,* edited by Don A. Dillman and Daryl J. Hobbs

† Available in hardcover and paperback.

About the Book and Editor

The Municipal Money Chase:
The Politics of Local Government Finance
edited by Alberta M. Sbragia

Gone are the days when the raising and apportioning of municipal monies was a relatively simple task, when ample income could be expected to meet projected needs and also fund a few additional projects. Now local officials are faced with shrinking budgets, tax revolts, decreasing federal support, increasing state and federal regulations—in short, genuine crunches that leave them pondering how sparse resources can ever be stretched to meet the multitude of actual needs.

This book stresses the political dimensions of local finance, emphasizing the local, intergovernmental, and private-sector constraints faced by municipal officials in their attempt to provide services while balancing the budget. Integrating the implications of the Reagan administration's new approach to federal spending into their analyses, the authors examine the impact of state regulations on local taxation and debt policies, the relationship between local governments and the municipal bond market, the political economy of New York City's fiscal crisis, and the impact of various tax limitation measures, including California's Proposition 13. They also study the effect of community development grants on local decisionmaking structures and the impact of urban congressional representatives on the allocation of federal grants. Their presentation is aimed especially at graduate and upper-level undergraduate students of urban politics, local finance, state and local government, and intergovernmental relations.

Alberta M. Sbragia is an associate professor of political science at the University of Pittsburgh. Her publications include "Borrowing to Build: Private Money and Public Welfare" (1979) and "The Politics of Local Borrowing: A Comparative Analysis" (1979).

The Municipal Money Chase:
The Politics of
Local Government Finance

edited by Alberta M. Sbragia

Westview Press / Boulder, Colorado

Copyright © 1983 by Westview Press, Inc.

Published in 1983 in the United States of America by
  Westview Press, Inc.
  5500 Central Avenue
  Boulder, Colorado 80301
  Frederick A. Praeger, President and Publisher

Library of Congress Cataloging in Publication Data
Main entry under title:
The Municipal money chase.
  Includes index.
    1. Municipal finance—United States—Addresses, essays, lectures.   2. Intergovernmental fiscal relations—United States—Addresses, essays, lectures.   I. Sbragia, Alberta M.
HJ9145.M89   1983   352.1'0973   82-17367
ISBN 0-86531-116-1
ISBN 0-86531-398-9 (pbk.)

Printed and bound in the United States of America

Contents

Tables and Figures

Figures

About the Contributors

Roger Friedland is associate professor of sociology at the University of California, Santa Barbara. He has written widely on the politics of urban renewal and is the author of *Power and Crisis in the City: Corporations, Labor Unions, and the Making of Urban Policy* (1982) and *The Power of Theory: Aspects of the State in Western Societies* (in association with Robert Alford; forthcoming).

Patricia Giles Leeds is a native New Yorker who was educated at Hunter College of the City University of New York and the University of Wisconsin, Madison. She has taught at the University of Texas at Austin and is presently in the Government Department at Cornell University. She is at work on a book dealing with urban fiscal problems, public sector labor, and pension fund investment.

Susan A. MacManus is associate professor of political science at the University of Houston. She has written numerous articles on state and local government politics as well as finance and is the author of *Revenue Patterns in U.S. Cities and Suburbs: A Comparative Analysis* (1978). She has served as a consultant to the Brookings Institution and to many city governments in Texas.

Raymond E. Owen, associate professor of political science at the University of Pittsburgh, has worked as a consultant for the National Science Foundation, the Brookings Institution, and numerous local government bodies.

James P. Pfiffner is associate professor of political science at California State University, Fullerton. He has worked in the Office of the Director of the U.S. Office of Personnel Management and has been a research fellow at the Brookings Institution. He is the author of *The President,* the Budget, and Congress: Impoundment and the 1974 Budget Act (Westview Press, 1979) and editor of *The President and Economic Policy* (forthcoming). He is currently writing a book on presidential transitions since 1960. He received his Ph.D. from the University of Wisconsin, Madison.

Alberta M. Sbragia, associate professor of political science at the University of Pittsburgh, has written on urban politics in Western Europe and the United States and has been a visiting research fellow at the Centre for the Study of Public Policy at Strathclyde University, Glasgow. She will spend the year 1983/84 teaching at the Harvard Business School and is currently working on a book comparing the relationship between local government and the financial community in the United States and Great Britain.

Herbert Wong received his Ph.D. in sociology from the University of California, Santa Barbara, and is currently employed by Santa Barbara Applied Research.

1
Introduction

Alberta M. Sbragia

The world of public finance often seems boring to students interested in government and politics. "Politics" has the allure and excitement implied by power, policy, and manipulation. "Finance," by contrast, carries no ring of excitement at all, for it implies the technicalities of accounting and the horrors of numbers. Students who are fascinated by the most intricate—and technical—details of how a political machine works become glassy-eyed as soon as the discussion turns to how local officials raise and spend the money that is the lifeblood of both government and political machines.

The purpose of this book is to convince students that the study of politics becomes *more* interesting when linked to the study of money. In fact, one is incomplete without the other. After all, most of government's efforts involve taxing people, asking other governments for money, deciding how to spend the money it receives, borrowing the money it hopes to receive later, paying people, and buying goods. Mayors spend a great deal of their time worrying about money—how to get it without making too many voters angry and how to spend it without making too many voters feel neglected. Students who want to study politics and public administration without studying finance are like medical students who cannot stand the sight of blood.

The links between government and finance are so complex that no book could cover all of them. But the contributors to this volume do analyze in some depth several issues of local government finance that most textbooks tend to skim, thereby encouraging students to consider the complex relations that concern local officials, the vagaries

of city finance, and the effects of fiscal appropriation and expenditure
on the distribution and exercise of political power at the local level.

The Politics of City Finance

The dilemma of municipal officials is that they are in the best
position to feel the effects of many wider economic and social trends
but in a poor position to affect them. They have to cope with urban
growth in the Sunbelt or urban decline in the Northeast and Midwest,
economic recessions, inflation, structural and cyclical unemployment,
flight from the public schools, the influx of refugees and illegal aliens,
and the lack of international competitiveness of some U.S. industries.
The courts, the international and national economy, the decisions of
private corporations, and the mandates of state and federal government
constantly shape—and limit—what local government officials can do.

Further, every elected official works within the legacy of choices
made by his or her predecessors, choices that have affected each city's
political culture and budget. Past choices often weigh heavily on officials
of declining cities. In Frostbelt cities, the policies of elected officials and
the expectations of their voters conspired over time to mold an urban
political culture disposed toward high levels of social service provision,
an acceptance (however begrudging) of the mobilization of both economic
and racial minorities, a recognition of the legitimacy of municipal
employee unions, a tolerance for local patronage systems, a suspicion
of the motives of businessmen, and an indifference to the maintenance
needs of the city's capital infrastructure.

As the number of private sector (especially manufacturing) jobs
shrank in such cities, officials presided over a replacement of private
sector jobs by public sector jobs. The difficulty was that the new public
jobs had to be paid for just as the taxable capacity of local industry
was waning; inevitably, taxes went up, probably accelerating the de-
parture of both employers and residents.

The financial problems of these local governments deepened as
the strength of public employee unions grew, although still unclear is
the extent to which unionization by itself became a major cause of
increasing costs. The threat of strikes by police and fire personnel led
local officials to agree to binding arbitration, and arbitrators did not
have to take account of the financial health of the cities. The unions,
particularly those representing uniformed personnel, obtained for their
members increasingly generous fringe benefits, especially in the form
of pensions. These pensions were usually not funded by annuities but
instead would draw on future tax revenues; as a result they did not
place an immediate burden on the budget. Local officials were thus

able to give benefits without having to worry about their short-term costs. Moreover, maintenance of water and sewer systems, bridges, tunnels, and roads was often deferred because the provision of "people services" was considered more pressing. And, finally, in some cities borrowed funds were used in ways that did not strengthen local finances.

By 1980 these choices had come home to roost. Taxpayers resisted high rates of taxation by voting for tax limitation measures (such as Proposition 2½ in Massachusetts) or by moving to lower-tax jurisdictions. Private sector jobs had left the Northeast and Midwest at an alarming rate for the so-called Sunbelt, attractive for its sunshine, low taxes, and probusiness climate. Millions of people had followed the jobs, leaving many older industrial central cities with sharply reduced populations. Arbitrators had given city employees such large wage and benefit increases that some mayors who had helped establish the arbitration procedure publicly called for its repeal. Pension costs had skyrocketed to the point that officials of most declining cities (as well as those of California cities hit by Proposition 13, especially Los Angeles) were seriously worried about how they were going to meet them. The capital infrastructure of older cities needed extensive repairs; local newspapers frequently reported leaking water systems, dangerous bridges, and damaged sewers. Finally, those who lend money through the municipal bond market to local governments began scrutinizing the credit-worthiness of prospective local borrowers more stringently—New York City's fiscal crisis had seen to that.

The legacy of decisions made, avoided, or postponed is a particular problem for mayors of declining cities. But their counterparts in the Sunbelt also have a historical inheritance to face. Here, it is the political culture of their cities and regions that limits them rather than the choices made by previous local leaders. More so than the Frostbelt, the South and West are suspicious of government intervention to help minorities and the poor, hostile to taxation, probusiness, reluctant to accept public (or private) sector unionization, and uncomfortable with collective as opposed to individual solutions to problems. These attitudes have been reinforced by the enormous influx of migrants from the Frostbelt who do not want to pay taxes anywhere near as high as they had to pay up north.

The migrants do, however, want to keep the amenities to which they have grown accustomed. Their migration has forced municipalities to provide more sewers, water systems, sidewalks, recreational facilities, schools, libraries, airports, and roads. Yet local officials, in providing them, are under extreme pressure not to raise taxes. Meanwhile, at least in some growing cities, minorities and the poor have become more assertive and politically important. They, too, are demanding services commonplace in the Northeast but not previously offered to them in the Sunbelt and, in many cases, not approved by those who have traditionally run local politics. Officials are under pressure by one segment of the population to provide services but are prevented from raising taxes by the rest of the community.

How have local officials coped with these pressures? Until the election of Ronald Reagan as president, mayors of both declining and growing cities were able to avoid making some hard choices by turning instead to the federal government. In fact, Washington became a crucial contributor to the budgets of all sorts of localities. Furthermore, where allowed by state law (primarily in the Sunbelt), city governments have annexed growing areas outside their boundaries in order to broaden their tax base and avoid the central city–suburb fiscal disparities that bedevil and hamstring cities unable to annex. City governments (again, when permitted by state law) have also levied taxes less "visible" than the property tax, which has aroused much hostility. They have turned to user fees and the "contracting out" to private firms of some services once performed by public employees. They have also simply cut back on services.

No matter what mayors do, however, the contradictory pressures upon them are not likely to cease. Local officials will have to make some very difficult decisions, confronted as they are by President Reagan's insistence on cutting the rate of growth in federal aid, the constraints put on state spending by voters in many states, taxpayer resistance to increases in the property tax, and the continued demand for high service levels. Not only will local governments receive less from both the federal and state levels, but economically disadvantaged residents of local jurisdictions will be given less federal and state money as well. Local governments thus face the prospect of decreased aid from both Washington and their state capitols *and* of greater demands for help from those citizens who were previously helped by state and federal government. The 1980s are not easy times in which to be a local official.

The stage for the problems of the 1980s was set by the trends and events of the previous decade. John Shannon has pointed out that, if one uses a Richter-like scale to examine the importance of various changes in the world of local finance, "the New York City fiscal crisis [falls in] the 5 to 6 category, and Proposition 13 and the 1980 election of Ronald Reagan and a Republican Senate both rate at least a 9."[1] The articles in this book analyze these shocks to the state-local governmental system and attempt to place them in a larger context.

Introduced in Chapter 2 is the tax revolt exemplified by Proposition 13, which was perhaps the most dramatic and publicly visible change to occur within the world of local finance in the 1970s. It was unprecedented for the entire citizenry of a state to vote on taxing and spending measures; previously, with the exception of school districts in some states, elected officials had been responsible for setting tax rates and voters had not been directly involved. The revolt spread, and attempts were made to limit taxing and spending at both the state and federal levels. The financial—and psychological—limits that citizens placed on state and local governments raised difficult new questions for officials: Although taxpayers wanted relief, they did not want a reduction in the quality of their services. They did want "efficient" government.

In Chapter 3, James P. Pfiffner further describes the tax revolt at the local, state, and federal levels and discusses its impact on budgets burdened with long-term commitments. He then argues that there is a basic problem in using spending limits to obtain efficiency in government, and he explores the ways in which cutbacks may actually reduce efficiency. Whatever the problems in implementing the tax revolt, it has certainly changed the very terms of the debate about local finance. Mayors are now stressing limits rather than opportunities, and those who argue for increased spending are forced to deal explicitly with the cost implications of their proposals.

The 1970s also put a spotlight on the previously obscure borrowing and repaying activities of local governments. New York City's moratorium on debt repayment and the visible role played by bankers in resolving the city's fiscal crisis taught the public that the municipal bond market existed. Cleveland's subsequent fiscal problems reinforced the fact that the bond market was intimately tied to the operations of local government. If nothing else, citizens became aware that the actions taken by their cities involved not only voters but a wide range of financial institutions as well. Local officials became explicitly constrained by the demands for credit-worthiness made by lenders; if a city's finances became too unsound, that city was denied access to the municipal bond market and not allowed to borrow until its financial cutbacks satisfied the terms of the major lending institutions.

Although the market has been mentioned often in newspapers and has been analyzed by economists, its actual operations remain a mystery to many of those interested in city politics. In Chapter 4, Alberta M. Sbragia describes the operations of the market, the actors within it, and the uses to which it is put and explores the political consequences of the municipal bond market for local government.

Whereas Sbragia provides a basic initiation into the general world of the market, Patricia Giles Leeds focuses in Chapter 5 on New York City's financing crisis and its relationship to the market. The Sbragia-Leeds chapters should be viewed as a "loose package," the purpose of which is first to give students an elementary introduction to the market and then to deepen that knowledge by exposing them to the specifics of a case. Readers are therefore urged to read Chapters 4 and 5 in succession.

Leeds describes how New York City, in the face of constitutional restrictions, was able to borrow the money it needed to sustain the stable politics of "fiscal crisis," and how the refusal of the market to lend further funds transformed that routine into the unstable politics of a "financing crisis." She outlines various actions taken by all levels of government to prevent the city from defaulting on its debts, focusing in particular on the decision to use the city's public employee pension funds to help save the city from bankruptcy.

Ronald Reagan's election and the political takeover of the Senate by Republicans will have, as Shannon notes,[2] an enormous impact on the state and local government sector. In a sense, the budget cutbacks are both the most visible and the most easily understood activities of the new order. If approved by Congress (which seems increasingly doubtful), President Reagan's strategy of returning power to the states by using block grants would be in many ways more revolutionary than that of simply reducing the growth of federal aid to states and cities. Block grants will shift the focus of intergovernmental politics from Washington to state capitols because state legislatures will decide, within broad guidelines, how to allocate money received from Washington.

Chapters 6, 7, and 8 take account of these changes in various ways. Because President Reagan and the Republican party generally favor the transferring of power to the states, it is especially important for students to know something about state-local relations. Even aside from current politics, the controls that states exercise over their municipalities are extremely significant, for they shape the options that local officials have in raising and managing their funds. The role of the state in local finance, however, is often downplayed by analysts in favor of discussing the more visible role played by the federal government.

Susan A. MacManus remedies this neglect by focusing in Chapter 6 on the role played by the state in local government finance. By comprehensively surveying the controls that states exercise over major aspects of municipal finance, she illustrates how state laws and policies set many of the boundaries within which city politics take place. She then goes on to analyze the impacts of such controls on the fiscal health of central cities. This analysis reveals how dependent municipalities are on state governments for the powers they need to maintain their fiscal health and to what extent the options from which city officials can choose are shaped by the state capitol.

The states will have even greater influence on local finance if they are given federal money in the form of block grants. In Chapter 7,

Raymond E. Owen puts the current emphasis of the Reagan Administration on block grants within a larger historical context. Stressing the tension that exists between politicians and managers in the spending of federal money, he suggests how that tension has been resolved in each phase of intergovernmental aid. Owen sees President Reagan's program as another round in the perennial battle between those who yearn for predictability and stability in federal spending (the managers) and those who are more comfortable with a more flexible system allowing for accommodation and bargaining (the politicians). He argues that because block grants allow the states to choose which programs to fund, politics necessarily shift to the state level. In brief, according to Owen, the president's program gives a "managerial" role to the federal government and forces *state* governments to deal with the "politics" of spending *federal* money.

In Chapter 8, Roger Friedland and Herbert Wong are concerned with a different kind of tension—that between local need and congressional politics in the allocation of federal grants. Their analysis of the allocation of urban renewal grants, which in the 1960s were given out at the discretion of officials in the federal bureaucracy, reveals the kinds of political resources that are most important for cities hoping to receive grants. Their argument, that the nature of a city's representation in the House of Representatives (from 1961 to 1968) was more important than local need in deciding what level of federal aid a city received, suggests that the House has not been as attentive to local needs as the opponents of block grants claim. Their study also reveals that the Senate (which was controlled by the Democrats throughout the 1960s) had little, if any, impact on the allocation of urban renewal funds. It ultimately leaves open the question as to whether a Republican Senate will have any greater influence, although the move to block grants necessarily implies a diminution of the role of both houses.

In conclusion, the contributors to this volume try to provide students with an understanding of the local, state, federal, and private sector pressures that affect the choices available to local officials. These constraints virtually force local officials to be creative if they wish to offer any leadership at all.

Notes

1. John Shannon, "The Great Slowdown in State and Local Government Spending in the United States: 1976–1984," Advisory Commission on Intergovernmental Relations, unpublished paper, 1 June 1981, pp. 7–8.
2. Ibid.

2
The 1970s:
A Decade of Change
in Local Government Finance

Alberta M. Sbragia

The 1970s saw a profound reshaping of the environment that affects local government finance. The relationship between local government, state government, and federal government changed dramatically, and those changes set the stage for the intergovernmental conflicts of the 1980s. Under the U.S. federal system, local governments are legally creatures of the state; they do *not* have the relationship to the state that the states, constitutionally, have to the federal government. This subordinate relationship, however, was substantially redefined in the 1970s.

In the 1960s federal money flowed directly only to a limited number of cities and counties; in the 1970s, however, those funds were extended to the vast majority of municipalities and to many other local governments as well. The nature of the federal system changed: Washington rather than the state capitol increasingly became the focus for local officials and they, in turn, began replacing state officials as the objects of federal attention. The figures tell the story: Federal aid "passed through" the states to the localities increased by 73 percent between 1972 and 1977, but direct aid to local governments increased by 264 percent.[1] By 1978, 28 percent of total federal aid went directly to localities, whereas in 1970 only 13 percent had.[2] A direct federal-local relationship developed, and the state's control over municipalities consequently weakened.

Local officials spent an increasingly large share of their time lobbying Congress and the federal bureaucracy. Federal aid to municipalities of all sizes came to be taken for granted: Whereas, in 1968, municipalities with populations under 100,000 obtained only 20 percent of all federal grants allocated directly to cities, by 1977 their share had risen to 46 percent.[3] Although local officials complained of excessive numbers of federal strings, they preferred spending federal dollars to raising local taxes or to becoming more dependent on often unfriendly state legislatures. Thus, when in 1981 the Reagan Administration began talking about returning power, autonomy, and money to the state governments, local officials were upset. They had been hoping that Washington would give *them* money with fewer strings than had been the case in the 1970s; indeed, their definition of "local autonomy" emphatically excluded the states.

How did this alteration of the federal system come about? What contributed to the system's transformation in the 1970s—a transformation so unpublicized that it went almost unnoticed by the general public until the changes proposed by the Reagan Administration highlighted it? In the first section of this chapter, we focus on two elements that played a critical role in altering the federal system: changes in the system of finance and competition among subnational governments.

The Federal System Redefined

Changes in the System of Finance

If we examine federal assistance to state and local governments combined, we find that between 1958 and 1978 it rose, on average, almost 15 percent per year.[4] By fiscal year 1978, the federal government was giving approximately $78 billion annually to states and localities, or roughly 17 percent of total federal expenditures. The increase in federal funding was most dramatic in the case of local governments, city governments in particular. Between 1969 and 1979, federal aid given directly to city governments increased from 5 percent of overall city general revenues to 15.4 percent in 1978–1979.[5]

Turning to state governments, we find that their financial role in the intergovernmental system changed significantly during the decade. State governments received a smaller percentage of federal aid in 1976–1977 than they had in 1971–1972, a greater percentage of what they did receive in 1976–1977 was "passed through" to local governments, and their own relative contribution to local finance generally declined during the 1970s. In 1971–1972, the states received 85.4 percent of all federal aid and retained 62 percent for their own use, but in

1976–1977 they received only 73.4 percent of all federal aid and passed through so much of the money to local governments that they kept only 54 percent of all federal aid. Thus, the local governments increased in importance as recipients of federal aid at the expense of the states: Local governments increased their *share* of all federal funds (including pass-through funds) from 38 percent in 1971–1972 to 46 percent in 1976–1977.[6] Nonetheless, states continued to be quite dependent on federal monies. In 1972 such monies were equivalent to 38 percent of the states' own-source revenue, and in 1978 that figure was estimated to be 39 percent.[7]

Although the states pass through federal funds to local governments, they also provide funds from their own treasuries. Net state aid to local governments was still much greater than net federal aid in 1976–1977, but the states' share of all intergovernmental aid going to local government had declined since 1971–1972. During these latter years, 70 percent of all intergovernmental aid was given by the states; 30 percent was given by the federal government. By 1976–1977, the states' portion of total intergovernmental aid was only 62.5 percent, whereas the federal government's was 37.5.[8] This decline was particularly noticeable at the city level: In 1978–1979, cities received 22 percent of their general revenue from state monies and 15.4 percent from the federal government.[9] Although the states gave nearly twice as much money to all local governments as did Washington, the latter's contribution had increased in importance, whereas the states' contribution had declined.

Between 1970 and 1978, municipal government became increasingly dependent on both federal and state aid: In 1968–1969, intergovernmental aid accounted for 30 percent of cities' general revenues, but by 1978–1979 that figure had risen roughly to 39 percent.[10] The year 1978, however, was a turning point for local finance. Federal aid began to slow significantly (in terms of constant dollars, it declined), and the tax revolt began to make itself felt. Beginning in late 1978, the federal government became less generous with state and local aid: Between 1978 and 1979, federal grants rose by only 6 percent.[11] But this change did not stop some cities from continuing to rely heavily on federal aid; in 1980 roughly 22 percent of Detroit's budget was dependent on federal assistance, as was 26 percent of Chicago's and 36 percent of New Orleans'.[12] Overall, however, local governments were becoming less dependent simply because federal monies were no longer gushing forth.

Part of the reason for the slowdown in federal aid was the expiration in 1978 of two federal programs that had significantly helped municipal budgets—those of big distressed cities, in particular—between 1976 and the middle of 1978. Both the Local Public Works program, with a $6 billion appropriation, and the Anti-Recession Fiscal Assistance program

(ARFA), with an appropriation of $3.5 billion, had been passed by Congress during the 1975 recession to stimulate local economies. Because Congress has always been more eager to combat recession than to help big cities with their financial problems, the programs were sold as ways of assisting the economy by aiding cities rather than as programs aimed specifically at bolstering cities in fiscal trouble. The programs were therefore labeled as "antirecession" or "countercyclical." Their effect, nevertheless, was to help financially troubled cities whose budgets had been badly battered by the most severe recession since the Depression. When the two programs expired on September 30, 1978, the national economy had recovered, long-term aid for cities with high structural unemployment (i.e., unemployment unrelated to the business cycle) was unpopular, and Congress did not renew either program in any form.

ARFA, in particular, was popular with state and local officials, for it replaced revenue lost due to recession. This program was "a kind of state and local insurance against recession"[13] and had few strings attached. However, its funds were allocated on the basis of unemployment figures, and argument soon arose over the relationship of those figures to recession. Powerful opponents, such as Representative Jack Brooks, chairman of the Government Operations Committee (which had jurisdiction over the program), argued that too much money went to cities suffering high structural unemployment and too little to cities suffering unemployment directly caused by recession. The program itself and various possible modifications were discussed in 1979 and 1980, but it never passed all the congressional hurdles. Cities consequently suffered through the 1979–1980 and 1981–1982 recessions without any prospect of the federal help they had received after the 1975 recession.

The loss of countercyclical revenue was felt most keenly by the larger distressed cities, for ARFA had essentially functioned as a form of revenue sharing for them. When the program was not renewed, mayors had to cut back even more than they had done during the previous years. Newark, for example, was forced to lay off 441 municipal employees, and the Treasury Department estimated that Philadelphia would have had to raise its property tax rate by $.67 (per $100 of value) to come up with the money the city would have received. Buffalo would also have had to raise its tax rate by $.50, Pittsburgh by $.66, and Baltimore by $.58.[14]

The idea of raising taxes, however, has made local officials nervous ever since Proposition 13 was passed in 1978 by referendum in California. It was "Prop 13," in fact, that sparked the tax revolt. Citizens in many states used the referendum process to take the overall taxing and spending policies of subnational government directly into their own hands. Property taxes were cut in some states (notably California and, in 1980, in Massachusetts), and in many other states, various taxing and spending limits were placed on the state and local governments. Thus, the tax revolt spread, notwithstanding the fact that by 1977, all the states had taken some kind of action to bring relief to property owners; twenty-six states, in particular, had devised so-called "circuit breakers," which prevented property taxes from taking up any unreasonable percentage of the homeowners' income. Further, by 1977 many states had finally allowed local governments to be more flexible about the types of taxes they imposed; cities in these states were, for example, permitted to levy sales and/or earnings taxes and therefore to decrease their reliance on the property tax.[15]

Nonetheless, the tax revolt captured the public's imagination, and even in those states in which measures to limit taxing and spending were not introduced or were defeated by the voters, state and local officials had been frightened and were now loathe to raise taxes. Between 1978 and 1980, reliance on the property tax as a way of raising local revenue declined significantly. Local officials coped in various ways with the decreases in federal aid and property tax revenues that characterized the 1978–1980 period: Between 1978 and 1979, state aid increased significantly, and between 1979 and 1980, user fees were raised sharply.

Local Response. The decline in federal aid and the impact of the tax revolt hampered the ability of city governments to balance revenues and expenditures. On average, city revenues did not keep pace with expenditures in 1979 and 1980. Some city governments had managed to accumulate surpluses in 1977 and 1978 sufficient to make up the difference; many cities, however, did not have the funds needed to balance their budgets.[16]

The gap between revenues and expenditures cannot be bridged unless the revenues are increased or the expenditures cut. In the 1980s, local officials will have to increase their revenues *and* cut back expenditures. Increasing their revenues by obtaining larger amounts of intergovernmental aid, however, is no longer a valid option. The federal government is currently limiting increases in its aid to cities even more sharply than it did in the 1978–1980 period, and state governments will be hard pressed simply to maintain their levels of aid. In brief, then, local officials will somehow have to balance their budgets by cutting expenditures for services, by improving their efficiency, by increasing property and nonproperty taxes (in those states where they are legally able to do so), and by increasing user charges and fees.

Balancing the budget, however, will be more difficult for some cities than for others. Cities not experiencing economic and population growth may find it particularly difficult to balance expenditures against revenues. Although scholars have only recently begun to study the differences among city-level financial management practices, as well as the political choices implicit in such practices, preliminary evidence suggests that some declining cities have managed their finances more effectively than have others.

It is true, as George Peterson points out, that declining cities have higher per capita costs than growing cities because of the "fixed overhead" costs of their large capital stock and of their public employee sector. To complicate matters, as population declines, the people left behind have socioeconomic characteristics different from those of emigrants. The empty houses resulting from the loss of residents may lead, for example, to an increased incidence of vandalism and housing fires, thus requiring higher public expenditures for policemen and firemen. Furthermore, it is politically attractive to create employment by increasing the number of public employees.[17]

Nonetheless, declining cities do seem to vary in their means of handling the "costs of decline." Decline in a city's population and economic base does not inevitably produce a fiscal crisis in which local revenues are insufficient to pay for local expenditures. Political leaders *can* adapt to such decline by refashioning their policies; after all, the needy don't make policy.[18] On the other hand, politicians may choose to ignore decline. Martin Shefter, Donald H. Haider, and the Temporary Commission on City Finances all argue that political decisions and processes that ignored decline were crucial to the emergence of New York City's fiscal crisis. As Haider in particular notes, although there were "ample signs to political leaders" that New York City was losing its tax base, local leaders created more public sector jobs and increased expenditures for the poor.[19] In essence, their spending policies ignored the city's economic decline.

To put it simply, political leaders, all faced with similar problems, have made differing choices. Cincinnati, for example, although located in the Midwest where many cities are in financial difficulty, had a budget surplus in both 1979 and 1980. The diversity of the city's economic base had certainly helped to maintain its fiscal health, but good management also contributed to this effect. In 1976 and 1977, when the city's finances seemed to be weakening, local officials quickly and sharply cut back on public employment and service levels. Pittsburgh had followed the same strategy in the early 1970s and thus, by the end of the decade, it too was fiscally much stronger than many comparable cities. By contrast, Cleveland—which is located in the same state as Cincinnati, has a similarly diversified economy, and is tied with Pittsburgh as the third largest corporate headquarters in the United States— defaulted on its debts in December of 1978. Similarly, Wayne County (encompassing Detroit) is widely thought to have had severe fiscal problems due to gross financial mismanagement.[20] Local politics and political culture, then, do seem to affect the outcome of fiscal management—that is, whether local officials are able to live within their respective cities' declining means as opposed to spending without much regard for their budgets' balance sheets.

Although much of the evidence concerning intercity variation in financial practices is subjective, systematic studies have been carried out that attempt objectively to identify distressed cities, to measure urban hardship or fiscal stress, and to explore differences in the responses of cities to decline and hardship.[21] Yet much debate and controversy surround not only these studies but also the question of how such studies should be carried out, what indicators and statistical procedures should be used, and even how such terms as "fiscal stress" should be defined. Moreover, the city characteristics under investigation vary from study to study, often resulting in findings that cannot be compared or that contradict one another.

However, we can conclude from several such studies that certain choices made by city officials do affect the budgetary health of a city. The extent to which city resources can be stretched seems to be, at least in part, a political and management decision. Per capita spending and taxing levels tend to reflect political choices concerning the number and remuneration of city jobs as well as the level of services that are offered to the public.

In some dramatic cases, voters have indicated that they did not support the political choices made by their city officials. The passage of Proposition 2½ in Massachusetts (which lowered property taxes to a maximum of 2½ percent of the full market value of the taxed property) was one such case. Although Boston's city auditor thought that "the city can afford to pay for its government," and although the mayor's chief financial advisor said, "I'm not sure that we're overtaxed as a society,"[22] Boston taxpayers, in voting for "Prop 2½," seemed to be disagreeing. They insisted that they could not afford their government, at least as it was currently being financed, and that they were indeed overtaxed. (Before Proposition 2½ was passed, Boston's property taxes were over 6 percent of the full market value, compared to a national average of 1½ percent.)

Just as cities vary in their spending and taxing policies, the dependence of some cities on federal and state aid is much greater than that of others. Although the average contribution nation-wide of intergovernmental revenues to city revenues is 39 percent,[23] some cities depend on intergovernmental revenues for over half of their budgets. One study, for example, found that the contribution of intergovernmental revenues to total local revenues ran from a low of 14 percent (in Amarillo) to a high of 64 percent (in Baltimore).[24] In short, some cities have had, and will continue to have, much greater difficulty than others in coping with reductions in federal and state aid.

Indeed, many cities may discover that they can keep their budgets in balance only by increasing taxes, reducing the number of public employees, and cutting service levels. Felix Rohatyn, however, argues that although these actions may help the budget, they have negative consequences in the long run:

> For us in the Northeast it is futile to try to cope with long-term structural problems by taking short-term actions that will only exacerbate our ultimate situation. Increased taxes, layoffs, and reduced services in a time of inflationary recession will accentuate our regional downturn and drive more and more taxpayers away. There will come a point when the hemorrhage is not reversible.[25]

To take Rohatyn's argument further, it may be that reductions in federal aid will push officials of declining cities into a no-win situation. On the one hand, cutbacks and increased taxes required to balance the budget may lead to further erosion of the tax base and to further general economic decline. On the other hand, if officials do not cut back and decide instead to maintain service levels in the face of inadequate revenues, operating deficits will expand. Increasingly large deficits may eventually lead to the inability to repay a given city's debts, with lenders consequently refusing to lend the city more money. In order to regain access to loans, the city government will then be forced to increase taxes and reduce services, leading in turn to a further decline in the economic base.

Although this analysis may seem excessively bleak, it does highlight the possible consequences over the long term of reduced federal aid for declining cities. The analysis also makes the crucial point that whereas a balanced budget may be a necessity, it is not synonymous with a "healthy" city.

Competition among Subnational Governments

The reduction of federal aid has taken place within an environment of increased competition for that aid among subnational governments. There are over 80,000 state and local governments, and nearly all of them became eligible during the 1970s for some form of federal aid; in the Johnson era, by contrast, only a relatively few larger cities and counties, school districts, and special districts received such aid. General Revenue Sharing (GRS) funds, for example, now go to 94 percent of those townships and 95 percent of those municipalities so small that they do not have even one employee working full-time.[26] With the allocation by formula of these funds, federal monies penetrated the local government system in an unprecedented fashion.

The change to formula distribution of federal funds altered the nature of competition among local governments in the 1970s, as compared with the previous decade. In the 1960s, cities (especially the larger ones) applied to the federal bureaucracy for funds, and federal officials generally decided which cities should be helped. Such decisions were often influenced by political factors. As Roger Friedland and Herbert Wong reveal in Chapter 8, central cities represented by Democrats in the 1960s were especially fortunate in obtaining federal money for urban renewal; that is, federal officials were responsive to the requests of Democratic members of Congress. In the 1970s, however, formulas devised by Congress began to be substituted for bureaucratic discretion. Because these formulas determine how much money, if any, each locality will receive, the battles over which variables the formulas should incorporate continue to be among the most heated in Congress.

Those formulas "targeted" to help the most needy areas substantially more than others, rather than spreading money around the majority of congressional districts, often do not survive in Congress. ARFA is a case in point. The monies allocated by ARFA's formula helped some cities far more than others, insofar as those with high rates of unemployment received the most money. Although Dallas represented an extreme case in that it received only $.04 per capita in ARFA funds, the figures for Houston ($1.56), Fort Worth ($.99), Nashville-Davidson ($1.63), Indianapolis ($3.52), Jacksonville ($3.87), Tulsa ($2.60), and Omaha ($2.21) were also very low. By contrast, Newark received $39.34 per capita in ARFA monies; Detroit ($28.11), New York City ($26.32), Buffalo ($18.59), Philadelphia ($21.25), San Francisco ($22.69), St. Louis ($20.18), and New Orleans ($20.25) also received substantial per capita allocations.[27] It is not altogether surprising that countercyclical assistance was not renewed.

When the executive branch proposed a new formula that tried to allocate monies more equally between cities while still taking account of need, just about everyone was enraged. And so, in the end, the program died. As one congressional aide concluded, "Political pressures dictate more equalizing of federal grants rather than a stress on meeting social needs. I think we are going to see this played out in more spreading of federal aid over the next decade."[28] Competition for funds thus led to an emphasis on helping all localities a little, rather than on selecting some areas as particularly needy.

The use of formulas increased the number of local governments that looked to Washington for aid. Compared to many nonformula-based programs, those based on formulas were not as focused on big declining northeastern and midwestern cities. The paperwork for many of them was much simpler than for other kinds of grants (project grants, in particular), so that even small municipalities could easily apply. Furthermore, because the money was distributed by formula, it was viewed more as an entitlement than as a handout.

The competition for federal funds has therefore become very tough. Counties, small rural municipalities, suburbs, small nonmetropolitan cities, prosperous cities with "pockets of poverty," and large declining central cities are all after a shrinking pot of federal money. Formulas are becoming increasingly complex as the pressures from the various local governments now in the fray become more intense. Computer printouts showing where funds would go under any proposed formula have therefore become indispensable to the members of Congress.

Due to the deluge of newly active local officials with an interest in the federal grant system, the nature of intergovernmental relations underwent a significant change in the past decade. The federal government had to begin dealing with a much more diverse set of localities than was the case in the 1960s. The dominance in federal-local relations of big declining central cities with deep-seated problems of structural poverty and physical decay began to fade. Local governments facing other types of problems began to clamor for federal attention. Organization followed. Not only are numerous associations currently lobbying in Washington for their state and local government members' interests, but at least thirty-one states, twenty-five counties, and over one hundred cities have opened some kind of Washington office to look after their specific interests in the labyrinth of congressional and bureaucratic corridors.[29] The world of local government in Washington has become extremely well-organized as well as diverse.

Such diversity, as well as the institutionalization of competition and representation, is also evident in Congress. The formation of the Northeast-Midwest Congressional Caucus (with over two hundred members), the Rural Caucus (with one hundred members), and the Suburban Caucus (with fifty-four members) indicates that members of Congress have begun forming coalitions based on geography and the type of local jurisdictions that they represent. Whether all such coalitions will actually be effective remains to be seen: The Northeast-Midwest Coalition, for one, has had some legislative victories.

In the 1980s, these groups will be struggling to find politically feasible answers to two basic questions: Given finite resources, how many of those resources should go to help localities experiencing economic and population growth, and how many should be directed toward those undergoing decline? Further, to what extent should the federal government help prosperous local governments assist their poor if those governments are not themselves making much of an effort in that direction? These questions will certainly dominate the politics of federal aid in the 1980s.

Growing versus Declining Cities. The question of whether growing or declining areas should have priority has become central to the politics of intergovernmental aid. Local governments in both types of areas claim that the federal government needs to—and should—help them. Both have been helped, but the balance has swung back and forth. In the 1960s, federal aid for highways, sewer construction, and home mortgage insurance helped growing areas. Although urban renewal grants and, later, the model cities program helped declining central cities, growing areas, on balance, were probably favored. In 1973, the general revenue sharing program allocated funds to roughly 40,000 local governments, many of which were not experiencing decline. In 1974, the Community Development Block Grant program included areas of growth as well as decline, but in 1976–1977, changes in that program helped declining areas at the expense of growing ones. The antirecession programs of 1976–1978, such as ARFA, also primarily helped declining areas. In 1978 President Carter chose to encourage rehabilitation and to discourage urban sprawl, including suburban shopping malls.

But by 1978, officials of growing municipalities had become both organized and vocal. They did not like President Carter's focus on rehabilitation rather than new construction. Claiming that a focus on rehabilitation would aid older cities, the officials of growing cities argued that the federal government should help them cope with growth.[30]

On the other hand, the infrastructure of many older declining cities is in an increasingly perilous condition. Although we do not have an exact picture of capital infrastructure needs, we do know that Buffalo, Boston, Newark, Detroit, Cleveland, East St. Louis, Pittsburgh, and New York City have serious deficiencies in their capital stock. Water systems, sewers, and bridges are a particular problem.[31]

In an era of limited resources, the quandary for the federal government is a difficult one. How much should it help maintain, replace, and repair the capital stock of older cities, and how much should it assist local governments forced to cope with an enormous influx of new residents who often demand far higher standards of service than did the "old-timers"? At present there is simply not enough money to go around, and Congress, through the types of formulas it approves, will ultimately decide what share of the federal aid available in the 1980s will go to declining and growing communities, respectively.

Achieving a consensus is intrinsically impossible, and arranging compromises will be very difficult: Buffalo hopes to receive money from Washington to upgrade its capital stock, and the cities of New Mexico hope to get money to build their stock. It will, indeed, be difficult for Congress to make both Buffalo and Albuquerque happy, especially since the Reagan Administration has slashed the budgets for sewage systems, waste water treatment systems, mass transit, economic development projects, and other programs dispensing federal grants for capital facilities. There would not have been enough money to meet all such needs even with significant increases in the federal budget, but, with sharply reduced appropriations, the competition between local governments for the relatively little money available will likely be ferocious.

The Poor amidst the Untaxed. An even more intractable question is how much federal aid should be allocated to help prosperous cities deal with their "pockets of poverty"—especially if those cities (and their respective states) are not taxing their own citizens to help the poor in their midst. The various lobbying groups representing growing cities are pressing for aid formulas that take more account of the existence of deep poverty alongside affluence. The representatives of declining cities with tax rates much higher than those of growing cities argue against increasing the share of aid received by growing cities on the grounds that, by and large, growing cities are keeping their taxes low by passing on the problems of the poor to Washington. Such a process, they argue, is unfair to taxpayers in other cities who are doing their share to cope with their own cities' poor.

Houston and Phoenix are sometimes singled out as typical of Sunbelt cities that are maintaining a low tax rate by shifting primary responsibility for their poor to Washington. Both cities have robust economies with an unemployment rate substantially below the national average, and their tax rates are low. However, they also have large areas scarred by the kind of poverty usually associated with the cities of the Frostbelt (Houston's pockets of poverty are largely caused by low wages rather than by unemployment).

Julia Vitullo-Martin described the ghetto in Phoenix as follows:

> Though part of the city, South Phoenix presents a startling picture of rural poverty. Much of the housing, hundreds of tiny hovels, is left over from the old cotton labor camps. Some shacks are painted, many are bare, many lack hot water or indoor plumbing, all are exposed to the vicious desert sun.[32]

And in 1979 now-former Houston Congressman Eckhardt described a section of his congressional district in the following fashion:

> Take Bordersville, as poor a black community as you ever saw. Corrugated tin roofs, rusting and leaking, no city services. The city did not supply water for years. You can travel on the small roads in my district and see grinding poverty.[33]

Houston's total 1976 budget represented an expenditure of $285 per person (compared to $506 in Atlanta and New Orleans, $996 in Newark, and $1,223 in Boston); in 1980 Phoenix had a per capita tax burden of only $137.[34] Yet, in spite of this low taxing and spending effort, per capita federal aid to Houston increased from $23.27 in 1973 to $143.47 in 1978, and aid to Phoenix increased by 500 percent between 1972 and 1978.[35] Total federal aid to Phoenix in fiscal year 1978 was equivalent to over one-third of the city's operating revenues.[36] In Houston, if federal funds used for operating purposes in 1978 had been eliminated, taxes would have had to be raised by $.31 for each tax dollar to maintain the same level of service.[37]

There is no doubt that much of the federal aid for both cities went to pay for social programs directed to the poor. In studies for the Brookings Institution, both Susan MacManus and John Hall concluded that federal aid to Phoenix and Houston permitted these cities to help their low-income populations without having to raise taxes.[38] Because tax increases are politically explosive issues in both cities, federal aid allowed local officials to avoid both neglecting the poor and upsetting the taxpayers.

Should Congress continue helping the poor so much in Houston and Phoenix? If it does not, it is unlikely that the city governments will step in to any significant degree (probably to a greater degree in Houston than in Phoenix). As Mayor Margaret Hance of Phoenix said in 1980, "The poor are a federal, not a local responsibility. If Washington cannot afford these programs, we certainly can't. Local people do not feel that welfare programs should be financed by local taxes."[39] (The program she was referring to provided federal money for such things as buses, clinics, sewers, streets, housing rehabilitation, and facilities for the mentally ill.)

Many Frostbelt citizens, however, argue that the federal government should concentrate on helping the poor in those cities in which the local government has shown through its taxing policy that it is willing to carry a reasonable share of the total burden. Now that federal aid is shrinking significantly, this argument maintains, Congress must force prosperous low-tax state and local governments to accept responsibility for their own poor. Supporters of federal aid for fiscally healthy cities with pockets of poverty, by contrast, claim that the poor are indeed a federal responsibility and that increased local taxes would not only be politically unacceptable but would also slow down the economic growth their cities so desperately need. After all, poverty levels are significantly higher in the Sunbelt than elsewhere, and the Sunbelt cities, their advocates argue, have as much claim on federal aid as northeastern cities that, despite higher per capita tax burdens, have less poverty.

Given that federal aid to localities will be sharply reduced under the Reagan Administration, the degree of financial responsibility that state and local governments should take for their poor will necessarily be even more hotly debated. Nonetheless, whatever share of total aid is allocated to low-tax cities, local officials will probably no longer receive enough federal money to avoid completely a clash between their poor's demand for services and their taxpayers' resistance to tax increases and welfare programs.

The Federal System of the 1970s Versus the System of the 1980s

In brief, then, the system of federal, state, and local relations in the United States underwent significant change in the 1970s. The federal government became an important source of funds not only for large declining cities but for most other local governments as well. It began to help the poor in Phoenix and Houston, as well as those in Newark. By the end of the decade, state aid was still much more important for localities than was federal aid, but it had declined in *relative* importance as the federal government increased its role. Local governments of all sizes and geographic location had become organized, had hired lobbyists, and had enlisted their representatives' help in an effort to maintain or increase their share of federal aid. All cities clamored for—and received— many more federal dollars in the 1970s than they had previously.

The world of local government had become integrated into the federal system to an unprecedented degree. The federal-local relationship, although wrapped in red tape, mandates, and restrictions, nonetheless offered local officials a chance to institute many new programs with relatively little state control. By 1980 local officials had enjoyed roughly a decade of being able, in fact if not in law, to modify the budgetary decisions of state legislators: If the latter would not pay for a certain program, cities could turn to the federal government and set up the program anyway. In essence, political power had become redistributed in the 1970s—away from state governments and toward Washington and local governments. Although the process had begun in the 1960s, when big cities had begun dealing directly with Washington, it blossomed in the following decade when smaller municipalities across the country had become part of a truly national system of government for the first time.

President Reagan's proposal to give federal monies for state *and* local governments to the states in the form of block grants disturbed the "balance of power" that had been achieved by the end of the 1970s between local governments, state governments, and the federal government. His proposal threatened the very system of direct federal-local relations that local governments had struggled to build. Although local officials complained bitterly about federal restrictions on their use of federal monies, they were otherwise happy with their status as newly arrived members of a national governmental system: They certainly wanted federal money, wanted it given to them directly, and wanted to spend it as they wished.

Although the president's budget cuts were a shock to local officials, many of them supported the cutbacks in the hope that they would in fact reduce inflation. However, the president's proposal to redistribute power back to the states received very little support and a great deal of condemnation. Big-city mayors were particularly skeptical. As Mayor Hance of Phoenix declared, "We are sick to death of being an administrative province of the federal government, and we want to avoid becoming administrative provinces of state governments."[40] Local officials worried that the states would not pass on funds from federal block grants. One council member, speaking at the 1981 Congressional-City Conference, expressed the views of numerous other members when, referring to federal aid, she declared, "We don't want it to go to the states unless it's specifically earmarked for cities."[41] "Local autonomy" to local officials meant being able to spend federal money as they saw fit—not as state officials saw fit.

Previously, local officials had been able to use federal aid to avoid making difficult political choices between services or between potential users. Now they feared that such aid would not only be substantially reduced but might also be allocated by the states in ways contrary to their wishes. Not surprisingly, the prospect of the states regaining substantial power over the policy activities of local governments disturbed many local officials. Their clout with the state legislature might often be less than it had been with Congress. Further, some of the groups that supported local governments' requests in Congress (blacks and representatives of the poor, for example) also had less influence with state legislatures than with Congress. If the trends that emerged in 1981 continue, in fact, the 1980s will be a decade in which state rather than local governments increase in power and prominence. This idea is enough to make local officials gloomy, for many vastly prefer to deal with Washington than with their own state governments.

The Economic Context

Parallel to changes in the intergovernmental system, the 1970s saw a shift in the relationship between local government and the private sector. Although local officials had long been aware of the importance of having a healthy tax base, the past decade brought their dependence on that base into sharp relief. A wave of plant closures occurred throughout the Northeast and Midwest during the decade, and over a million manufacturing jobs went either to the West and South or abroad. Seymour Sacks estimates that between 1970 and 1975 the job loss for northeastern cities averaged 2 percent per year and 1.6 percent per year for cities in the Midwest, whereas southern cities averaged an employment gain of 3.2 percent and western cities saw the number of jobs rise by 1.6 percent.[42] To take one example of the effects of such an enormous shift in employment: If since 1969 New York City had obtained new jobs at the prevailing national rate rather than losing jobs, its deficit would easily have been avoided.[43]

Many Frostbelt cities, including New York City, substituted city jobs for the private sector jobs that were leaving. In fact, Alfred J. Watkins has found that between 1958 and 1972, "among Frostbelt cities, local government employment represented the second largest source of new jobs. In Sunbelt cities, the local public sector was the least important source of additional employment."[44] This policy drove up the tax rates in the Frostbelt,[45] which in turn encouraged further shifts to the Sunbelt, and the slow growth of city jobs in Sunbelt cities helped keep tax rates low, thus sustaining the economic attractiveness of the area. However, the severe 1974–1975 recession, taxpayer resistance to increased tax burdens, declining federal aid, and the impact of high pension costs that had been built into municipal budgets in the 1960s and 1970s had, by the end of the decade, led to a nation-wide slowdown in the growth of municipal employment.

The slackening of public employment coincided in many cities with an increased focus by local officials on private sector jobs. The focus on private employment has been strong in the Sunbelt for several decades, but the Frostbelt has often taken its private sector for granted. Although some programs, such as urban renewal, have been directed at revitalizing business areas, many cities have not been particularly concerned about creating a probusiness climate, and businessmen have often felt unappreciated and misunderstood if not actually under attack.[46] However, when the private sector declined so much that the fiscal condition of Frostbelt cities was seriously affected, city officials began to realize that business played a vital role in the U.S. economic system.

It was needed both as an employer and as a taxpayer. City budgets, to put it simply, depended heavily on private sector jobs.

Frostbelt officials have also recognized that in a federal system that allows state and local governments to differ in how they tax, regulate, and accommodate to business, firms can—and do—shop around for the most favorable conditions. Officials have consequently joined the competition to attract new jobs and have begun to court firms and employers in ways that previously had been used primarily by Sunbelt officials. The contest for jobs pits the Frostbelt against the Sunbelt, to be sure; however, Frostbelt officials often also compete against one another, as do those from the Sunbelt. Officials "raid" other states and municipalities, promising firms a better business climate, lower housing costs, a more skilled work force, more sophisticated cultural attractions, and whatever else they can think of to entice those firms to relocate.[47] And, of course, states and cities with employers likely to be wooed try to keep them from moving away. For example, the governor of California asked the state legislature to appropriate $7.6 million to establish a major research institute in the microelectronics field at the University of California at Berkeley, an attraction he hoped would discourage the state's constantly wooed high-technology firms from moving.[48]

In addition to advertising their supposedly unique virtues, states and localities have adopted a variety of specific policies designed to attract employers. Although the effectiveness of tax incentives in attracting employers has not been proven, tax laws in such states as Wisconsin and New York were changed to create a more favorable business climate. Municipalities borrowed money, which they lent at below-market rates to businesses; they offered property tax abatements; they promised new public investments, such as access roads and sewers; and they worked with financial institutions, especially banks, to help new and expanding businesses.

In particular, cooperation between city officials and banks has become increasingly widespread. The city of Baltimore, for one, formed a partnership with its banks that resulted in the offering of 20-to-25-year bank loans to small- and medium-sized businesses—even though the banks usually preferred to deal with larger business firms and to lend for shorter periods of time. By 1981 roughly 3,000 jobs in the private sector had been created through such public-private cooperation.[49] Similar cooperation between banks and city government is occurring in numerous other municipalities; Toledo and Pittsburgh are two examples.[50]

Whereas in the 1960s Frostbelt officials talked about the "urban crisis," referring to such social problems as racism, poverty, and alienation, the "fiscal crisis" in the next decade forced them to think about the economic trends to which cities are subject. The private sector was no longer either ignored, attacked, or taken for granted; rather, it was viewed as the foundation upon which local finance rested. The decline of federal aid in the late 1970s reinforced the dependence of local budgets on local economies: At the beginning of the 1980s, the revitalization of declining economies and the maintenance of healthy ones were the top priorities for most local officials.

This emphasis on the health of local economies led to a concern with investment and to the recognition that economic growth requires large infusions of capital. The substantial loans made by New York City's municipal employee pension funds to the city government during its fiscal crisis turned the attention of state and local officials in the Frostbelt to pension funds as sources of capital. Pension funds are a tempting source of capital for the stimulation of local economies; they control many billions of dollars that typically are invested for the highest possible yield, which is then paid out to retired pension fund members. The size of certain individual funds is enormous. In 1979, for example, the California Public Employees Pension Fund controlled $15.4 billion; New York State, $10.5 billion; Ohio State Teachers, $4 billion; and Ohio Public Employees, $4 billion.[51] State and local officials have thus begun searching for investments that will both yield a good return for retired citizens and stimulate their cities' or states' economies.

Although the investment of public pension funds in ventures that strengthen the local economy appeals to officials of declining Frostbelt cities, no consensus has yet been reached on whether the funds should be invested with the primary objective of aiding the local economy rather than of obtaining the highest possible yield for retired individuals. Whether municipal employees will want their funds invested for purposes other than yield is unclear, except perhaps to the fire union chief in Hartford who resisted suggestions that his union's pension fund be invested in mortgages in Hartford by saying, "God, get them away from our money."[52] As Patricia Leeds points out in Chapter 5, the purpose for which pension funds should be invested promises to become a major political issue in the 1980s and 1990s. The fact that the issue has emerged at all, however, indicates how concerned local officials have become about the health of their local economies.

The Eternal Triangle: Local Government,
Federal Government, and the Private Sector

The federal government has not been idle while local officials have been competing for private sector jobs. In fact, many localities have also gone after federal aid that would help them to compete more effectively for private sector development. Local government, federal government, and the private sector have become locked into a closely knit triangular relationship.

Roughly seventy federal programs gave grants to help local jurisdictions with economic development. The Commerce Department's Economic Development Administration (EDA) and HUD's urban development action grant (UDAG) program (authorized in 1965 and 1977, respectively) were particularly important, in that they tried to help local governments furnish the elements needed for private investment, such as land and sewers.

The Reagan Administration has attacked both programs, and President Reagan has proposed eliminating EDA altogether. Such attacks highlight the differences between those who see the decline of the Frostbelt as the natural and inevitable consequence of market forces and those who view it more as a result of federal government policy. The Reagan group considers economic development assistance to be economically inefficient, whereas its advocates see it as a counterweight to federal government activities, such as patterns of defense spending, that have hurt the Frostbelt and helped the Sunbelt.

President Reagan's supporters ignore the important role of federal government policy in stimulating the boom in the Sunbelt. For example, although Connecticut is a major beneficiary of defense spending, most defense funds are spent in the Sunbelt. Mainly because of this imbalance, the Frostbelt states between 1975 and 1979 paid $165 billion more in federal taxes than the federal government spent in those states, whereas the federal government spent $112 billion more in the Sunbelt states than it received from them in federal taxes.[53] On the other hand, those officials who argue that the federal government has an overriding obligation to help Frostbelt cities attract private sector jobs ignore the fact that Frostbelt cities accelerated the exodus of employers and middle-class residents, particularly by allowing local taxes to rise rapidly and by not worrying about efficient government. The decline of the northeastern cities was certainly not entirely the federal government's fault.

The debate over how much the federal government has influenced the decline of the Frostbelt has highlighted the sheer complexity of urban growth and decline. It has also encouraged local policymakers to analyze the probable impacts on urban areas of new federal legislation affecting the private sector. Federal corporate tax policy can be particularly important for local governments and their budgets. For example, George Peterson of the Urban Institute has found that the Reagan Administration's initial proposals for an accelerated business depreciation write-off for investment in new plant and equipment would hurt the Frostbelt (as well as central cities generally). Across-the-board federal tax incentives for local capital investment "encourage industrialists to abandon aged or near-obsolescent plant equipment, most frequently located in older urban centers, and to build anew in suburbs or lower-cost states."[54] The executive director of the Northeast-Midwest Institute claims that the Reagan Administration could encourage capital investment without hurting the Frostbelt by instituting "a 'bonus' depreciation allowance for firms that invest on-site in their communities."[55] The fact that local officials are worrying about depreciation allowances indicates that they have learned a good deal in the last decade both about the dynamics of the private sector and about how those dynamics affect various types of local governments.

Recession and Inflation

Although local budgets are affected by the pattern of defense spending, private sector investment choices, and such arcane factors as the business depreciation allowance, they are also shaped by recession and inflation. Unfortunately, we have only inconclusive data on the impact of either recession or inflation on local revenues and expenditures and even more inconclusive analyses of how the two interact. None-theless, the subject is important enough that students should be aware at least of the general constraints imposed by such economic trends over which local officials have no control.

Recession hurts local revenues; income-elastic tax yields such as those from the sales tax are especially hit. The Advisory Committee on Intergovernmental Relations (ACIR) concluded that "because of the 1975 recession, state and local governments lost 8.4 percent of own-source revenues in fiscal year 1975."[56] Recession also affects expenditures: During a recession, expenditures climb a bit, but during the recovery, expenditures will be cut somewhat more than they climbed during the recessionary period. On balance, therefore, expenditures seem to decline in response to recessions.

Some cities suffer more from recessions than aggregate figures would indicate. Roy Bahl and his colleagues have concluded, on the basis of a preliminary analysis, that employment in central cities suffers more during recession and gains less during recovery than does em-ployment in other areas. Further, some central cities suffer more than others—the "sufferers" being primarily in the Northeast and Midwest.[57] Similarly, in examining the revenue loss suffered by *state* governments during recessions, the ACIR concluded that some had lost less than 5 percent of their own-source revenues, whereas others had lost more than 20 percent.[58] Although state revenue systems differ from those of local government, such wide disparities in the consequences of recession reinforce the thesis that recession hurts some local governments far more than others.

Inflation also shapes local budgets. Although inflation increases expenditures, it has also generally increased tax revenue, as indicated by increases both in the market value of property and in people's salaries and wages. The ACIR estimated that in fiscal year 1976, inflation pushed up local government revenue $7.8 billion, or 8.4 percent.[59] New York City officials, for example, found it much easier to balance the city's budget in the early 1980s because high inflation brought in more revenue from the sales tax and personal income tax than had been expected.

There seems to be little consensus, however, about whether gains in revenue induced by inflation balance expenditure increases that are also attributable to inflation. Whereas one study found a net loss in purchasing power in the years 1972–1974, an ACIR study, by contrast, concluded that between 1973 and 1976 "inflation generally added more to state and local government revenue collecting potential than it took away in lost purchasing power."[60] However, most observers, including local officials, think that the persistently high inflation of the late 1970s and early 1980s increased expenditures more than it increased revenues.

To make matters even more complicated, recession and inflation have occurred simultaneously in the 1970s. How do the two intersect? The ACIR concluded that, as a consequence of recession and inflation, local governments in 1976 had a net aggregate decline of only 3.7 percent in own-source general revenue.[61] That percentage takes on added meaning when we realize that it has been calculated on the basis of figures for *all* local governments—including, for example, those in Texas, which are relatively insensitive to recessions.[62] Some budgets suffered far more than the ACIR figures indicate. Although the intersection between inflation and recession is extremely complex, the uneven impact of recessions suggests that in periods of simultaneous inflation and recession, the budgets of Frostbelt cities are hurt more than those in growing areas of the country.

Even if national economic trends affected all areas equally, however, their impact on local budgets could not be uniform, for municipal tax structures vary in the extent to which they reflect both inflation and recession. Cities, such as Boston, that rely almost entirely on the property tax will be affected differently from those, such as New York City, that are more dependent on sales and income taxes. It is politically difficult for local officials to adjust the property tax rate (or assessments) to keep up with inflation; the sales tax, by contrast, brings in added revenue in inflationary periods at no political cost. On the other hand, in times of recession, cities dependent on the sales tax may suffer far more than those relying on the property tax.[63]

Conclusion

It is clear that local finance in the 1970s was affected by numerous factors that intersected with one another in complex patterns. The migration of jobs and taxpayers to the Sunbelt, uneven impact of recession and recovery, fluctuation in intergovernmental assistance, differences in urban political culture and constituency expectations, use of formulas in allocating federal grants, new constraints on taxing powers, changes in the political party control of the presidency and senate, and increased competition for federal monies all affected local finance in intricate ways. Certainly, each local government—each municipal government, in particular—is a special case and has its own peculiar constellation of pressures to face. Yet most of these pressures are at work in all cities; what differs is merely their relative force. Thus, in the 1970s local officials began to cope with problems that did not disappear, but instead usually worsened, with the advent of the 1980s. Some cities were fortunate in finding a basic financial equilibrium and may well be able to sustain that balance in this decade. Those less successful, however, will find the 1980s a time of serious testing.

Notes

1. Advisory Commission on Intergovernmental Relations, *Recent Trends in Federal and State Aid to Local Governments*, Washington, D.C., 1980, p. 11.

2. U.S., Congress, Joint Economic Committee, *State and Local Finances and the Changing National Economy, Hearing before the Special Study on Economic Change of the Joint Economic Committee.* Prepared statement of Roy Bahl, 96th Cong., 2nd sess., 1980, p. 12.

3. James W. Fossett and Claire C. Osborn, "Federal Grants in Large Sunbelt and Frostbelt Cities: An Overview," *Texas Business Review* 54 (March–April 1980):74.

4. George F. Break, "State and Local Finance in the 80's," *Taxing and Spending* 3 (Summer 1980):36.

5. U.S. Department of Commerce, Bureau of the Census, *City Government Finances in 1978–79*, Washington, D.C., p. 1. "City" is defined in this instance as any municipality with a population of over 30,000.

6. Advisory Commission on Intergovernmental Relations, *Recent Trends in Federal and State Aid to Local Government*, p. 8.

7. Advisory Commission on Intergovernmental Relations, *The Federal Role in the Federal System: The Dynamics of Growth*, Washington, D.C., 1980, p. 127.

8. Advisory Commission on Intergovernmental Relations, *Recent Trends in Federal and State Aid to Local Governments*, p. 9.

9. Bureau of the Census, *City Government Finances in 1978–79*, p. 7.

10. Advisory Commission on Intergovernmental Relations, *The Federal Role in the Federal System: The Dynamics of Growth*, p. 127; U.S. Department of Commerce, Bureau of the Census, *City Government Finances in 1968–69*, Washington, D.C., p. 5; *City Government Finances in 1978–79*, p. 7.

11. John Shannon, "The Great Slowdown in State and Local Government Spending in the United States: 1976–1984," U.S., Congress, Advisory Commission on Intergovernmental Relations, unpublished paper, 1 June 1981, p. 5; John E. Petersen, "Financial Roundup for State and Local Governments," *Resources in Review* 3 (March 1981):4; George F. Break, "State and Local Finance in the 80s," *Taxing and Spending* 3 (Summer 1980):36.

12. Rochelle L. Stanfield, "What Has 500 Parts, Costs $83 Billion, and Is Condemned by Almost Everybody?" *National Journal*, 1 March 1981, p. 6.

13. John P. Ross, "Countercyclical Revenue Sharing," in *Fiscal Crisis in American Cities: The Federal Response*, ed. L. Kenneth Hubbell (Cambridge, Massachusetts: Ballinger, 1979), p. 259.

14. U.S., Congress, Senate, Committee on Finance, *Targeted Fiscal Assistance to State and Local Governments, Hearings Before the Subcommittee on Revenue Sharing, Intergovernmental Revenue Impact, and Economic Problems on S.200 and S.566*. 96th Cong., 1st sess., 1979, pp. 127–129.

15. David B. Walker, "Localities Under the New Intergovernmental System," in *Fiscal Crisis in American Cities: The Federal Response*, p. 34.

16. U.S., Congress, Joint Economic Committee, *Trends In the Fiscal Condition of Cities: 1978–1980, A Study Prepared for the Use of the Subcommittee on Fiscal and Intergovernmental Policy*. 96th Cong., 2nd sess., 1980; U.S., Congress, Joint Economic Committee, *Trends In the Fiscal Condition of Cities: 1979–81, A Staff Study*. 97th Cong., 1st sess., 1981; see also John E. Petersen, "City Finances, 1978–1980: The JEC/MFOA Survey Results," *Governmental Finance* 9 (June 1980):4.

17. George E. Peterson, "Finance," in *The Urban Predicament*, eds. William Gorham and Nathan Glazer (Washington, D.C.: The Urban Institute, 1976), pp. 44–51.

18. As Martin Shefter points out, "unemployed men and fatherless children do not, after all, have the authority to appropriate monies or float municipal bonds." Martin Shefter, "New York City's Fiscal Crisis: The Politics of Inflation and Retrenchment," in *Managing Fiscal Stress: The Crisis in the Public Sector*, ed. Charles H. Levine (Chatham, N.J.: Chatham House, 1980), p. 71.

19. Donald H. Haider, "Fiscal Scarcity: A New Urban Perspective," in *The New Urban Politics*, eds. Louis H. Masotti and Robert L. Lineberry (Cambridge, Mass.: Ballinger, 1976), p. 210; see also Roy W. Bahl, Alan K. Campbell, David Greytak, *Taxes, Expenditures, and the Economic Base: Case Study of New York City* (New York: Praeger, 1974), pp. 4–6; and *The City In Transition: Prospects and Policies for New York, The Final Report of the Temporary Commission on City Finances* (New York: Arno, 1978).

20. Iver Peterson, "In Cincinnati, Last Doesn't Mean Least," *New York Times*, 12 April 1981, p. 13; Lorna Crowley Ferguson, "Fiscal Strain in American Cities: Some Limitations to Popular Explanations," in *Urban Political Economy*,

ed. Kenneth Newton (London: Frances Pinter, 1981), pp. 170–172; "Cleveland Striving to Polish Its Image," *New York Times*, 12 October 1980, p. 59; Iver Peterson, "Detroit and Environs Face a Predictable Fiscal Crunch," *New York Times*, 12 October 1980, p. 2E.

21. See, for example, Richard P. Nathan and James W. Fossett, "Urban Conditions—The Future of the Federal Role," *Proceedings of the National Tax Association* 71 (1978):30–41; Terry Nichols Clark and Lorna Crowley Ferguson, "Fiscal Strain and American Cities: Six Basic Processes," in *Urban Political Economy*, ed. Kenneth Newton (London: Frances Pinter, 1981), pp. 137–155; Ferguson, "Fiscal Strain in American Cities: Some Limitations to Popular Explanations," pp. 156–178; James M. Howell and Charles F. Stamm, *Urban Fiscal Stress: A Comparative Analysis of 66 U.S. Cities* (Lexington, Mass.: Lexington Books, 1979); Charles F. Stamm and James M. Howell, "Urban Fiscal Problems: A Comparative Analysis of 66 U.S. Cities," *Taxing and Spending* 3 (Fall 1980):41–58; for a study comparing per capita expenses and property taxes in Boston (a city that Howell and Stamm identified as suffering serious fiscal stress) with those of roughly comparable cities, see Michael Brody, "No Tea Party: Prop. 2½ Has Both Boston and State at Bay," *Barron's*, 9 March 1981, p. 24; for a good general discussion and critique of the various "fiscal distress" studies, see Roy Bahl, "State and Local Government Finances and the Changing National Economy," in *Special Study on Economic Change, Volume 7: State and Local Finance: Adjustments in a Changing Economy*, U.S., Congress, Joint Economic Committee, 96th Cong., 2nd sess., December 1980, pp. 32–39.

22. Brody, "No Tea Party," p. 29.

23. Bureau of the Census, *City Government Finances in 1978–79*, p. 7.

24. Howell and Stamm, *Urban Fiscal Stress*, p. 109.

25. U.S., Congress, Joint Economic Committee, *State and Local Government Finances and the Changing National Economy*, p. 35.

26. G. Ross Stephens, "The Great Reform in Federal Grant Policy or What Ever Happened to General Revenue Sharing," in *Fiscal Crisis in American Cities: The Federal Response*, p. 101.

27. Ross, "Countercyclical Revenue Sharing," pp. 266, 286.

28. Rochelle L. Stanfield, "Playing Computer Politics with Local Aid Formulas," *National Journal*, 9 December 1978, p. 1980.

29. Lisa B. Belkin, "For State and Local Governments Washington Is the Place to Be," *National Journal*, 9 September 1980, pp. 1485–1487.

30. See, for example, Rochelle L. Stanfield, "Federal Aid Comes Out of the Closet in the Mountains and Desert West," *National Journal*, 15 December 1979, p. 2098.

31. George E. Peterson, "Capital Spending and Capital Obsolescence: The Outlook for Cities," in *The Fiscal Outlook for Cities: Implications of a National Urban Policy*, ed. Roy Bahl (Syracuse, N.Y.: Syracuse University Press, 1978), pp. 63–65; David A. Grossman, "The Infrastructure Blues: A Tale of New York and Other Cities," *Governmental Finance* 9 (June 1980):9–13.

32. Julia Vitullo-Martin, "A City That Can Take Federal Money or Leave It," *Fortune*, 28 July 1980, p. 76.

33. Rochelle L. Stanfield, "Pockets of Poverty—The Other Side of Houston," *National Journal*, 24 March 1979, p. 477.

34. Ibid.; Vitullo-Martin, "A City That Can Take Federal Money or Leave It," p. 77.

35. Susan A. MacManus, "The Economics and Politics of Federal Money in Houston," *Texas Business Review* 54 (March–April 1980):80; John Stuart Hall, "Local Politics and Federal Aid in Phoenix," *Texas Business Review* 54 (March–April 1980):98.

36. Hall, "Local Politics and Federal Aid in Phoenix," p. 99.

37. MacManus, "The Economics and Politics of Federal Money in Houston," p. 81.

38. Hall, "Local Politics and Federal Aid in Phoenix," p. 98; MacManus, "The Economics and Politics of Federal Money in Houston," p. 82.

39. Vitullo-Martin, "A City That Can Take Federal Aid or Leave It," p.77.

40. Mara Adams, "Reagan's New Federalism: Where Are the Cities?" *Nation's Cities Weekly*, 9 March 1981, p. 16.

41. Ibid.

42. Cited in Roy Bahl, Bernard Jump, Jr., and Larry Schroeder, "The Outlook for City Fiscal Performance in Declining Regions," in *The Fiscal Outlook for Cities: Implications of a National Urban Policy*, ed. Roy Bahl (Syracuse, N.Y.: Syracuse University Press, 1978), p. 9.

43. Ibid., pp. 8–9. The link between economic growth and the local budget, however, varies from city to city, depending on the municipal revenue structure. Cities that are allowed by the state government to impose taxes on sales and income as well as on property and that share the revenue from certain state taxes are better able to capture the benefits accruing from economic growth and revitalization than are cities primarily reliant on the property tax. Boston is an oft-cited example of a city that, notwithstanding a healthy, service-oriented economy, is suffering severe fiscal stress partially because the state, rather than the city, government receives many of the tax revenues generated by Boston's revitalized downtown and waterfront areas. Portland, Maine, is in much the same position as Boston. The Mayor's Alternative Revenue Task Force in that city found that "for every $100 of new sales of taxable merchandise, the State government receives $4.80 in new revenues and the City government receives $.02" (Coalition of Northeast Municipalities, *Can Community Economic Development Meet the Fiscal Needs of Municipalities? Economic Growth and Fiscal Stress in Three Northeast Cities*, New England Municipal Center, September 1980, p. 46).

44. Alfred J. Watkins, "Employment Changes in Frostbelt and Sunbelt Cities," *Texas Business Review* 54 (March–April 1980):69; see also Peterson, "Finance," pp. 112–115; Bahl, Campbell, and Greytak, *Taxes, Expenditures, and the Economic Base: Case Study of New York City*, pp. 4–6; Haider, "Fiscal Scarcity: A New Urban Perspective," pp. 171–216.

45. Donna Shalala concludes that "service sector and public sector jobs replacing manufacturing job losses do not generally produce equivalent tax

yields" (U.S., Congress, Joint Economic Committee, *State and Local Government Finances and the Changing National Economy*, p. 44); see also Bahl, Campbell, and Greytak, *Taxes, Expenditures, and the Economic Base*, pp. 108–114.

46. According to a congressional study, the attitude of the city government toward business seems to be an important element of the so-called "business climate" and to have a strong influence on the decisions businesspeople make about relocating. In a survey of business firms in ten major cities, the Joint Economic Committee received 1,290 usable replies that throw some light on the loosely used term "business climate." When business leaders were asked to rank twenty-six variables in terms of the degree to which they affected relocation decisions, the attitude of the city government toward business was ranked as the most important. (Crime levels, the quality of the city's schools, and cultural attractions were also considered significant variables.) U.S., Congress, Joint Economic Committee, *Central City Businesses—Plans and Problems, A Study Prepared for the Use of the Subcommittee on Fiscal and Intergovernmental Policy*, Joint Committee Print, 95th Cong., 2nd sess., 1979, p. 24.

47. Doug McInnis, "Going After High Tech," *New York Times*, 19 July 1981, p. 6F.

48. State of California, *1981–82 Governor's Budget*, p. A-47.

49. John Sower, "Baltimore Plan Offers Small Firms the Capital Necessary for New Plants," *Nation's Cities Weekly*, 19 January 1981, p. 9.

50. Michael Barton, "Commercial Banks Team Up with Cities to Aid Development," *Nation's Cities Weekly*, 19 January 1981, p. 7.

51. Neal R. Peirce and Jerry Hagstrom, "Unions, Frostbelt Seek More Control Over Pension Fund Investments," *National Journal*, 27 January 1979, p. 147.

52. Ibid.

53. In 1980, Congress, led by the Northeast-Midwest Congressional Coalition, repealed the Maybank Amendment, which had prohibited the Defense Department from "targeting" its purchases so as to help distressed communities. In 1981, $3.4 billion were to be spent in areas with unemployment 20 percent above the national average. Lawrence Zaber, "Get your City's Share of Defense Dollars," *Nation's Cities Weekly*, 23 March 1981, p. 2. Because the Reagan Administration is slowing down federal aid to cities while increasing the proportion of the federal budget allocated to defense, some Frostbelt officials will probably try to help their cities' firms win more defense contracts above and beyond those targeted to distressed cities. Increased defense spending in the Frostbelt could partially cushion the effects of the slowdown in federal aid.

54. Discussed in Neal R. Peirce, "Economic Dunkirk," *Nation's Cities Weekly*, 12 January 1981, p. 5; see also Mary Fitzpatrick and Peter Tropper, *Tax Cuts for Business: Will They Help Distressed Areas?* Northeast-Midwest Institute, September 1980.

55. Peirce, "Economic Dunkirk," p. 5.

56. U.S., Congress, Advisory Commission on Intergovernmental Relations, *State-Local Finances in Recession and Inflation: An Economic Analysis*, Washington, D.C., 1979, p. 28.

57. Roy Bahl, Bernard Jump, Jr., and Larry Schroeder, "Federal Policy and the Fiscal Outlook for Cities," in *Fiscal Crisis in American Cities: The Federal Response*, pp. 12–13; see also Robert D. Reischauer, "The Economy, the Federal Budget, and the Prospects for Urban Aid," in *The Fiscal Outlook for Cities: Implications of a National Urban Policy*, ed. Roy Bahl (Syracuse, N.Y.: Syracuse University Press, 1978), pp. 94–96; Watkins, "Employment Changes in Frostbelt and Sunbelt Cities," pp. 72–73; U.S., Congress, Joint Economic Committee, *State and Local Government Finance and the Changing National Economy*, p. 45; Bahl, "State and Local Government Finances and the Changing National Economy," pp. 65–72.

58. Advisory Commission on Intergovernmental Relations, *State-Local Finances in Recession and Inflation*, pp. 78–79.

59. Ibid., p. 32.

60. Ibid., p. 33; for the opposite point of view, see David Greytak and Bernard Jump, *The Effect of Inflation on State and Local Government Finances: 1967–74*, Occasional Paper No. 25 of the Metropolitan Studies Program of the Maxwell School of Citizenship and Public Affairs, Syracuse University, 1975; on this general topic, see also Ferguson, "Fiscal Strain in American Cities," in *Urban Political Economy*, ed. Kenneth Newton (London: Frances Pinter, 1981), pp. 167–170.

61. Advisory Commission on Intergovernmental Relations, *State-Local Finances in Recession and Inflation*, p. 35.

62. John A. Burghardt, "Sensitivity to the National Business Cycle Among Major Metropolitan Areas in Texas," *Texas Business Review* 54 (January–February 1980):7–8.

63. Terry Nichols Clark and Lorna Crowley Ferguson, "Fiscal Strain and American Cities: Six Basic Processes," in *Urban Political Economy*, ed. Kenneth Newton (London: Frances Pinter, 1981), pp. 138–139.

3
Inflexible Budgets, Fiscal Stress, and the Tax Revolt

James P. Pfiffner

The big yell comes nowadays from the taxpayers. . . . No matter what you pay for taxes, high, low, or medium, the yell is always the same, 100 per cent.

Will Rogers[1]

U.S. Governments and Inflexible Budgets

Governments in the United States are suffering from inflexible budgets. An increasing percentage of expenditures at the federal, state, and local levels is nondiscretionary because of prior commitments and mandates from other levels of government. Moreover, the controllable portion of budgets is often difficult to change due to powerful political pressures. Thus, elected executives and legislators seem to have less and less control over budgetary outlays each year. In contrast to the 1960s, declining productivity and slowed economic growth in the 1970s and 1980s have made economic allocation decisions more nearly zero-sum. That is, increases in resources for one group come at the expense of decreases for other groups.[2]

At the same time that spending discretion is decreasing, pressure from the electorate for tax relief is mounting. Twenty-three states enacted fiscal limitations between 1970 and 1980, sixteen of them after 1975.[3] Although the more drastic types of tax reduction were not widely adopted, expenditure levels were popular ballot items. At the national levels, proposals for a constitutional convention to consider an amendment requiring an annual balanced budget gained the support of thirty of the thirty-four states necessary. In short, the tax revolt and inflexible budgets are meeting head-on and are putting government officials— elected and appointed, federal, state, and local—in the difficult position of trying to satisfy demands for more spending with increasingly constrained budgets.

I will begin this chapter with a description of the fiscal binds in which federal, state, and local governments find themselves. The trends are uncontrollability, rigidity, and increasing centralization of control. I will then consider the origins of the tax revolt in the United States and its success in imposing taxing and spending limitations on governments, with special emphasis on both California's experience with Proposition 13 and the proposed balanced budget amendment to the U.S. Constitution. Finally, I will outline the consequences of inflexible budgets, the tax revolt, and reduced growth rates of government budgets. My argument will be that there are important organizational costs that must be considered explicitly in deciding how to reduce governmental expenditures responsibly.

The Federal Budget and Uncontrollable Spending

Although the amount of money spent by the federal government has been steadily increasing, the percentage of the national budget that is discretionary or "controllable" has been decreasing. In a literal sense, of course, all spending is discretionary because Congress could refuse to honor the fiscal commitments of the U.S. government. But if Congress does choose to honor previous commitments, its discretion over spending in any one year is drastically reduced.

When applied to a budget, the term "uncontrollable" refers to those expenditures that must be made because of existing law or contracts entered into previous to the current fiscal year. Most claimants to these funds have a legal right to them that is enforceable in court. Payment for capital construction (such as dams, sewer systems, and public buildings) and defense procurement (such as missile systems, planes, and ships) are accomplished through long-term contracts. When contracts for these purposes are entered into, the actual expenditure is usually not made until years after the initial commitment. But when the bills come due, the United States has a legal obligation to pay them. The estimated cost for such contracts for fiscal year 1980 was $7.9 billion, or 16.5 percent of total outlays.[4]

In order to pay its bills, the U.S. government borrows money by selling bonds; the interest on such debt must be paid in order to avoid default. This expenditure is a fixed cost that must be paid each fiscal year.

The largest category of uncontrollable spending, however, consists of payments to individuals; most of these payments are *entitlements.* Included among programs providing these payments are social security, federal and military retirement benefits, unemployment insurance, veterans' benefits, medicare, and public assistance. If a person is included within the definitions of eligibility for one of these programs, that person is entitled to payments from the federal government. These entitlement payments for individuals made up almost half of the total outlays for fiscal year 1980.[5]

One of the main problems with such entitlements is that the amount of money spent on them depends on the state of the economy, particularly the levels of inflation and unemployment. For instance, a rise in the unemployment rate may cost the federal government more in unemployment compensation, as well as increasing the number of people receiving Aid to Families with Dependent Children (AFDC) payments. Thus a 1 percent increase in unemployment may result in a total of $7.3 billion in increased outlays.[6] In addition, automatic cost of living increases are built into many of these programs, including the civilian and military retirement, railroad retirement, and social security programs. When the Consumer Price Index (CPI) rises, so do benefits for these programs. A 1 percent increase in the CPI may cost the treasury an extra $2.1 billion.[7] Consequently, the size of each year's budget is linked directly to the state of the U.S. economy, which, despite the efforts of our best economists, cannot easily be controlled.

As a result of these uncontrollable expenditures (fixed costs, contracts, and entitlements), roughly 75 percent of the U.S. budget is locked in and uncontrollable in the short run. Of the $38.2 billion increase in outlays President Carter requested for fiscal year 1980, $33.9 billion was the result of costs in uncontrollable programs.[8] Although federal spending increased from $196.6 billion to $531.6 billion between 1970 and 1980, an average of 87 percent of the increase in this spending was due to uncontrollable expenditures.[9]

Uncontrollable spending has increased greatly over the past twenty years for several reasons. Congress has expanded coverage of the programs to more people and has increased benefits. When some of these programs were created, future cost was difficult to foresee. For instance, when medicare for the elderly and medicaid for the poor were enacted in 1965, the cost was less than $1 billion. Although Congress expected only moderate growth for both programs, in 1981 medicare cost over $35 billion and medicaid cost $16 billion.

Furthermore, in 1972 Congress indexed social security payments to the CPI. Other programs indexed since that time include supplemental security income, railroad retirement, food stamps, child nutrition, and military and civilian retirement. Indexing has accounted for about half the increase in cost of retirement systems in the 1970s.[10]

There are important obstacles to any major short-term solution to the problem of uncontrollable expenditures. One obstacle is the nature of entitlements. In order to ensure that payments to individuals are equitable, Congress has defined, by formula in statutes, the rights to such payments. Anyone qualifying has a legal right to be paid. Congress is unwilling to leave to the discretion of administrators the decision as to who gets which benefits. Another obstacle is that certain beneficiaries of popular entitlement programs have political clout, as several presidents discovered when they proposed cuts in social security payments.

Given these obstacles, how was President Reagan able to win such striking victories in the early months of his administration? Specifically, why were his proposals to cut social programs and to increase defense spending accepted by Congress? Simply put, the elections of 1980 provided the political backdrop for this major reversal in the fiscal priorities of the preceding two decades. Perhaps just as important as Reagan's presidential victories was the Republican capture of the Senate, which was fully supportive of Reagan's early initiatives. The Democrats lost seats in the House, and many felt that the mood of the electorate gave them little leeway in which to oppose the president's budget proposals. There was no major organized opposition to the Reagan proposals, and conservative Democrats joined with Republicans in the House to support many of the budget cuts.

Furthermore, the 1974 Budget Act provided a tool with which Congress could consolidate all of the budget cuts into one package. This "reconciliation process" allowed the budget committees to set ceilings in budget categories and to instruct other committees to make whatever cuts were necessary to come in under the ceilings. Effective opposition to individual program cuts was thus quite difficult.

The combination of electoral victories in the presidency and the Senate, favorable public opinion, pressure from the economy, and a skillful and coordinated administration strategy gave President Reagan the momentum he needed to achieve budget cuts that would have been considered impossible before his election. Victories in early battles, however, did not ensure final victory for the whole economic program: By mid-1982, his program was already under heavy attack.

State Governments: Caught in the Middle

Although in the 1970s state governments were in generally good fiscal shape, with many of them accumulating surpluses, governors and state legislatures were nonetheless subject to fiscal constraints from above and below. As aid from the federal government increased, so did the strings attached to the aid and the necessity to match those grants with state dollars. Furthermore, demands for more help from fiscally strapped local governments grew louder, and states responded by allotting more aid to local governments.

Looking over the past several decades, we find that states have greatly stepped up their fiscal activity. State spending increased from $8.9 billion in 1949 to an estimated $150 billion in 1980.[11] This rise in spending was made possible by the two main sources of state revenues: the personal income tax and the sales tax. In 1950 twenty-nine states levied a general sales tax and thirty-one states levied a personal income tax. By 1979 the numbers were forty-five and forty-one, respectively, and the number of states with both taxes was thirty-seven.[12]

The sales tax, which provided about 30 percent of state revenues in 1978, and the income tax, which provided about 26 percent, are relatively elastic.[13] That is, as economic activity increases, revenues from these taxes grow automatically, in the absence of any policy decision to increase tax rates. Thus, the great increase in state tax revenues in the 1970s was due primarily to economic growth and inflation. In addition to the sales and income taxes, federal grants have provided a growing share of state revenues. In 1948 the amount of federal aid was equivalent to 21.9 percent of the general revenues that states had raised from their own sources. By 1964 this figure had increased to 33.5 percent, and by 1977, to 38 percent.[14] Thus, even though states were spending more, they were also depending upon the federal government for more of their money.

Much of that federal money, however, was made available on the condition that the states match the federal money with a certain ratio of state money. Moreover, many federal grants require a maintenance of effort by the state. In California, for instance, $2.4 billion of the $7.9 billion in grants received from the federal government contained maintenance-of-effort requirements.[15] These requirements provide that if a state receives federal funds for a certain purpose, it cannot reduce its own spending for that purpose—a provision that is meant to prevent the state from substituting federal funds for its own. If there is any drop at all in state spending, the entire amount of federal aid will be cut. Thus, any attempt to reduce spending across the board could jeopardize receipt of these federal funds.

The federal government has also provided fiscal aid with relatively few strings attached to the states. The General Revenue Sharing (GRS) program enacted in 1972 and renewed in 1976 was intended to give states and local governments the leeway to spend the money according to their own priorities. In 1979 state governments received $2.3 billion, whereas local governments received $6.9 billion in GRS funds.

The states' share of revenue sharing became an issue when GRS legislation came up for renewal in 1980. State governments were enjoying budget surpluses, were cutting taxes, and were in generally good fiscal shape. At the same time, thirty state legislatures had called for a constitutional amendment requiring the federal government to balance its budget. Many members of Congress felt that one good place to start cutting spending was in the states' share of revenue sharing. Their proposals were temporarily defeated in 1979, however, because of strong lobbying from governors and mayors who pointed out that up to 40 percent of the states' share of GRS funds was being passed on to local governments.

In 1980 GRS was reauthorized for fiscal years 1981 to 1983. The states' share was dropped for fiscal year 1981 but authorized at $2.3 billion for fiscal years 1982 and 1983, on the condition that Congress appropriate the money. The catch was that states had to give up an equal dollar amount of categorical funds for any GRS funds that Congress appropriated for them. As a consequence, GRS funds would have few strings attached but would be "substitute" rather than "add-on" money. The reauthorization provided a mandatory entitlement of $4.6 billion annually for local governments for fiscal years 1981 to 1983. Inflation, however, cut the spending power of the money to about two-thirds of what it had been when GRS was first enacted.

Many states must allocate their own funds to legally mandated purposes, such as education, local tax relief, and welfare programs, that may be automatically indexed to the cost of living. There are also "earmarked" taxes—those that must be spent on a specific function rather than going to the general fund, from which most expenditures are made. For instance, the state of California has 260 categories of earmarked funds. The most significant of these is motor vehicle taxes, which amounted to over $800 million in 1979 and which must be spent for transportation. In 1979 total earmarked funds in California amounted to $3.1 billion.[16] As is the case with federal officials, state policymakers have discretion over a decreasing proportion of their budgets.

State funds have also increasingly gone to local governments: State aid to local governments was $5.7 billion in 1954, rising to an estimated $71.5 billion in 1979.[17] The increase in state expenditures, therefore, did not indicate an increase in discretion. Deil S. Wright has calculated that of the $45 billion in increased revenues collected by the states from 1958 to 1972, less than 25 percent was free to be used at state policymakers' discretion; the rest was used to satisfy the priorities of other levels of government.[18] Of course, state governments could reject the "free money" from federal grants or refuse to increase aid to local governments, but political pressures against doing so were generally overwhelming.

In the late 1970s, although many states were accumulating surpluses, the federal government was going further into debt and local governments were feeling severe fiscal stress. This trend was due in part to the elasticity of state revenue sources. As mentioned earlier, most states have adopted *both* a sales tax and an income tax. So long as the economy was growing and inflation was continuing state coffers continued to fill. In addition, most states have split their capital budgets from operating budgets. Thus, the money borrowed for capital construction by selling bonds does not show up on their books as an operating deficit (as it does in the case of the federal government), for which reason state year-end reserves in the late 1970s averaged above 8 percent.

In the context of the states' strong fiscal position, the tax revolt had an important impact. Eighteen states enacted spending or tax limitations between 1977 and 1980; twenty-two cut sales taxes; thirty-six cut income taxes; and nine states indexed their tax systems.[19] At the beginning of the 1980s, however, the states had to face the consequences of their tax cuts along with a slowed U.S. economy. In 1980 eighteen states were forced to raise taxes, and year-end balances had dropped to an estimated 3 percent by 1981. The combination of the tax revolt, a slowed U.S. economy, and the proposed Reagan Administration cutbacks in federal aid left all but a few energy-rich states in vulnerable fiscal positions.

The Reagan budget proposals called for consolidating many of the more than 500 categorical grant programs into several major block grants with few strings attached. In contrast to the many federal programs that funneled money directly to local governments, the block grants would go to state governments to be allotted at their discretion. This type of flexibility had long been advocated by governors. However, the states were not as enthusiastic about Reagan's proposal to cut overall federal aid by 25 percent. They felt that some services would have to be cut and that a strengthening of state bureaucracies might be required in order to implement programs previously administered at the federal level.

Although local governments had complained about the many strings attached to categorical grants, they were reluctant to permit federal aid (which had been going directly to the local governments) to be allocated to state governments for distribution at their own discretion. Large urban areas, in particular, felt that the priorities of state legislatures were unlikely to reflect adequately the needs of the urban poor. Furthermore, if federal aid were shifted from direct grants for local governments to block grants for states to pass through, states could attach strings of their own.

Local Governments and the Fiscal Crisis

The budgets of the federal government have been growing increasingly rigid, but local governments have fared even worse. Faced with continuing demands for increased quality and quantity of services, local governments have had to switch from heavy dependence on the overworked property tax to increasing dependence on state and federal financing.

The property tax, at one time the main source of revenue for local governments in the United States, has supplied an ever-decreasing proportion of such revenue through the years. In 1927, 73.9 percent of local revenues was provided by the property tax.[20] In 1942 the proportion was slightly over 60 percent, and in 1977 the proportion was 34 percent.[21] Yet, although the property tax pays for a much smaller portion of local expenditures, it is still the main tax source for local governments: In 1978 the property tax provided about 80 percent of all local tax collections.[22]

Given that local government spending has increased greatly (to 8.6 percent of the gross national product [GNP] in 1978)[23] and that the property tax is providing a smaller (34 percent) portion of the funds, where is the money coming from? Part of it is coming from charges, fees, and other taxes (a few cities have sales or income taxes). But most of the money is coming from the federal government and state governments. In 1948 the amount of federal and state aid was equivalent to 44 percent of locally raised revenues; by 1978 the figure had increased to 77 percent.[24] Thus, local governments are now heavily dependent on other governments for operating expenses, and many policy areas that were traditionally handled by local governments are now heavily subsidized by the federal government.

With this increasing involvement comes increasing federal control in the form of strings attached—that is, requirements, or mandates, with which the local government must comply. One of the problematic effects of these mandates is their high cost, most of which must be paid by the local government affected. Mandates represent a forced expenditure for local governments, which diminishes their own control over their jurisdictions. In order to comply with mandates, local governments must reallocate existing internal resources or raise the overall tax burden in order to meet the cost.[25]

There are now a great number of legal mandates that necessitate local spending. For example, New York City must comply with forty-seven state and federal mandates, the cost of which amounts to $6.25 billion in expenses and $711 million in capital expenditures. One example of a costly mandate is Section 504 of the Rehabilitation Act of 1973. The regulations implementing this law require total accessibility of transit systems to handicapped persons, which involved physical alterations to the New York City subway system costing $1.3 billion. Mayor Koch argued that it would be cheaper to provide taxi service for every severely handicapped person.[26]

Mandates are not the only form of federal involvement, however. The lure of federal money requiring matching expenditures is often too great for local officials to resist. Aside from necessitating the expenditure of funds, these matching requirements have the effect of displacing local priorities in favor of national ones.[27] They also have the stimulative effect of taking local governments into new-found areas of service or of expanding existing services.[28] Thus, new or expanded constituencies for these services are often created at the local level, making it difficult to scale down or terminate the services once they have been established.

The Tax Revolt

The United States is the land of tax revolts, yet it spends a smaller proportion of its GNP through its governments than do most other industrialized nations. Public sector spending peaked at about 35 percent of the GNP in 1975 and has declined since then. U.S. spending for social security insurance places it in the lowest quarter of the nineteen most affluent democracies in terms of spending for social services. Total U.S. tax collections as a percentage of the GNP are lower than those in Denmark, Sweden, West Germany, France, the United Kingdom, and Italy.[29] Despite these comparisons, however, many taxpayers feel that the tax burden in the United States is much too heavy.

The political culture and values of the United States have always reflected a distrust of governmental power, along with the strong feeling that as much economic activity as possible should be relegated to the private sector. These values have been manifested from time to time in political hostility toward governmental taxes, a tradition that includes the Boston Tea Party in 1773, Shay's Rebellion in 1786–1787, and the Whiskey Rebellion of 1794. Many states have limited the property tax, which was subsequently left to local governments.[30]

The most recent tax revolt began in the mid-1970s. One of its first major accomplishments, Proposition 13, was preceded by significant shifts in public opinion regarding governmental institutions in general and taxes in particular. Since the 1960s, public trust in U.S. institutions had been falling. The Vietnam War, Watergate, instances of corruption in Congress, the resignation of Vice President Agnew, and unpopular decisions by the Supreme Court—in addition to the economic squeeze of inflation and unemployment—all contributed to this distrust. The percentage of people who trusted the government to do right always or most of the time dropped from 77 percent in 1964 to 34 percent in 1976.[31] Those who thought the federal government wastes a lot of money rose from 48 percent in 1964 to 80 percent in 1978.[32] In 1961, 47 percent thought that the income tax was "too high"; by 1978 the proportion had increased to 70 percent.[33] Many people thought government was too big, and 52 percent thought property taxes could be cut by 20 percent without a serious reduction in local government services.[34]

The tax revolt may also reflect a public disenchantment with the growth of government spending in the United States, which increased an average of 9 percent a year from 1929 to 1979.[35] Federal government spending grew most rapidly from 1929 to 1949, after which the growth of state and local government spending exceeded that of the federal level. The rate of public employment was also on the increase. State and local employment have shown the greatest increases, tripling between 1949 and 1979. Federal employment, however, has not increased since 1969: Federal government employees, as a percentage of all employees, have decreased in number since the early 1960s.[36]

Although these data do show that government spending and employment have been increasing, other factors are undoubtedly affecting public attitudes about government. Frustration with inflation and governmental regulations is one important factor. However, although voters cannot vote against inflation or regulation, they are increasingly being given the opportunity to vote against taxes.

Although certain tax limitation devices were enacted in the 1970s, the tax revolt was really ignited by Proposition 13, which was passed in June of 1978. In November of that year, just six months later, there were a total of twenty-three taxing and spending limitation proposals on the ballots in eighteen states. The voters in thirteen states approved one or more of those measures.[37] In 1979 one-half of all states had fiscal limitation laws; sixteen of these states had adopted such laws since 1975.[38]

Types of Fiscal Limitations

Fiscal limitations have taken a variety of specific forms, but they can be broadly classified into (1) limits on taxes, (2) limits on spending, and (3) changes in the fiscal policymaking process.[39]

California's Proposition 13 approach is one way to limit the property tax. It rolled back property assessments to the 1975–1976 market value and limited tax rates to 1 percent of that value. Assessments can increase only 2 percent per year; in the case of change of ownership, assessment can reflect full market value. Other property tax limits have also been popular. Between 1970 and 1977, fourteen states imposed some type of property tax restraint on local governments, and since the passage of Proposition 13 in 1978, at least fourteen other states have done the same.[40] In 1980 Massachusetts voters limited property taxes to 2½ percent of property values (from a state-wide average of 3.4 percent). The measure reduced property taxes by 75 percent in Boston and 30 to 40 percent in many other areas.[41]

"Circuitbreakers" and "indexing" are two other important ways of limiting taxes. Circuitbreakers go into effect when the property tax amounts to a certain percentage of a taxpayer's income. In 1979 twenty-nine states included circuitbreaker protection in their laws.[42]

Whereas circuitbreakers mitigate the effects of the property tax, indexing is a response to the effects of inflation on tax obligations. Inflation-induced salary increases push taxpayers into higher tax brackets, such that a greater percentage of their salaries is taken in taxes. Thus, although the taxpayers are paying more in taxes, they are not improving their financial positions in real terms. Moreover, although this feature of the income tax has allowed federal and state revenues to grow without increasing tax *rates*, it has put taxpayers in a difficult squeeze with the recent high inflation rates. Several states have responded by enacting full or partial indexing measures that require yearly adjustments of tax brackets according to rises in the consumer price index (CPI). In 1978 Arizona, Colorado, and California indexed their income taxes; in 1979 Wisconsin, Iowa, and Minnesota did also.[43] By 1981 nine states had indexed their tax systems, and indexing had been proposed at the national level.

In addition to curtailing taxes, fiscal limitations can be implemented by restricting expenditures—that is, by requiring that spending be limited by the increase in some economic indicator or specified rate. For instance, the Gann initiative (Proposition 4) required that California state and local spending not increase beyond a percentage determined by a combination of population increase and the CPI. Before Proposition 13 was passed, four states had limits on state spending. In the following two years, at least eight more states adopted such limits.[44]

Another major type of spending limitation—a more democratic type, perhaps—may prove to have more far-reaching implications than those of the direct taxing and spending limitations. Some states have chosen to change their fiscal policymaking processes in such a way as to make the enactment of taxing or spending measures more difficult. One change has been to remove from elected officials the authority to make certain fiscal decisions. For instance, Proposition 13 forbids local governments to raise taxes or to create new ones without the approval of two-thirds of the qualified electors. New Jersey requires a referendum before local government spending increases can exceed 5 percent.

Another approach is to require a two-thirds majority vote of elected officials in order to raise taxes. Proposition 13 requires this of the California legislature. A different change in procedures is Florida's full disclosure law, which requires extensive publicity and public notice before a local governing council can raise more in property taxes than had been raised in the previous year.[45]

A Rand Corporation study discerned three major trends in taxing and spending limitations, ultimately concluding that these trends are moving in a more restrictive di.ection. The first trend concerns limits on property taxes (the most common type of limit), which are changing from merely limiting the tax rate to limiting total tax revenues. By 1979 twenty-four states had limited revenues; twenty of these had enacted the restrictions in the 1970s.[46]

The second trend is the imposition of fiscal controls on state governments rather than on local governments. Nine states imposed such controls between 1976 and 1979, including limits on revenues and expenditures and indexing of the income tax.[47] Finally, the limits being imposed across the nation are becoming more. rigid, because recent limits are often embedded in constitutions rather than enacted by statute. Of the eight fiscal limitations approved in November of 1978, seven were constitutional limits.[48] Futhermore, since the passage of Proposition 13, there has been an increase in the number of limitations initiated by groups of citizens rather than by legislatures.[49]

The California Experience

Why were the conditions for the overwhelming passage of Proposition 13 ripe in 1978 and not at some other time? In both 1968 and 1972, California residents had the chance to vote for similar property tax limitations, yet they rejected those initiatives. Then-Governor Reagan supported a proposal in 1973 that would have held state taxing and spending rates to a certain proportion of personal income, but the proposal lost. What happened differently in 1978?

First of all, the economic factors discussed earlier had been affecting California as well as the rest of the country. Federal, state, and local spending had been increasing; governments were becoming involved in more aspects of people's lives; citizen trust in U.S. institutions was eroding; people thought government was wasteful and spent too much money; and the property tax was seen as the "worst tax." In addition to these general causes, however, there were factors unique to, or particularly bad in, California that paved the way for the passage of Proposition 13.

Although tax collections had been rising throughout the nation, the rate of increase in California was even higher. The combination of increasing taxes and a high rate of inflation was reducing people's purchasing power, despite the fact that total personal income was also rising.

Real estate values in California were undergoing a tremendous boom, particularly in certain highly desirable geographical markets. Property values had been increasing by more than 20 percent per year, with increases in some areas almost 40 percent. The property tax burden per capita increased by 42 percent between 1972 and 1977.[50] In many cases, property tax bills had risen by two or even three times between 1975 and 1978. Although total personal income was also rising, those on fixed incomes were extremely hard hit, and certain people had to pay lump sum tax bills twice as large as those of the previous year.

The irony, here, is that the property tax traditionally has been less elastic than other taxes and has not increased as quickly as economic conditions or the cost of local government. This contrast is generally due to the lag between rises in economic activity and rises in property values, as well as to the administrative lag in property assessment.

These factors, however, did not hold true in California during the mid-1970s. The booming real estate market resulted in drastically increased property values, and assessment practices in California were particularly efficient. The State Board of Equalization held local tax assessors strictly accountable for keeping property tax rolls up to date. Although many states have been criticized for unprofessional assessment practices, California assessors kept property assessments generally up to date and accurately reflecting current market values. As a result, local governments received increasing revenues each year without having to make politically unpopular decisions to raise tax rates. They could even reduce rates and receive more revenues.

These details were not ignored by those taxpayers who had put much political pressure on the legislature to relieve the growing tax burden. Governor Jerry Brown and the state legislature, however, were never able to agree on a tax relief measure, and thus the way was left open for citizens to take matters into their own hands.

Proposition 13. Enter Howard Jarvis and Paul Gann, an unlikely pair of elderly populists. Railing against dishonest politicians, bloated budgets, bureaucratic waste, and big government, they gathered over 1,250,000 signatures (500,000 were needed) to put Proposition 13 on the ballot. There were dire predictions from their opponents that thousands of workers would be laid off and essential services drastically cut. But the voters were unconvinced by such predictions. A majority of voters felt that local governments were inefficient, and 38 percent believed that the same level of state and local services could be provided even if funds were cut back by 40 percent.[51]

Predictions of disaster met with skepticism for the additional reason that California had a surplus of from $3 billion to $4 billion. State officials could not seem to agree on just how large the surplus was. (Later, the figure was determined to be $3.8 billion.) Even though the property tax was levied locally, people may have foreseen that the political pressure for a state bailout of local governments would be overwhelming.

On June 6, 1978, voters in the same state that had rejected tax cut proposals in 1968, 1972, and 1973 amended the California constitution by adopting Proposition 13, 65 percent to 35 percent. Voting turnout, about 65 percent of the registered voters and 43 percent of eligible adults, was at the highest rate in a state-wide primary since 1958.

The constitutional amendment enacted by the voters in 1978 reduced the property tax rate to 1 percent (from a state average of 2.7 percent) of the full market value in 1975–1976, with the exception of rates necessary to pay off previous bonded indebtedness. In addition, the 1975–1976 assessed value was not allowed to rise any higher than 2 percent per year, unless the property changed hands—in which case it could be reassessed to reflect its full current market value. In addition, the measure prevented local governments from imposing new taxes or increasing existing ones without the approval of two-thirds of the qualified electors, also preventing the state government from levying a new tax unless two-thirds of each house of the legislature voted for it.

The cut in the property tax rate amounted to $7 billion, which constituted 57 percent of all property taxes or 20 percent of all local revenues. Because different types of local governments in California depended on the property tax to varying degrees, the impact on their revenues was different. School districts were hardest hit, losing $3.5 billion or 23 percent of total revenues, and cities lost $8 billion, amounting to 15 percent of their revenues.

At first glance it would appear that California homeowners were the main beneficiaries of the tax savings from Proposition 13, but a closer examination of the incidence of tax savings yields some unexpected results. About 33 percent of the initial tax relief went to owners of homes who actually lived in them. About 58 percent went to owners of rental, commercial, industrial, and agricultural properties. About 9 percent were savings to the state due to reduced tax relief to localities. Thus, contrary to popular opinion, California home owners did not receive most of the tax relief from Proposition 13.[52]

Further analysis reveals that they did not even get the full initial 33 percent. In fact, the federal government received $2.2 billion of the total $7 billion tax cut. Because property taxes are deductible from federal and state income taxes, Californians had to pay more in federal taxes ($2.2 billion) and state income taxes ($.4 billion).[53]

The requirements of Proposition 13 will also probably cause the incidence of property taxes to shift gradually from business to residential property. The reason for this is that any property that changes hands is reassessed at its full market value, and since homes are sold more often than businesses, a greater portion of the property tax will be paid by owners of residences. The Orange County Tax Collector-Treasurer reported that in 1977–1978, 57 percent of the property tax was paid by businesses and 43 percent by residential owners. In 1978–1979, after the passage of Proposition 13, the proportions were reversed (i.e., to 43 percent and 57 percent), and the gap continued to widen.[54]

Given the $6 to $7 billion loss in revenues to local governments in California, significant cutbacks might have been expected, even if the opponents of Proposition 13 had been exaggerating. But this eventuality ran up against political reality. The governor and legislature, sitting on a huge surplus of state funds, were not going to cut their political throats by letting local governments bear the full brunt of the tax cut. On June 23, 1978, the legislature passed Senate Bill 54, which allocated $4.2 billion of the state surplus to replace revenues lost by local governments. Most of the lost revenues were thus restored by the state bailout.

Proposition 4. When the predicted terrible effects of Proposition 13 failed to materialize because of the state bailout, California voters were in no mood to pull back on their incipient tax revolt. Proposition 4, the "Gann Plan," was their next chance to express themselves on the topic. Although then-Governor Reagan's spending limitation initiative had been defeated in 1973, Paul Gann's Proposition 4 was strongly endorsed by California voters in November of 1979. Both measures were designed to limit spending by California governments. Although Reagan's Proposition 1 had provoked acrimonious debate in the state, Gann's Proposition 4 passed without significant opposition.

Whereas Proposition 13 had placed a limit on tax collections, Proposition 4 limited *spending* by California governments at all levels— cities, counties, special districts, and state.[55] Article XIII B of the California Constitution now limits the rate of growth of governmental appropriations to the percentage increase of population and of the CPI (or growth of personal income in California, if it is lower). The limit is fairly inflexible. Voters can increase the limit, but not for more than four years at a time. In the case of an emergency, the limit may be exceeded for one year, but the limits for the following three years would have to be reduced to make up for the excess spending. If revenues of a government for a fiscal year exceed appropriations, the excess has to be returned to taxpayers by lowering rates for the next two years.

Opponents of Proposition 4 pointed out several of its possible negative consequences. The spending limit formula might, for instance, act as a deterrent to economic development not tied to increased population. That is, if a city were to build a new shopping complex, it would also incur certain costs for services such as construction of sewers and roads, police protection, traffic control, and so on. But the city would not be able to increase spending to cover these added costs unless its population also increased. Similarly, cities that depend on tourist, convention, or commuter business would have no incentive to increase business activity, because they could not increase expenditures to handle the rising demand on city services. Any additional revenues from the activities generated by the sales tax would have to be used for property tax relief.

Proposition 9. The third major tax revolt measure on the California ballot in two years did not fare as well as Propositions 13 and 4. Proposition 9 ("Jarvis II" or "Jaws II" to its opponents), which called for halving the California state income tax, was decisively defeated in June of 1980. Estimates by official sources concerning the probable revenue loss ranged from $4.9 to $5.1 billion. The entire loss would have come from the general fund budget. Approximately 20 percent ($4.6 billion) of the 1978–1979 state budget was spent on traditional state expenditures such as higher education, the legislature, the governor's office, prisons, mental hospitals, and so forth. The other 80 percent ($14.7 billion) was spent at local government levels for such purposes as education, property tax relief, and health and welfare services. This latter figure included $4.8 billion in bailout funds provided in the wake of Proposition 13. Thus, the revenue loss from Proposition 9 would have been larger than the cost of the state functions funded by the general fund in 1978–1979.[56]

How can the defeat of Proposition 9 be explained, given the overwhelming victories of Propositions 13 and 4, as well as the sizable sums spent on the campaign by its proponents? Seymour Martin Lipset and William Schneider argue that the defeat of Proposition 9 did not signal the end of the tax revolt so much as prompt the voters' realization that futher cuts in tax revenues in California would directly lead to reductions in services or to other taxes being raised. According to public opinion polls, many people who voted for Proposition 13 but against Proposition 9 believed they were right in voting for Proposition 13.[57] Such voters may have felt that, even though there was still significant waste in government spending, further cuts in taxes would not eliminate the waste.

Even with the defeat of Proposition 9, California was not in a strong budgetary position in 1981. Its 1980–1981 budget proposal showed a deficit of $1.7 billion, which had to be funded by the state surplus. In 1982, California began feeling the full effects of the tax revolt—for, by that time, the state's surplus had been spent.

In the debate over the 1981–1982 budget, however, many legislators seemed unable to acknowledge that the state's fiscal profile had been fundamentally changed by the tax revolt. As State Finance Director Mary Ann Graves noted, "What we still haven't faced is the fact that while we now stand about midpoint in terms of taxes collected, we are still spending as if we were leading the nation. We have to face up to the fact that we can no longer support the kind of government services we are used to."[58] Thus, even though California is one of the richest states in the country, the combined impact of the fallout from Proposition 13 and the cuts in aid to the states proposed by President Reagan left it in a difficult financial situation at the beginning of the 1980s. In fact, when Governor Deukmejian took office in January of 1983, halfway through fiscal year 1982–1983, the state faced a $1-2 billion deficit.

Balancing the Budget

At the same time that state and local governments were bearing the brunt of the tax revolt, momentum was gathering for spending reductions and cutbacks at the national level. One of the most significant aspects of the national tax revolt was the campaign to adopt an amendment to the U.S. Constitution requiring the federal government to balance its budget each year.

The Proposed Constitutional Amendment. In the late 1970s, public opinion polls indicated that 70 to 80 percent of the U.S. public favored a "budget-balancing" amendment to the U.S. Constitution. In 1981 thirty of the thirty-four necessary state legislatures had passed resolutions calling for a constitutional convention to formulate the amendment. The idea of requiring a balanced budget has intuitive appeal, but there are serious drawbacks to this method of cutting government taxes or spending.

Most ordinary citizens feel the need to balance their checkbooks every month and think that the federal government should do likewise. But this seemingly common sense notion overlooks some crucial facts. Most middle-class people spend more than they earn: Homeowners often have mortgages, and credit card use is widespread. Businesses routinely borrow money to expand or modernize. In effect, only the poor really have to balance their budgets in the short run because they cannot obtain credit. The crucial consideration is the ability to repay, which depends on income, cash flow, and earning capacity. This is not to argue that borrowing is always wise, but, rather, that the decision to borrow should depend on economic circumstances. The ability of the United States to repay its debts depends on the productivity of the U.S. economy and the ability of the government to raise taxes.

Some people are alarmed at the accumulated deficits—that is, the national debt—which passed $1 trillion in 1981. This is truly a staggering sum, but it must be put into perspective. At the same time as the national debt has been increasing, the economy has been growing at a faster rate. In 1951 the national debt was 79 percent of the GNP, but by 1976 it had fallen to 37 percent. In addition, private debt has increased to a level over four times as large as the public debt. By 1980 the high level of debt and low level of investment had become major problems in an inflationary economy. But it must be noted that the federal government was not exclusively to blame: In 1978 the federal debt was only 19 percent of total debt.[59] Business, household, and state and local borrowing accounted for the rest.

Whereas proponents of the balanced budget amendment argue that deficit spending is necessarily inflationary, others claim that whether or not deficit spending is inflationary depends on the economic circumstances in which it is undertaken. Most economists agree that there is no necessary link between deficit spending and inflation, the latter having many economic causes.[60] Deficit spending *may* be inflationary, however, under certain economic conditions. The Johnson Administration's policy of "guns and butter" in the late 1960s is generally considered to have been inflationary. On balance, then, whether deficit spending is inflationary or not depends on the state of the economy. If the economy is running at or near full employment, the link is likely. If, however, there is low demand and resources are slack in the private sector, deficit spending may increase demand and boost a lagging economy out of a recession.

The latter possibility leads us to the strongest argument of all against a rigid balanced budget requirement. Such a requirement would deprive the United States of one of the only weapons available to fight a recession that might spiral down into a depression. If the budget had to be balanced in the face of a recession, little could be done to short-circuit the downward spiral of fewer revenues, thus leading to less spending, which in turn leads to reduced demand in the economy. If taxes were raised to balance the budget, private sector demand would be decreased further. Reduced federal spending may be a laudable goal, but the balanced budget amendment is a dangerous and uncertain way to achieve that goal. As Senator Muskie put it, "We don't need fiscal handcuffs to wipe the deficit out. We need fiscal discipline. If we have that will, no formula is necessary. If we don't, no formula will work!"[61]

The Elusive Balanced Budget. Presidents and Congresses have been chasing the elusive balanced budget for most of the twentieth century.[62] The federal budget has been in surplus only seven times since 1930, and the national debt passed $1 trillion in 1981.[63] President Carter promised to balance the budget in his fourth year in office, and in June of 1980 Congress passed a first concurrent resolution that showed a surplus for fiscal year 1981. It soon became obvious, however, that the assumptions underlying this resolution were unrealistic: The final deficit was $58 billion. The culprit was not the initiation of new programs but a poorly performing economy. The combination of historically high inflation, high unemployment, and high interest rates combined to defeat the best efforts of Congress and the president to balance the budget.

Although President Reagan campaigned for the presidency on a platform of drastically reduced federal spending, his budget for fiscal year 1982 projected a deficit of $45 billion due to large increases in defense spending and a large tax cut. Nevertheless, he also promised a balanced budget by 1984: A large tax cut was intended to spur the economy sufficiently to increase tax revenues and produce a balanced budget by 1984. However, the Congressional Budget Office, among others, was skeptical about the optimistic assumptions built into the Reagan scenario for 1984. It argued that the proposed tax cuts would not boost the economy as much as the Reagan Administration's "supply-side" economists predicted and that inflation would be higher and tax receipts lower than the Reagan projections.

A deepening recession in 1981 and 1982 made balancing the budget by 1984 impossible. The actual deficit for fiscal year 1982 turned out to be over $110 billion. Nevertheless, when the Senate passed a resolution proposing a constitutional amendment to require an annual balanced budget, President Reagan endorsed it while presiding over the largest deficit in U.S. history.

Thus far we have examined the dynamics of fiscal stress in federal, state, and local governments in the United States. Budgets at all three levels are becoming more difficult to control. An increasing portion of the federal budget is committed to be spent unless basic laws and entitlements are changed. Increasing portions of state budgets are committed to be spent because of mandates from the federal government, state laws earmarking funds for certain purposes, and demands from local governments for tax relief. At the local level, as the property tax has become increasingly strained, governments are becoming more dependent on states and the federal government.

Budgetary rigidity makes flexible responses to changes in economic circumstances more difficult. It also accentuates both the increasing interdependence that characterizes U.S. governments and the continuing centralization of power. As more money flows from higher levels of government, strings are inevitably attached to that money.

Although the taxing and spending limitations spawned by the tax revolt have reinforced the structural rigidities of government budgets, there is no reason to believe that voters have changed their minds. Opinion surveys indicate the public belief that much "fat" exists in government organizations at all levels. The political campaigns for Proposition 13, the balanced budget amendment, and the presidential campaign of 1980 have had a profound effect on governments in the United States. The final section of this chapter will examine the political and organizational consequences of the tax revolt and of fiscal stress in U.S. governments.

The Impact of Government Cutbacks

The revenue and budget constraints discussed earlier have serious implications for the distribution of power in the U.S. federal system and for the quality of public service in the United States. In this section I shall first consider how revenue reductions at the local government level may add to the trend toward increased centralization of political power and policy. Next, I shall examine the management implications of budgetary cutbacks, in addition to various strategies for personnel reductions. Finally, I shall discuss organizational morale. Although the morale factor is difficult to define, much less measure, it is real and can be ignored only at great risk to an organization.

Centralization

Catherine Lovell has argued that the increasing fiscal dependency of local governments, in combination with federal- and state-imposed mandates, is severely threatening the autonomy of local governments. In what she calls the "fiscal dependency syndrome," local governments have vastly expanded the amounts and proportions of funds received from states and the federal government. She concludes that "cities no longer depend on their own revenue sources to pay for locally delivered services."[64] The tax revolt has exacerbated this trend toward centralized control and away from local autonomy.

Because many of the taxing and spending limitations resulting from the tax revolt affect local governments, and because the fiscal squeeze is greatest at the local level, local governments have little choice but to pressure state governments for aid. Only with difficulty can state officials resist such potent political pressure. This was evident in the willingness of Governor Brown and the California state legislature to use the state surplus to bail out local governments after the passage of Proposition 13, despite early statements that they would not do so.

State aid, however, often diminishes home rule and increases the centralization of control at higher levels of government, for there is a tendency for those who control financing to try also to control policy.[65] Money without strings attached is rare. Spending priorities are eventually decided in state rather than in local political arenas. The debate over California's bailout of its local governments took place in the state legislature, where state-wide interest groups attempted to influence outcomes. Since the interests of any particular local community may not coincide with the interests of the major participants in state legislative battles, control of local decisions is further removed from the individual citizen.

The trend toward more centralized control in policymaking is in part a result of increasing interdependence in our modern industrialized society. Broader coordination is necessary, and the consequences of systems failure are more disruptive. The administrative costs of taxation also contribute to this trend. The sales and income taxes are more efficiently administered by higher levels of government, and the economic distortions are fewer. Thus, the centralizing effects of the tax revolt are not a reversal but rather an extension of broader historical trends. It is ironic that most proponents of taxing and spending limitations would favor decentralization of governmental power, yet the diminishing ability of local officials to raise revenues leads them to seek more funds from higher levels of government and often to accept more centralized control.

Organizational Effectiveness

The avowed purpose of the tax revolt is to "cut the fat" out of government. Undoubtedly, there is slack or "fat" in large governmental agencies, just as there is slack in all large organizations, public or private.[66] The means advocated to cut that fat in governments involves the limiting of taxes and spending. But will this method achieve the desired ends? The answer is problematic.

In deciding the best way to implement these cutbacks, we must consider several factors. First, the choice must be made between across-the-board cuts and selective cuts. If the cuts are deep enough to necessitate personnel reductions, the choice becomes one between natural attrition and the laying off of employees. Both of these dilemmas and some of the tradeoffs involved in the available choices will subsequently be examined.

"Meat-Ax" versus Selective Cuts. Budgets can be reduced by "meat-ax" or across-the-board decreases in spending. But these reductions will apply to fat and lean alike. The surgeon's scalpel of good management, rather, is the appropriate and effective way to reduce programs where fat exists. Good management can, and ought to, determine which organizational units and programs can be cut with the least impact on the overall organizational mission. A good manager will know which units are superfluous. The elimination of whole units may be more rational than cutting both the essential and the less essential by equal percentages. In fact, with an across-the-board cut, the most efficient unit will be hurt most. Because, by definition, the most efficient unit has the least slack or fat, equal cuts will affect the efficient missions more significantly than those with much fat that can be pared with little effect.[67]

Fundamentally, any large organization is only as good as its managers. Management techniques and systems may help rationalize or routinize decisionmaking, but control systems can be carried only so far in most governmental systems. At some point, centralized control becomes inappropriate because local circumstances are not always adequately covered by central rules. In such cases, managers must use judgment and vision in order to deal with the changing environments of their organizations.[68] Unfortunately, in a time of budget cuts, it is difficult to recruit effective managers given the problems involved in offering higher salaries, promotions, or larger programs as rewards for their effective budget cutting.[69]

Another problem with cutting the fat is that power in organizations is not necessarily clustered specifically around those functions that produce the organizational product or accomplish its mission. Certain organizations are often observed to be top-heavy with administrators and expensive staffs. When budgets are cut, it will be the most powerful employees, rather than the most essential ones, who will best be able to protect themselves. The only way to get around this problem and to overcome entrenched power centers is to have effective managers at the top who are willing to make tough decisions.

Further, most people can point to some function of an organization they consider to be wasteful. Elimination of function is accomplished not by cutting the organization's budget but by convincing the responsible manager that the function is indeed wasteful. But a more important consideration, perhaps, is that one person's fat is another's meat and bone. That is, differences in policy priorities and political values often underlie assertions about fat in government programs. Whether it be the granting of welfare-like subsidies for poor people or the issuing of revenue bonds that benefit certain businesses, the presence of such unwanted activities leads to the conviction that governments contain fat that could be easily eliminated. It may be impossible, therefore, for governments to satisfy the political demands of the tax revolt. Although most people want to lower taxes and government spending, there is no consensus on which government activities ought to be eliminated toward this end.

Personnel Reductions. Dealing with personnel administration is the major problem in cutback management, particularly in local governments, whose major expenses are payroll costs. Given budget cuts of sufficient size, reduction of the number of employees becomes inevitable. The short-run concern is how to limit hiring and lay off workers. The longer-range issues related to these policies are future recruitment and retention of skilled people; problems with collective bargaining and affirmative action; and loss of morale, which may lead to poor performance among workers.

The first step in budget reduction is often the imposition of a hiring freeze. If it is to be effective, this action must be taken with dispatch. If rumors of a freeze have begun to circulate, agencies may engage in "preemptive hiring"—that is, filling all open positions as quickly as possible in order not to be caught short-handed when the freeze takes effect. Preemptive hiring is the reason that President Reagan gave when, upon taking office, he imposed a hiring freeze and made it retroactive to his election. A hiring freeze may, however, increase the use of part-time employees and of contracting with outside organizations for needed services. In the first case, less skilled people may end up doing the job, and, in the second, services may be more expensive, especially at professional levels.

The use of natural attrition to reduce employees is the next step in personnel reduction. In this case, employees who voluntarily have left the organization are not replaced. The major problem here, however, is that vacancies seldom occur where management would choose. Thus, people whose skills are essential to the organization may leave, with workloads increasing for those who remain.

In times of organizational cutback, natural attrition is liable to be augmented by employees who quit. Organizations suffering cutbacks are not attractive places to work: Pay may be frozen, workloads may have increased, and uncertainty may reduce organizational morale. In such situations, the people who are most occupationally mobile will be the first to go. These are people who most likely have specialized skills in high demand. Such people may also have attractive options and thus might leave for better paying jobs in other governments or in the private sector.

Jack Stumpf and Paul Terrell, for example, found that after the passage of Proposition 13, attrition was abnormally high in California's local government health services. As a result of low salary levels, increasing caseloads, and lower organizational morale, the younger and better qualified employees were leaving public agencies. Doctors and nurses were leaving in record numbers, and there were problems retaining good managers, planners, and skilled clerical employees. Those whose skills were most in demand and most easily transferable to the private sector left first.[70] Peter J. May and Arnold J. Meltsner also found that persons with marketable skills such as high-level managers, skilled clerical employees, nurses, and doctors sought other opportunities and left behind those who were less employable and often less productive.[71] All large organizations are likely to have some "dead wood" or non-productive employees. When payrolls are cut by attrition rather than by management decisions, the dead wood is likely to remain.

Such attrition also results in an accentuation of the "Peter Principle," according to which organization employees are said to be promoted until they reach a position they cannot handle, where they tend to stay. When management positions are left vacant and, due to a hiring freeze, recruitment cannot be accomplished from outside the organization, the positions must be filled with persons already on board. However, inside candidates for these jobs may not have the appropriate skills and experience necessary for the positions in question, and the organization may be weakened by ineffective managers in key positions.

In the federal government, the procedure for laying people off for budgetary reasons is called a reduction in force (RIF). When an agency determines which units are to be eliminated or reduced and what types of positions have to be cut, it establishes a retention register that ranks employees according to their right to keep their jobs. The criteria for these lists include type of appointment (career or temporary) and length of service. Those low on the list and subject to being laid off may be able to "bump" other employees in the organization who have even fewer tenure qualifications.

Needless to say, RIFs can greatly disrupt an organization. Tremendous uncertainty is created as to how many people will be laid off and who will be bumped from one job into another. People become much more concerned with keeping their jobs than with carrying out the agency mission.

For these reasons, agencies will usually avoid RIFs if at all possible. One alternative to an RIF is forced placement, in which management forces those units with vacancies to accept employees from a section that is undergoing an RIF. The problem, here, is that the good workers subject to RIF are immediately snapped up by alert managers, leaving the "turkeys." No manager wants to be forced to accept a turkey, especially in an important management position. One tactic for avoiding this outcome is to "hide" vacancies in the hope that top management will not discover the unfilled positions and require the acceptance of inadequate employees.

It can be argued that a forced placement system is less disruptive than an RIF, because an RIF may involve bumping three or four other people for each one position that is RIFed. Thus, the number of potentially disgruntled employees might be multiplied by a factor of three or four. Forced placement may alienate those managers required to accept less qualified personnel, but fewer employees are displaced overall.

The long-run consequences of cutbacks for organizations may well be negative. Bright young managers and professionals are less likely to be attracted to organizations in decline. If such people are not assured of a positive career path in one organization, they will search for another able to offer such assurance. Thus, one of the most unfortunate consequences of governmental cutbacks is the difficulty in recruiting tomorrow's managers. The most promising young people may choose to pursue other careers.

Personnel reductions in governmental agencies may be necessary because of budgetary cutbacks, but they are inevitably difficult to carry out and often entail many negative consequences for the organizations involved. Public managers must weigh all such factors when deciding how to cut back government organizations with the least damage to the public good.

Organizational Morale. Although difficult to measure, the effect of budget reductions on organizational morale can be significant. The effects of decreasing morale may not be precisely quantifiable, but they are real. Different units within the organization may begin to position themselves so that the burden of cutbacks will not fall on them. When the prospect of layoff occurs, workers may begin to see their co-workers not as partners but as rivals for scarce organizational resources. Disputes from the past may take on the added weight of uncertainty about the future. People may begin to fear the worst, interpreting innocent actions as tactical moves in the organizational struggle. Latent animosities may rise to the surface.

Simply put, morale is difficult to maintain in periods of decline. Organizations require leaders, people with vision who can give the workers a sense of direction and mission. But, unfortunately, leadership is more easily provided in a situation of growth than in one of decline. When there are new missions to accomplish and opportunities to make significant contributions, people are generally motivated to attain organizational goals. On the other hand, if an organization is retrenching, leadership is more difficult to come by. When budgets are being cut, increased workloads, personnel cutbacks, and low morale are likely. Given these factors, it is a fair question to ask whether good leadership can thrive in organizations that are cutting back.

Organizational goals and service to the client are almost certainly lost in the shuffle of such decline. Personnel and organizational survival take precedence over accomplishing the goal or task at hand. This is not to say that symptoms of "bureaupathology" do not exist in many organizations under normal circumstances, but that the self-interest syndrome is accentuated during times of cutback. Nor is it implied that organizations should not be cutting back. The point is that organizations bear real costs in cutting back—costs that must be considered when deciding how to implement such cuts.

The political demands of the tax revolt, therefore, may be impossible to satisfy. May and Meltsner have described a "vicious circle" that may characterize the dynamics of governments under fiscal pressure.[72] In their scenario, declining public confidence in government leads to the various manifestations of the tax revolt. Taxing and spending limitations lead to revenue gaps and situations in which governments must cut back on existing services and spend less overall. The organizational results of these cutbacks are often austerity measures, uncertainty, increased workloads, and a general decline in morale. Organizational morale problems and loss of key personnel can easily lead to reduced organizational effectiveness, which in turn leads to further decline in public confidence in governmental programs and to the desire to cut them back.

The potent political pressures of the tax revolt to cut government taxing and spending cannot be ignored. Yet, at the same time, the consequences of budget cutting must be seriously considered. Citizens must consciously decide which governmental services are to be cut, rather than permitting those in power to escape the burdens of cuts at the expense of politically weak, yet important, governmental functions. We must also guard against the negative personnel consequences of organizational cutbacks and drops in morale that may lead to deteriorating performance of organizational missions. The only way to accomplish these tasks is through good management and wise political leadership. Both of these commodities are in short supply, but if U.S. governments are to respond responsibly to citizen demands for governmental cutbacks, they are indeed essential.

Conclusion

The tax revolt has had a great impact as a result of the actions of elected officials and of the voters themselves. The consequences of these actions began to be felt in 1981. State fiscal revenues had dropped to low levels, eighteen states were forced to raise taxes, and voters began to reject tax cut measures that might have passed in the heyday of the tax revolt. California had used up its surplus and was compelled to come to terms with the fiscal effects of Proposition 13. Local governments in Massachusetts had proposed the laying off of thousands of workers to cope with Proposition 2½. The tax revolt was not dead, but it was injected with a new sense of reality. If taxes were seriously reduced, services would also have to be cut. Cutting taxes did not produce the free lunch for which voters had hoped.

The political implications of these budgetary changes provide American governments with possible pitfalls and potential opportunities. On the negative side, the new stress on fiscal conservativism could lead to increasingly rigid budgets. A rigid requirement to balance the federal budget could reinforce a downward economic spiral. The consequences of the tax revolt and of the Reagan cuts in federal aid might kill the concept of home rule for local governments and further centralize policymaking at the federal or state level. Cutting back governmental organizations could lead to declines in morale and, in turn, might produce the poor quality of public service that the tax revolt posited as characteristic of all American governments.

But the above negative outcomes are fortunately not foreordained. U.S. governments have the capacity to turn all of these trends in positive directions. The tax revolt marked a resurgence of citizen participation in the political process, particularly at the local level. This new activism can build on the lessons learned from the tax revolt experience and result in citizens much better informed about their governments.

The Reagan Administration budget cuts may bring a new sense of fiscal austerity and efficiency to public employees. If the truly needy are protected, the willingness to attack the uncontrollable expenditures in the federal budget may bring spending under control and cause Congress to be more careful about the future costs of proposed legislation. The block grant approach to fiscal federalism may foster a new independence in state and local governments, and the tax revolt may have scaled down citizen expectations about what governments can or ought to do.

Although budgetary procedures in U.S. governments are undoubtedly in a state of flux, some overall directions can be discerned. The political actions of citizens and governmental officials will ultimately determine whether these changes are opportunities or pitfalls.

Notes

1. *Will Rogers* (Claremore, Okla.: Will Rogers Co., 1969), p. 39.

2. Lester Thurow, *The Zero-Sum Society* (New York: Basic Books, 1980).

3. Anthony H. Pascal et al., *Fiscal Containment of Local and State Government* (Santa Monica, Calif.: The Rand Corporation, R02494-FF/RC, Sept. 1979), p. 7.

4. Jane Gilbert, "Federal Expenditures: The Impact on the Economy," paper presented at the American Political Science Association Convention, 1979.

5. Ibid., p. 3.

6. Ibid., pp. 20, 27, 29.

7. Ibid., p. 20.

8. Ibid., p. 12.

9. Ibid., p. 5.

10. Timothy B. Clark, "How Do You Control the Budget When Benefit Programs Keep Growing?" *National Journal*, 16 August 1980, p. 1344.

11. U.S., Congress, Advisory Commission on Intergovernmental Relations (ACIR), *Significant Features of Fiscal Federalism, 1979–80* (Washington, D.C., October 1980), p. 4.

12. ACIR, *Significant Features of Fiscal Federalism, 1978–79* (Washington, D.C., May 1979), p. 51.

13. Ibid., p. 53.

14. Ibid., p. 79.

15. *Los Angeles Times*, 8 May 1980, part 1, p. 3.

16. *Los Angeles Times*, 17 January 1980, part 1, p. 3.

17. ACIR, *Fiscal Federalism 1978–79*, p. 169.

18. Deil S. Wright, *Understanding Intergovernmental Relations* (North Scituate, Mass.: Duxbury Press, 1978), p. 112.

19. *The Washington Post*, "State Governments Facing Financial Crunch," 10 May 1981, pp. 1, 6.

20. James A. Maxwell and J. Richard Aronson, *Financing State and Local Governments* (Washington, D.C.: Brookings, 1977), p. 136.

21. ACIR, *Fiscal Federalism 1979–80*, p. 76.

22. Ibid., p. 79.

23. Ibid., p. 6.

24. ACIR, *Fiscal Federalism 1978–79*, p. 79.

25. Catherine Lovell et al., *Federal and State Mandating on Local Governments: An Exploration of Issues and Impacts*, Final Report to the National Science Foundation (June 1979), p. 232.

26. Edward I. Koch, "The Mandate Millstone," *The Public Interest* (Fall 1980), p. 45.

27. Lovell et al., *Federal and State Mandating*, p. 193.

28. Charles Levine and Paul L. Posner, "The Centralizing Effects of Austerity on the Intergovernmental System," paper presented at the American Political Science Association Convention, 1979, p. 9.

29. Harold Wilensky, "Taxing, Spending and Backlash: An American Peculiarity?" *Taxing and Spending* (July 1979), p. 6.

30. Pascal et al., *Fiscal Containment*, pp. 63, 102.

31. "The National Mood," *Public Opinion* 1 (American Enterprise Institute, July–August 1978):31.

32. Ibid.

33. Ibid.

34. Ibid., p. 33.

35. Pascal et al., *Fiscal Containment*, p. 9; see also ACIR, *Fiscal Federalism 1978–79*, p. 9.

36. Pascal et al., *Fiscal Containment*, pp. 11–14.

37. *Congressional Quarterly Weekly Report*, 25 August 1979, p. 1749.

38. See Anthony Pascal and Mark David Menchick, "Fiscal Containment: Who Gains? Who Loses?" (Santa Monica, Calif.: The Rand Corporation, R-2494/1-FF/RC, September 1979), p. 7.

39. James N. Danzinger, "Rebellion on Fiscal Policy: Assessing the Effects of California's Proposition 13," *The Urban Interest* 1 (Spring 1979):65.

40. Jane F. Roberts, "States Respond to Tough Fiscal Challenges," *Intergovernmental Perspective* 6 (Spring 1980):16.

41. Jane F. Roberts, "Fiscal Issues Dominate as States Meet the Eighties," *Intergovernmental Perspective* 7 (Winter 1981):20.

42. *Congressional Quarterly Weekly Report*, 25 August 1979, p. 1750.

43. *Tax Revolt Digest*, September 1979, p. 6.

44. See Roberts, "States Respond to Tough Fiscal Challenges," p. 16.

45. Pascal et al., *Fiscal Containment*, p. 60.

46. Ibid., p. 65.

47. Ibid., p. 69.

48. Ibid., p. 70.

49. Ibid., p. 77.

50. Danziger, "Rebellion on Fiscal Policy," p. 59.

51. Mervin Field, "Sending a Message: Californians Strike Back," *Public Opinion* 1 (American Enterprise Institute, July–August 1978):6.

52. See Congressional Budget Office, "Proposition 13," p. 4.

53. See Jack Stumpf and Paul Terrell, "Proposition 13 and California Human Services," National Association of Social Workers, Inc. (February 1979), p. 4.

54. *Los Angeles Times*, 22 February 1980, part 2, pp. 1, 6.

55. The proposition exempts spending for several purposes: tax refunds, costs incurred in order to comply with state or federal mandates, and debt service payment for debt existing prior to January 1, 1979, or voter-approved bonded debt passed after that date.

56. Senator Albert S. Rodda (chairman of the California Senate Finance Committee), "Fiscal Implications of Jarvis II for the State of California and

Agencies of California Local Government, Including the Schools, as Viewed from the Perspective of a Practical Politician" (January 15, 1980), p. 19.

57. Seymour Martin Lipset and William Schneider, "Is the Tax Revolt Over?" *Taxing and Spending* (Summer 1980), p. 78.

58. *Los Angeles Times*, 15 March 1981, part 1, p. 3.

59. *Congressional Quarterly Weekly Report*, 17 February 1980, p. 271.

60. See Otto Eckstein, *Public Finance*, 4th edition (Englewood Cliffs, N.J.: Prentice Hall, 1979), p. 93; David J. Ott and Attiat F. Ott, *Federal Budget Policy* (Washington, D.C.: Brookings, 1977), pp. 123–127.

61. *Congressional Quarterly Weekly Report*, 17 February 1980, pp. 268–269.

62. For an account of budget pressures that led to the Budget and Accounting Act of 1921, see James P. Pfiffner, *The President, the Budget, and Congress: Impoundment and the 1974 Budget Act* (Boulder, Colo.: Westview Press, 1979).

63. *Budget of the U.S. Government, Fiscal Year 1982*, p. 613.

64. Catherine Lovell, "Evolving Local Government Dependency," *Public Administration Review* 41 (January 1981):196.

65. Irene Rubin, Charles H. Levine, and George Wolohojian, "States' Role in Local Fiscal Stress: Observations from Six Localities," paper presented at the Midwest Political Science Meeting, Cincinnati, Ohio, April 1981, p. 24.

66. See Richard Cyert and James March, *A Behavioral Theory of the Firm* (Englewood Cliffs, N.J.: Prentice Hall, 1964).

67. See Charles H. Levine, "Organizational Decline and Cutback Management," *Public Administration Review* 38 (July–August 1978):316–325, and "More on Cutback Management: Hard Questions for Hard Times," *Public Administration Review* 39 (March–April 1979):179–183.

68. Russell Stout, Jr., *Management or Control?* (Bloomington: Indiana University Press, 1980), Chapter 1.

69. Levine, "Organizational Decline and Cutback Management" and "More on Cutback Management."

70. See Stumpf and Terrell, "Proposition 13 and California Human Services," pp. 57–63.

71. Peter J. May and Arnold J. Meltsner, "Limited Actions, Distressing Consequences: A Selected View of the California Experience," *Public Administration Review* 41 (January 1981):176.

72. Ibid.

4
Politics, Local Government, and the Municipal Bond Market

Alberta M. Sbragia

The investment community has an important role in local government finance, as became apparent when it precipitated New York City's fiscal crisis by refusing to lend the city more funds. Because local governments borrow much of the money they need both to construct buildings and to attract private sector employers, complex relationships have developed between local governments in their capacity as borrowers and the network of financial institutions, securities dealers, and individual investors that act as lenders. These relationships provide opportunities for, and set constraints upon, local officials; under certain conditions, they establish the limits within which the officials may act.

This chapter hopes to alert students of local government and politics to the existence of important links between the investment community and local policymaking. Focusing first on a general descriptive overview of the dynamics, processes, and uses of a capital market that in 1980 lent state and local governments nearly $80 billion,[1] it then sketches four sets of relationships between government and market. These relationships indicate that local finance, the very structure of local government, local politics, and the financial community are intertwined in ways that significantly affect the governance of cities.

Local Government Borrowing

State governments and, above all, local governments, whether they be municipalities, counties, special districts, or statutory authorities, borrow funds for three major purposes: to build public and quasi-public facilities, to lend the borrowed funds to various institutions in the private sector, and to cover cash flow problems.

Until the 1970s, a large proportion of all borrowed funds was used to pay for capital facilities regarded as "public" and traditionally provided by local government, such as schools, roads, libraries, sewer and water systems, parks, and police and fire stations. Since the mid-1970s, however, fewer capital facilities of that type have been financed by loans because significant amounts of federal aid have been available for such projects. In 1970 roughly 50 percent of state and local public capital expenditures were financed by borrowing, as compared to only 22 percent by Washington; by 1977 borrowing accounted for only 32 percent of such expenditures, whereas federal aid accounted for 43 percent.[2]

Local borrowing has, however, continued to climb, now directed toward purposes not traditionally associated with local government. These quasi-public purposes include hospitals, public power projects, private sector housing, industrial pollution control, convention and sports centers, and various types of private sector development. In fact, certain purposes for which state and local governments borrowed heavily in 1980 had been insignificant in 1960. In 1980, for example, roughly $3.7 billion was borrowed for hospitals, whereas very little was borrowed for this purpose in 1960; similarly, $9.5 billion was borrowed to help industry in 1980, as compared to only $100 million borrowed for that purpose as late as 1970.[3]

Many of these relatively new purposes involve borrowing funds and then lending them either to other governments or, more commonly, to private firms or households. State and local borrowers are therefore borrowing not so much to build capital facilities for their own use as to allow others to build facilities for theirs. John E. Petersen concluded in 1981 that an increasing percentage of long-term debt was issued "for purposes of acquiring financial as opposed to real assets."[4] State and local governments are thus increasingly acting as brokers in their borrowing and lending of funds. According to Petersen, government "acts as a financial intermediary . . . a conduit for supplying funds to private sectors in the economy. The capital spending financed . . . is not reflected in the acquisition of a physical capital asset, but rather a financial asset such as a mortgage or a lease agreement."[5]

Yet another reason for borrowing is to have the cash on hand required to pay day-to-day bills. Such borrowing is intended to improve cash flow and generally is backed by revenue (from the property tax, for instance) that the city knows it is going to receive. The loans allow the city to spend from anticipated revenues as the bills come in, and city finances thereby run more smoothly. Sometimes, however, such borrowing is used to make up an actual shortfall in revenue, a situation often indicating that the borrower is in fairly serious trouble.[6]

Funds borrowed for capital facilities and for the use of the private sector are repaid over a long period of time—commonly from fifteen to thirty years, although even forty-year loans are not unknown. Although borrowing for these purposes is typically long-term, officials deal with cash flow problems by borrowing funds that they repay within a year. Because local governments collect their various types of revenue (such as property tax payments) at least once a year, short-term borrowing allows them to borrow money that carries them from one collection date to the next. Short-term borrowing is also often used to provide "working capital" for a capital project until long-term funds are acquired.

Amount of Borrowing

The borrowing activities of state and local governments have become an important aspect of public sector borrowing. Indeed, state and local debt has increased since World War II at a proportionately greater rate than has federal government debt. In fact, state and local governments had an outstanding debt in 1975 of approximately $225 billion.[7] (This figure had grown by 1979 to roughly $300 billion.) In the late 1960s, the governments borrowed between $13 and $15 billion a year in long-term loans; in 1975, the figure had risen to $31.5 billion, and in 1980 it rose to $53.3 billion.[8] The net amount borrowed (that is, the gross amount borrowed less the amount repaid on previously acquired debt) in 1978 was approximately $30 billion.[9] Short-term borrowing has also fluctuated: It was high in 1974–1975, declined after New York City's fiscal crisis, and then increased substantially in 1980 when roughly $26.5 billion was borrowed on a short-term basis.[10]

Aggregate state and local borrowing is dominated by local borrowing, for local governments spend more capital funds and borrow a higher percentage of such funds than do state governments. Accordingly, this chapter will concentrate on local borrowing, although most of the analysis is applicable to state borrowing as well.

Cost of Borrowing

Obviously, borrowed funds have to be repaid, and interest charges on loans have to be met. Interest payments represent a drain on a local government's budget, for they cannot be spent instead on services and certainly do not attract votes. In the mid-1970s, the "full debt service"—debt repayment and interest charges for both long- and short-term borrowing—claimed about 20 percent of the funds raised by state and local governments from their sources.[11]

The rate of interest paid on a loan is important—and small differences in interest rates are therefore noticed. Because local governments often borrow millions of dollars and pay interest on those millions for many years, an interest rate variation as small as $\frac{1}{100}$ of a percent can have significant consequences. To the layperson, a difference of 1 percent on the interest rate paid on a loan may not seem worth worrying about; however, when applied to the large amounts often involved in local borrowing, the difference in dollar amounts can be staggering. For example, New York City in the mid-1960s borrowed approximately half a billion dollars per year. One percentage point difference in the interest rate would have represented at least $30 million per year—equal at that time to the cost of hiring three thousand policemen or of building ten schools.[12] Even when much smaller amounts are borrowed, a percentage difference in interest rate can amount to millions of dollars. When Richmond, Virginia, wanted to borrow $43.8 million in 1980, each percentage point of interest was worth roughly $4.5 million over the period of the loan.[13] Even $\frac{2}{10}$ of a percent increase in the interest rate that Boston paid in 1980 for its $50 million annual borrowing program would probably have involved an additional interest payment of $1 million over twenty years.[14]

Interest rate levels are also important to the users of various capital facilities. In the case of public housing, for instance, an increase of 1 percent in the interest rate has meant an increase of $25 per month in the rents charged in public housing projects.[15] And in March 1980, when Midland, Michigan, wanted to borrow $26 million over a thirty-year period for a new water plant, each additional ½ percentage point added $2.27 per month to the average resident's water bill.[16]

The Municipal Bond Market

The Borrowers

State and city governments are perhaps the most prominent and visible borrowers, but they are by no means alone. In some states, in fact, they may be in the minority. The explosion of borrowing for such purposes as hospitals, utilities, stadiums, pollution control, and industrial development has been accompanied by the formation of many new governmental units established in order to borrow money for such purposes. These units have joined forces with the other special districts and, in particular, the statutory authorities created after WWII to provide schools, reservoirs, and sewers, as well as with those authorities created in the 1960s as a consequence of metropolitan growth.[17]

Just as the structure of state government has become a bewildering array of quasi-governmental agencies with the legal power to borrow, so too the structure of government at the local level has been transformed. Local government, rather than being confined simply to municipalities and counties, is now also composed of thousands of special-purpose governments—statutory authorities especially—whose defining characteristic is the right to borrow money independently of any general-purpose government. The proportion of borrowing carried out by these authorities has increased dramatically in the past fifteen years, and such governments now dominate the aggregate borrowing carried out by local government. Whereas statutory authorities accounted for only 26 percent of all new bond sales between 1966 and 1970, in the years 1977 through 1979 they accounted for 45.5 percent.[18]

State and local officials established both special districts and statutory authorities not only because their boundaries cut across numerous municipal boundaries and thus allowed services in an area to be provided without duplication, but also because of debt limitations imposed on general-purpose governments by state constitutions. As Susan MacManus points out in Chapter 6 (Table 6.3), half of the state constitutions restrict at least moderately the borrowing powers of their municipalities. For example, some constitutions limit the amount of debt a municipality can accumulate under its guarantee and the interest rate it can pay.[19] By creating authorities with independent borrowing capacities, local officials are able to circumvent these limits, which are otherwise difficult to change. Similarly, state legislators, by allowing the creation of authorities, are able to avoid the difficult and complex process involved in altering constitutional provisions.

Furthermore, since authorities rely heavily on revenue produced by their activities rather than on taxing powers, [20] *they can acquire debt without having to obtain voter approval.* By contrast, in over forty states, general-purpose governments have to obtain such approval in a referendum (sometimes even with a two-thirds majority) before they can borrow for certain purposes.[21] Again, by establishing authorities, local officials can circumvent voter constraints as well as state restrictions on the nature of their debt.

The creation of special-purpose governments changed the type of debt characteristic of the state and local sector: In the 1970s, debt that could be acquired without voter approval dominated the borrowing scene, whereas in the 1960s, debt was typically approved through the electoral process and backed by the taxing power rather than by the revenue-producing capability of the borrower.[22] In brief, the importance of public authorities in the current local government system cannot be overestimated, a point to which we shall later return.

Borrowing Instruments

State and local governments do not borrow most of their short-term (much less long-term) funds by taking out a bank loan as you and I might do. Rather, they usually borrow by issuing and selling borrowing instruments known as *municipal bonds* (used to acquire long-term funds) and *municipal notes* (used for short-term funds). Notes and bonds are "certificates which pledge that the issuer will pay back the money borrowed by the date of maturity and make the specified interest payments periodically through the term"[23] of the security. When investors buy a municipal security, they are giving a loan to the state or local government that sold the security. They are, in essence, investing by lending.

Municipal notes are backed by money that local governments expect to receive either from specific taxes due to be collected in the near future (these notes are known as tax anticipation notes or TANS), from intergovernmental aid (revenue anticipation notes or RANS), or from funds to be borrowed in the long-term market (bond anticipation notes or BANS). Municipal bonds, by contrast, are backed by the taxing power of the borrower or by revenue expected from a specific project or service.

The oldest type of municipal bond is the general obligation bond, which is considered guaranteed debt in that it is backed by the "full faith and credit" of the borrowing unit (i.e., by its taxing powers). General obligation (GO) bonds are issued by general-purpose governments and school districts and often need voter approval for their issuance.

Revenue bonds, a more recent type of municipal bond, are backed by the income expected from a project being constructed or a service being provided. They are considered nonguaranteed debt and generally offer slightly higher interest rates than do guaranteed securities. Issued by both general-purpose governments (for their revenue-producing enterprises) and special-purpose governments, they do not usually require voter approval. Revenue bonds have been very useful in circumventing state limits on guaranteed debt.[24]

One type of revenue bond first issued in 1960 by New York State and now extensively used—the "moral obligation" bond—represents an attempt by states to give some kind of guarantee to a revenue bond issued by one of their (usually quasi-governmental) agencies. It might be thought of as a "hybrid" bond. As Robert Lamb and Stephen P. Rappaport put it, "the state provides a moral pledge or payment in the event that an authority is unable to make timely debt service. However, unlike the GO pledge, the moral obligation bond does not require voter approval and does not have the state's official pledge of its full faith and credit."[25]

General obligation bonds are ordinarily used to finance tax-supported facilities such as roads, libraries, and schools; revenue bonds, by contrast, finance facilities for which a user charge is levied, such as turnpikes, sewer and water systems, hospitals, airports, harbors, and public power projects. Whereas general obligation bonds previously dominated the municipal bond market, the 1970s saw a greatly increased use of revenue bonds: In 1968, 60 percent of all municipals were general obligation bonds; by 1978, however, only 37 percent fell into this category, and by 1980 the figure had dropped to 30 percent.[26]

The Market

Municipal notes and bonds are bought and sold in what is called the municipal bond market. That market, simply put, is the forum within which state and local governments borrow by selling their notes and bonds and in which investors lend by buying the securities. Perhaps the best description of this market for the layperson was that given by the Twentieth Century Fund Task Force on Municipal Bond Credit Ratings:

> The municipal bond market is not confined to a single location such as an exchange for listed securities. Rather, it is a nation-wide network of investors, investment institutions, securities dealers, and governmental borrowers. In this setting, hundreds of new and outstanding municipal securities are traded each business day.[27]

This market provides most of the funds borrowed by all but the smallest local governments.[28] It is divided into two segments: the primary market and the secondary market. The former deals with new issues of both bonds and notes, whereas the latter refers to that network of dealers who buy and sell older securities before they reach maturity. Much larger than the primary market, the secondary market is extremely important, for it allows municipal notes and bonds to be relatively "liquid." That is, an investor holding a bond maturing in the year 2000 can convert that security into cash in, say, 1990 by selling it to a buyer in the secondary market. Many municipal notes, too, are almost as liquid as actual cash.

When a local government wants to borrow long-term money in the bond market, it issues a whole set of bonds totaling the amount to be borrowed, which is collectively referred to as a *bond issue*. Local officials then deal with a group of investment and/or commercial banks known as a *syndicate*. The syndicate buys the whole set of bonds from the borrowing local government (known as the *issuer*) and then sells those bonds to institutional and individual investors. (In some bond sales, various syndicates compete against each other; the syndicate offering the best terms to the issuer gets to buy the bonds. Other sales are "negotiated"; in such cases, the issuer asks a single syndicate to handle its bond issue.) The process of buying the bond issue and then selling the various bonds that make up the issue is known as *underwriting;* each member of the syndicate is known as an *underwriter.*[29]

The Role of Risk. All capital markets operate with reference, on the one hand, to the "risk" involved in making a loan to a particular borrower and, on the other, to the interest rate that the lender will receive. Because lenders want above all to be repaid, the lower the likelihood of repayment, the higher the interest rate they will charge relative to other less risky loans. Different local government borrowers, therefore, do not necessarily pay the same interest rate. Each borrower's rate is influenced by the general level of interest rates in the municipal bond market (these are linked to the interest rates prevailing in the other financial markets in which the U.S. Treasury and private firms borrow), the type of investor active in the municipal bond market at the time the loan is being sought, *and* the ability of the local government to repay the loan. The risk of nonpayment may be viewed as so great that lenders simply refuse to lend, regardless of how high an interest rate the would-be borrower offers to pay.

Ratings and Rating Agencies. Since the degree of risk varies with the borrower, assessment of risk necessarily plays a crucial role in the municipal bond market: Local governments differ widely in terms of the circumstances that could affect their ability to repay a loan, and investors need a reliable guide to the degree of risk they are assuming by lending to any particular borrower. Lenders essentially need to know the risk involved in lending to, say, the city of Birmingham, Alabama, in order to be able to demand an interest rate roughly proportionate to rates demanded for loans to other cities carrying a different degree of risk. Further, they must have some idea of how Birmingham's bond is likely to do in the secondary market over the long term. Evaluating the risk of lending to Birmingham is known as *credit analysis*, and *ratings* are the product of such analysis.

Ratings, in fact, are the heart of credit analysis, for they categorize risk. Essentially a shorthand way of letting investors know the degree of risk they are incurring in buying a particular municipal bond, ratings have a significant impact on the final interest rate the issuer of the bond will be asked to pay. Generally speaking, the lower the rating, the more the borrower will have to pay in interest charges.

Ratings are important, therefore, to both local governments and lenders. They influence how much of the local budget has to be set aside for interest payments; without them, in fact, lenders would find it impossible to evaluate the credit-worthiness of all the various local governments that borrow in the market at one time or another. Those who determine ratings thus wield a great deal of power in the market. Their impact makes the world of credit analysis important to the world of local finance.

The two major private investment advisory firms, Moody's Investors Service and Standard & Poor's Corporation, are known simply as "the rating agencies." They have been the preeminent credit analysts on Wall Street, and their influence, although weakened by their failure to spot New York City's problems, is still significant. Their importance has been reinforced by a lack of competition: Before 1975 the rating agencies held a monopoly on ratings because most investment and commercial bankers on Wall Street did relatively little in-house credit analysis. Further, various federal and state laws used the judgments of the rating agencies as references against which to assess the prudence of investments carried out by, for example, bank trust departments. Most financial institutions, in fact, are forbidden by law to buy bonds in either the primary or secondary market if the bonds have been given low ratings by the two agencies. The combination of tradition, federal and state laws that have explicitly recognized their ratings, and the absence of competing assessments has made the rating agencies influential in the market.

The agencies give ratings in the form of letters. The basic distinction is between those securities considered "investment grade," for which risk ranges from very low to medium, and those considered "speculative," for which risk ranges from medium to very high. Bonds carrying a Moody's rating of Aaa, Aa, A, or Baa or a Standard & Poor's rating of AAA, AA, A, or BBB have been judged to be very likely to pay interest and to repay principal on time. Aaa bonds "carry the smallest degree of investment risk and are generally referred to as 'gilt edge.' "[30] Bonds rated Ba, B, Caa, Ca, or C by Moody's or BB, B, CCC, or CC by Standard & Poor's are considered to be speculative investments in that the likelihood of their paying interest and repaying principal is rather weak.

Generally speaking, and under most conditions, the lower the rating given by Moody's and Standard & Poor's, the higher the interest rate the issuer has to offer in order to find buyers for its bond issue. Changes in ratings are therefore of widespread interest. When Standard & Poor's dropped Chicago's rating from AA to A+ in 1979, headlines were made. Bond dealers estimated the reduction would increase the city's interest cost on a $29 million bond issue by $3.6 million over the life of twenty-five-year bonds.[31]

The two agencies rate a borrower each time it comes to market. Because coming to market with an unrated bond makes it far more difficult to find lenders, the borrower pays the agencies to evaluate its credit-worthiness.[32] Both agencies periodically review outstanding bonds, and the original ratings on those bonds will be modified if the issuer's finances change.

The two agencies do not, however, always agree in their ratings, for they weigh various criteria differently in determining such ratings. Although they both analyze a locality's economic base and the quality of management practiced by the borrower, Moody's counts prior debt most heavily and places very high priority on the borrower's general debt history. Standard & Poor's, on the other hand, has become particularly concerned with a borrower's economic base, and therefore weighs heavily such indicators as per capita income levels, employment mix, population dynamics, and building activity. Yet, in spite of these differences, it is rare to find that one agency has given a bond a rating of A when the other has specified a rating of AAA.[33]

The impact on ratings of stressing the economic base of a city may be illustrated by the experience of Dayton, Ohio, with Standard & Poor's rating. In 1979, Dayton's rating slipped from AAA to AA-. Although the agency acknowledged that the city was fiscally well-managed and decidedly within its debt limit, the agency officers argued that because Dayton had lost both population and jobs, it no longer deserved a AAA rating. Whereas in 1977 Dayton officials had managed to convince the agency to keep the city's AAA rating, by 1979 their argument that new building and business activity were strengthening the city's economic base no longer sufficed.[34]

One might suppose that since cities in economic decline have trouble getting top ratings, rapidly growing cities would do extremely well. Yet, for example, Phoenix, Denver, Albuquerque, and Anchorage did not have an Aaa rating in 1980. It is the concern of the rating agencies that, as local governments with booming economies provide infrastructure in anticipation of the growth often accompanying a boom, they will incur debt that existing taxpayers will have to repay should the growth occur more slowly than anticipated. It is thus rare for such local governments to be given an Aaa rating.[35]

Mutual "Lobbying." Due to the significant impact of agency ratings, local officials often "lobby" the two agencies by presenting arguments and analyses to their credit analysts in the hope of getting an improved rating or, at least, of retaining the current one. The list of prominent and not-so-prominent governors, mayors, controllers, and cities' financial advisors who present their cases to the rating agencies each year is extremely long. All such officials want their governments to be given the highest possible ratings, and their hope is that by making "pilgrimages" to Moody's and Standard & Poor's, they will impress the agencies with their professionalism and commitment, as well as with the budget figures presented. This preoccupation with the rating agencies is often expressed by local officials in comments such as "Let's hope Standard & Poor's doesn't hear about this" and "If we weren't doing something right, Moody's wouldn't even be talking to us."

State and local officials often try to lobby the two agencies; in turn, Moody's and Standard & Poor's have been known to warn officials that certain decisions will hurt their cities' credit rating. Such warnings are particularly sharp if the possibility of default exists. When the mayor of St. Louis threatened to withhold interest and principal payments due on January 1, 1980, as a weapon in his political feud with the city's comptroller, the two rating agencies publicly warned the mayor that such action would mean that all the city's outstanding bonds would be given a rating below investment grade. Such a default rating would have seriously hurt St. Louis bonds in the secondary market and made it very difficult for the city to borrow in the future.[36] In brief, the rating agencies often react, as well as listen, to local officials.

The Agencies' Competitors. The nature of credit analysis changed after 1975 because the two agencies began to have serious competition. Although their ratings still have an important impact on interest rates and are officially acknowledged legally, the agencies' failure to identify the New York City crisis before the banks and other investors did so severely damaged their credibility. The agencies lagged so far behind the market's judgment of the city's fiscal condition that their ratings were shaken from their pedestal: Bankers "unloaded" their securities and lenders refused to lend, even though both agencies listed the city's securities as investment grade. The agencies' judgments still sometimes lag behind those of investors; in fact, one interviewee referred to these judgments as "lag indicators."

Following the New York City fiscal crisis, the major commercial and investment banks on Wall Street decided that they had to have more information than the rating agencies were giving them. They strengthened their own in-house municipal research departments, certain employees of which now speak rather contemptuously of the rating agencies. This is not to say that the ratings given by Moody's and Standard & Poor's do not influence the in-house analysts: They do, but they are nonetheless viewed skeptically. When Standard & Poor's gave a BBB (investment grade) rating to New York City bonds in 1981, a credit analyst in the municipal research department of a very prestigious commercial bank declared scornfully, "The city really gave S & P's a song and dance." He then went on to list the reasons for which he believed New York City bonds were not yet investment grade.

In-house analysts have become crucial, particularly now that the secondary market is so important. If a city gets into financial trouble, the value of securities that lenders have already bought drops; investors thus often try to outguess each other, hoping to determine that the city is in trouble in advance of other analysts so that they can sell their bonds before the price drops. Decisions have to be made quickly, with the most up-to-date information available. As one analyst put it, "Unless you're immersed in credit analysis every day, you don't know what's going on." In sum, the deficiencies in the rating agencies' judgment and the importance and complexity of the secondary market have combined to strengthen the influence of the in-house credit analysts.

The diffusion of credit analysis has implications for local government. Although officials lobby the two major agencies, that lobbying, even when successful, is not as effective vis-à-vis the overall market as it had been before 1975. The "internal ratings" of various financial institutions are now a factor to be considered. Such ratings can help or hurt local governments—but they cannot be ignored.

State and local officials therefore try to give a generally good impression of their city's finances to as many credit analysts and investors as possible. For example, they may attend luncheons and dinners with members of various Wall Street firms or address seminars attended by the financial community; occasionally, they might even go on speaking tours across the country to boost their bonds' chances.[37] In short, many mayors, governors, and other officials find it necessary to be bond salesmen as well.

Financial Advisors. The New York City crisis dramatically illustrated how important credit analysis can be: The assumption that lending to local governments was almost free from risk came to be severely shaken. As a consequence of the crisis, borrowers came under a much greater degree of scrutiny after 1975 than they had been before. As the number of credit analysts grew and as credit analysis became more complex and sophisticated, the relationships between local governments and the investment community became much closer and more sustained. Many cities, counties, and authorities hired investment and commercial bankers as financial advisors. It became taken for granted not only that cities in financial trouble would have advisors, but also that most cities of any size would have advisors as a matter of course. Smaller cities often set up advisory committees composed of local bankers, accountants, and lawyers, whereas larger cities usually hired nationally known firms. It was the purpose of such firms to help a city deal with syndicates, to "sell the city" to Wall Street, to warn officials of impending difficulties for their securities, to provide the city with technical advice on structuring bond issues, and so forth.

Complex relationships began to develop among the various firms involved in the municipal bond market, with some firms at times counseling their local government clients to avoid exposing their weaknesses to other Wall Street firms. In the case of one large city in a northeastern state that needed to borrow funds, its financial advisor counseled local officials to borrow from a bank rather than to go to market, basing this recommendation on the advisor's own credit analysis. The reason was straightforward. The Moody's and Standard & Poor's ratings for that city were not very high, and conditions had deteriorated since the city had last issued a general obligation bond. The advisor was worried that if the city went to market and thus exposed itself anew to the rating agencies, it stood a good chance of having its securities rated as "speculative." Borrowing from a local bank would entail very high interest rates, but at least the city's financial weakness would be kept from public view a while longer. The implicit hope, of course, was that the city's fiscal health would eventually improve, at which point it would seek to borrow in the bond market without having to live down the stigma of once having had its securities rated as extremely risky.[38]

Furthermore, the reputation of a city's advisor affects that city's general image on Wall Street. One analyst went so far as to say that "Wall Street is down on City X because it has a rotten advisor." The prestige of a city's advisor is one of those intangibles that cumulatively affect interest rates. Indeed, if a large city does not hire a major (at least prestigious) investment or commercial bank as an advisor, the financial judgment of the local officials tends to be questioned by the big Wall Street firms.

Disclosure and Accounting. Before New York City's problems indicated to investors that they needed more complete and verifiable information than they had been getting, the amount of information disclosed by borrowing governments to investors was minimal. George Peterson concludes that "until 1975, when some local governments began to issue prospectuses describing their financial situation in greater detail in order to insulate themselves from the market resistance bred by New York City's crisis, virtually no information was routinely provided by local authorities to the public regarding the issuing authority's financial condition."[39] Essentially, investors lent to local governments because they assumed that the risk of default was almost nonexistent.

Since 1975, when New York City's problems in repaying its debts revealed the risk involved in lending in the municipal bond market, investors have demanded far more information before buying bonds than they had done previously. The result has been sharp improvement in the quality of information disclosed in official statements. Both investors and rating agencies now have a better idea of the financial health of any given borrower.

Of course, before such information can be disclosed, local governments must have accounting procedures that let them know where they stand financially. New York City did not have such an accounting system, and many other cities were in a similar position. As late as 1979, for example, Arizona's Maricopa County (encompassing Phoenix), with a budget of nearly $300 million, had such an archaic accounting system that the county controller was quoted as saying, "We don't know where we stand at any point in time. We know we have enough money to pay our bills—hopefully."[40] Accordingly, accounting standards have been the focus of a good deal of attention since 1975, and even Maricopa County was supposed to have a modern accounting system by the end of 1980.

Accounting standards came into their own with particular force in 1980: Standard & Poor's formally stated that accounting would be taken into consideration when ratings were being determined. The agency declared, in particular, that generally accepted accounting principles had to be used and that financial statements should be independently audited (in fact, independent audits became increasingly widespread after 1975). Standard & Poor's even threatened to withdraw its ratings if local governments did not give the agency financial information on schedule—a fate that San Francisco suffered in 1980.[41]

In sum, both disclosure and accounting standards are improving, and audits are becoming more comprehensive, routine, and rigorous. But, as Standard & Poor's noted, "it is a slow, agonizing process, muddled in politics, legalities, and the desire of states to reject any tampering with sovereign rights and powers."[42] Investors will continue to push for more information and better accounting procedures, whereas many local governments will resist demands for changes that might threaten the strategies they have used in the past to be financially creative. Nonetheless, a continuation of the trend toward more standardized accounting and disclosure standards seems inevitable.

Short-term Borrowing. Since the occurrence of New York City's financial crisis, investors have been worried about cities' short-term borrowing as well as about their accounting standards. New York City's (and later Cleveland's) fiscal crisis involved an inability to repay notes rather than bonds, a problem that investors are continuing to scrutinize with particular care. (In fact, after 1975 such borrowing declined sharply.) Of special concern is the practice that New York City had elevated to a fine art—namely, the "roll-over" of debt. If a city is to have sound finances, its short-term debt should be repaid in the year in which it is issued. However, New York City (and, on a smaller scale, many other cities) had for several years been borrowing to repay notes as they matured; outstanding short-term debt increased and short-term money was actually being transformed into long-term debt. In 1971 and 1975, for example, New York City borrowed $1 billion more in short-term debt than it repaid.[43] Since the New York City case, investors have viewed the extension of short-term debt as a sign of weak local finance.

Short-term debt is worrisome because cities with large amounts of such debt are absolutely dependent on maintaining their access to the market in order to renew that debt or to convert it into long-term debt. The crises in both New York City and Cleveland, for example, were triggered by an inability to find lenders willing to lend those cities the short-term funds they needed to repay previously acquired short-term debts. If, for some reason, cities should find it difficult to attract investors, they are in trouble. Essentially, short-term borrowing renders borrowers vulnerable to conditions over which they may have no control but which can very quickly affect the municipal bond market and the fate of borrowers in it.

Default. Default occurs if a borrower is unable to repay a loan when it falls due. In the New York City case (discussed in more detail in Chapter 5), investors had been worried for some months about the increase in the city's outstanding short-term debt; then, in Cleveland, in an atmosphere of vitriolic political feuding, the banks refused to roll over a mere $14 million worth of notes. It follows that the point at which investors withdraw support is both crucial and unpredictable. Given that only two cities (with rated bonds) have recently defaulted,[44] it is impossible to generalize about the probable circumstances attendant upon such a crisis. Some thoughts on the subject are nevertheless in order.

Because investors are affected by symbols and ambiance as much as (if not more than) anyone else, it is difficult to explain or predict, except in fairly broad terms, the actual timing of crisis. The market is not a very precise judge of a city's fiscal condition. Although most observers agree that New York City had for some time been spending more than its declining economic base could finance, it is not clear why the city got into trouble with lenders—that is, why the city's fiscal crisis exploded—precisely when it did. The argument could be made, on the basis of evidence *then available*, that the investors were either premature or tardy in their decision to "pull the plug" on the city. The investors could have refused to lend well before they actually did, or they could have hung on, assuming that the 1974–1975 recession would soon be over and that New York City's budget would then be strengthened.

Perhaps all that can be concluded at this point is that financial markets are terribly vulnerable to fear. Once such fear is stimulated by, say, New York City banks (seen by many investors as leaders in the secondary market) selling huge quantities of securities, it is almost impossible to stop. The banks' own decisions about selling in the secondary market are based upon their analysis of a city's condition; however, as the Securities and Exchange Commission's report on New York City indicated, numerous factors enter into such a decision, rendering its timing unpredictable.[45] The investors' lack of confidence, therefore, cannot usually be pinned down to any particular aspect of a city's financial condition; rather, confidence is eroded by numerous events, facts, rumors, and fears, which cumulatively lead to a complete collapse of confidence.

Cleveland's default was very different from New York City's fiscal crisis—as were its lessons. Cleveland's bond anticipation notes were held exclusively by local banks and not by other types of investors. Moreover, the city's default was particularly messy, for the mayor was feuding not only with the banks and business community as a whole, but also with much of his city council—which backed the banks.

The question surrounding Cleveland's default is whether the banks' refusal to roll over notes was due solely to the city's lack of creditworthiness or to political reasons. Regardless of whether Cleveland suffered from a "political default," however, we can see the process leading to the denial of credit as indicating the kinds of questions and issues surrounding debt in a city that has financial problems and lacks public-private sector cooperation.

Although Moody's had lowered the city's rating to Ba and Standard & Poor's had entirely suspended its rating for Cleveland securities by July 1978, and although Moody's had lowered its rating still further to B on November 30, 1978, Cleveland's mayor charged that the banks' refusal to roll over $14 million of notes due on December 15, 1978, was politically motivated. Specifically, he accused the banking community (and Cleveland Trust Company, in particular) of trying to dictate city policies by requiring that the city sell the municipally owned power company as a condition for extending the notes. The mayor also claimed that the bankers sought to get the power company sold because they were closely tied to a privately owned utility that, in turn, wanted the municipal enterprise out of the way.[46] These charges were made in an atmosphere of extreme bitterness between the mayor and the business community (which had been actively involved in an effort to recall him).

In the case of Cleveland, then, shaky finances and mutual hostility combined to force a "showdown" that ended in the city's default. Although Cleveland Trust's decision to ask for repayment could, according to a Federal Reserve study, be "supported as having been made on factors related to the city's creditworthiness,"[47] it seems clear that the bank probably would have agreed to extend the notes *if* the relationship between the mayor and the banks had been better. As Brock Weir, the president of Cleveland Trust, admitted, "There has to be initial civility. That is one of the basic requirements." He and other business leaders had felt attacked when, to use Weir's words, they were "characterized in public and in print by the current city administration as being 'blood-sucking vampires.' "[48] The refusal by banks to extend further credit may thus reflect not only a judgment on the city's finances but also the state of relations between the city government and the business community.

New York City's inability to meet its debt on short-term loans in 1975 changed profoundly and permanently the psychology of the municipal bond market.[49] Without doubt, the city's crisis marked a watershed in the market's evolution: It made investors aware that city governments could not, or would not, automatically raise taxes high enough to ensure that their debts were repaid on time. Cleveland's problems, and its default, reinforced the sense that municipal governments might not always and under all conditions repay lenders on time.

The New York City crisis also set a precedent that has shaped the thinking about municipal defaults: Specifically, the market learned that municipal defaults were manageable. In New York City's particular case, Washington as well as Albany stepped in; default was then technically avoided through a series of legislative actions at both the state and federal levels. Moreover, the city did take significant and politically difficult steps aimed at restoring its credit-worthiness. Although New York City first raised the specter of default, the public sector's reaction as well as those of such other actors as commercial banks and pension funds encouraged the feeling that even if default did occur, bondholders would eventually be taken care of without suffering an enormous loss. Although Cleveland's default did not inspire the level of federal and state involvement generated by New York City's crisis, this city's agreement with the banks, roughly two years after default occurred, reinforced the notion that nonpayment of debt charges, even if it did occur, would likely be temporary.

With the experience of these two cases behind it, the market now seems to operate on the implicit assumption that default, at least of rated borrowers, will be rare and that when it does occur, it will be temporary. Although a city's financial condition is of concern to bond dealers (if only because it affects the fortunes of that city's bonds in the secondary market), the possibility that bondholders will simply lose all or even most of their principal and interest payments is not seen as even a remote possibility. Although repayment may be late or otherwise modified, as was the case in New York City and Cleveland, Wall Street tends to work on the assumption that local officials, over the medium to long term at least, will raise taxes and retrench on services in order to meet their debt charges. As we shall later see, the need of local officials to borrow in the market is so great that they are unlikely to refuse to redeem debts and thereby shut themselves off from credit. Thus, Wall Street analysts now seem to regard municipal default as both rare and manageable.

Bankruptcy—entailing a formal declaration in court of inability to pay lenders and creditors (as discussed in more detail in Chapter 5)— is regarded by analysts as so unlikely, and perhaps so complicated, that no one interviewed on Wall Street had thought seriously about the implications flowing from a local government borrower filing for bankruptcy. Because Cleveland did not file and because, in fact, no rated local borrower has done so since the Great Depression, the prospect of bankruptcy is not at the forefront of Wall Street's concerns. However, if a major borrower does file, this prospect will quickly become a benchmark, as was the case with New York City's fiscal crisis.

Although bankruptcy is not widely analyzed, and although municipal defaults are now essentially regarded as manageable, the possibility of default by a state government is not merely of concern but deeply disturbing to Wall Street.[50] Although default was not an issue in the 1970s, several major states (Michigan, in particular) began facing severe budgetary pressures in 1981. Default by these states was not probable, but it was possible.

What troubled analysts was that although state governments can ordinarily be counted on to step in, if only minimally, to help municipalities in default (Ohio, for example, set up a board with broad powers to assist Cleveland's reentry into the market), no similar help can be relied upon for state governments in financial trouble. Especially under the Reagan Administration, Washington was unlikely to help such states in any significant way. Wall Street credit analysts consequently began to think more seriously about state financial problems than they had ever done before. If a state should default, the municipal bond market would be shaken to its very core: The effects of New York City's troubles had sharp although relatively temporary financial repercussions throughout the market, but the effects of a state default would very likely be more permanent.

Investors

The distinguishing feature of municipal bonds is that the income investors receive from them is *tax-exempt*. That is, whereas interest received on a bond issued by a private firm or by the federal government is subject to federal taxation, interest paid on a municipal bond is not; moreover, it is often exempt from state and local taxation as well. The factor of federal tax exemption sets the municipal bond market apart from other, taxable, financial markets. It also permits issuers of municipal bonds (sometimes referred to as "tax-exempts") to pay lower interest rates on their bonds than private firms or the U.S. Treasury pay on theirs. Although the differential between interest rates in the taxable markets and those in the municipal bond market fluctuates, the latter are always lower than the former.

Investors buy municipal securities precisely because of their tax-exempt status: They find that the after-tax yield of municipal securities is higher than that of taxable bonds. As one investment banker put it, "The municipal bond market is a tax market." Thus, the most successful investors in the market are those institutions and individuals whose tax position is such that they benefit more by investing in tax-exempt municipals than by investing in other securities.

Because tax considerations are so important, the investors in this market are fewer in number than those in other financial markets. For example, pension funds are important buyers of taxable securities but nonbuyers of municipals: Since pension funds are taxed at low rates, the relatively low yield on municipals makes them unattractive.[51] In fact, although municipals are occasionally bought by life insurance companies, foreign investors, and corporations, they are principally attractive only to three types of investors: commercial banks, fire and casualty insurance companies, and relatively wealthy individuals or households. These groups are attracted to tax-exempts because of their need for tax shelters.[52] If, for some reason, none of them should be interested in investing in municipal bonds, local governments would find themselves in deep financial trouble indeed.

The narrow range of investors is not the only problem for local government borrowers, however. As Ronald W. Forbes and John E. Petersen point out, "municipal bonds are not the preferred investment of any of the three chief buyers."[53] That is, each invests in municipals with residual funds only. The market is therefore particularly affected by economic conditions and by alternative investment opportunities, because these factors significantly influence the amount of residual monies available to the bond market's major investors.

Commercial Banks. The impact of such conditions and opportunities on the investment patterns of commercial banks is of particular importance to the market. Although bank investment in this market fluctuates, it is always significant. The withdrawal of banks from the market can make it difficult and more expensive for local borrowers to find long-term money.

In an economic climate of tight credit, commercial banks will not buy many municipals, for their first priorities are to maintain their required reserves and to meet the loan demands of their customers (corporations, in particular). In times of "tight money," their residual funds disappear and their investment in municipals drops, sometimes dramatically.[54] For example, in 1966, 1969, 1974–1975, and 1976, commercial bank investment in municipal bonds dropped sharply. In 1969, in fact, bank buying dropped so sharply that many local government borrowers could not sell their bonds and had to turn to short-term borrowing.[55] Furthermore, in times of volatile interest rates, banks tend to buy municipal bonds with shorter maturities; that is, they are no longer willing to lend funds for twenty to thirty years. By the end of 1980, for instance, after a year of roller-coaster interest rates, banks were becoming extremely wary of buying bonds with maturities beyond ten years.[56] Such a policy will make it more difficult and expensive for localities to sell the fifteen-to-thirty-year bonds they have traditionally sold.

The tendency to buy tax-exempts after loan demand from customers has been met is reinforced in federally chartered banks by the bank examinations carried out by the Office of the Comptroller of the Currency. Bank investments are checked by bank examiners to ensure that those investments are in the "community's interest." Examiners tend to be skeptical if a high proportion of a bank's investment securities are municipals: Buying municipals is not seen as necessarily in the community interest. Even if a bank has a high proportion of its investments in the bonds of the city in which it is located, examiners will usually advise the bank to be more cautious in the future. In addition, they will almost invariably be skeptical about investments in municipals issued by a local government perceived to be in financial trouble. At the extreme, this attitude can lead an examiner to question (unofficially) an Idaho bank's investment in a bond issued by, say, New Haven, on the general grounds that New Haven is in a declining region of the country. The influence of bank examiners is often informal, but it is clear that their recommendations do have an impact on the investment decisions of at least some banks.

Individual Investors. When commercial banks' buying of municipals declines, as it did in 1975 and 1976, individual investors usually take up much of the slack. However, as Forbes and Petersen point out, "individuals are attracted to the tax-exempt market under conditions least favorable for state and local borrowers."[57] Because individuals are generally attracted to municipals when the differential between tax-exempt and taxable interest rates is relatively small, local borrowers generally suffer when individuals rather than banks are lending.

Although individuals may demand higher interest rates than banks, they are important, valued, and wooed sources of capital for local government. When one has only three major types of investors, one is well advised to keep them all interested. Not surprisingly, local government borrowers become concerned when alternative investment opportunities divert household investment from the tax-exempt market, for local governments may then find it difficult to attract lenders.

Researchers (and even some policymakers) have, in fact, been worried for some time about the lack of investor diversity. The narrowness of the market's appeal is held at least partially responsible for the market's problems, one of which is "excessive volatility in tax-exempt interest rates and flows of credit."[58] Nonetheless, all proposals to broaden the market's appeal have been defeated with the help of local officials. Attracting more investors would require a fundamental transformation of the market, and local officials view such change as undesirable. Officials are willing to put up with relatively few types of investors in order to maintain the market's present structure.

The Role of the Federal Government

Local officials do not favor policies that might lessen their overall dependence on the market by involving Washington more extensively in local borrowing. Insofar as local borrowers are subject to the criteria of the investment community and have almost no alternatives to the private market for loans, it might be thought that local officials would approve of efforts to reduce their dependence. One solution would be to have the federal government act as a major lender. But this stratagem runs counter to a major preoccupation of U.S. local officials: the fear of federal intervention in the area of local borrowing. Most local finance officials, as far as can be judged by their writings and verbal presentations, strongly defend the basic set of relationships that now exists. Even though many officials from cities with previous trouble in the market have supported the establishment of a national public bank (usually referred to as URBANK), other officials have opposed it.[59] In an interview, a prominent local finance officer from a financially healthy Midwestern city stated the view of many: "Either a project is fiscally sound or it is not. If it is, the private market will fund it. If it isn't, then it should not be funded period."

Although local officials are basically satisfied with the tax-exempt market, the U.S. Treasury is not: The Treasury has been the chief initiator of proposals to change fundamentally the nature of that market and to extend Washington's role in local borrowing. In particular, it has often proposed that Congress remove the tax-exempt status from municipal bonds and then appropriate subsidies for the higher interest charges localities would have to pay. The Treasury defends its position on the grounds that the tax exemption narrows the range of investors and that it constitutes an "invisible subsidy" costing the federal government in foregone tax revenues while benefiting investors. Appropriately large direct subsidies would help localities as much as the tax exemption does, without permitting investors to reduce their tax burdens at Washington's expense.

Nearly all local officials have vehemently—and very successfully—opposed this argument for a taxable municipal bond market complemented by congressional subsidies. They see the proposals as encouraging massive congressional involvement in an activity that has traditionally been left almost entirely to state and local government. Such fierce opposition is partially rooted in the fear that Congress might not appropriate the funds that a subsidy program would require.[60] The opposition is also based on the fear that congressional subsidies might entail federal regulations and controls—and, in the worst case scenario, the eventual requirement that Washington approve all local borrowing.

The tax-exempt status of municipals is viewed as critical for the maintenance of local government autonomy in the area of borrowing. Losing the tax exemption and becoming dependent on subsidies appropriated at the whim of Congress is almost universally regarded as a giant step toward centralization. In essence, the private capital market as it currently functions is seen as a protection against federal intervention.

"Public Purpose." Much to the Treasury's regret, direct congressional involvement in local borrowing is currently restricted to deciding which state and local activities serve a "public purpose" and thereby qualify as activities for which tax-exempt bonds can be issued. Until 1968 Congress generally regarded all activities of subnational governments as serving a public purpose, and thus its involvement in this area was minimal. However, as localities increasingly became *lenders* of funds borrowed at tax-exempt rates, Congress became a bit more restrictive in its definition. In 1968 (as discussed in greater detail in the next

section) Congress limited the amount of money borrowed in the tax-exempt market that local governments could lend to private firms. In the late 1970s, congressional concern with the definition of public purpose became even more intense, and Congress imposed limits on the ways in which tax-exempt funds could be used to assist home-buyers.

Encouraged by intergovernmental competition for jobs and tax-payers, local governments have increasingly stretched the definition of public purpose in order to lend funds cheaply to various sectors of the economy. Congress, on the other hand, has become increasingly worried about the financial and public policy implications of defining public purpose in such a way so as to provide an "invisible subsidy" (which deprives Washington of tax revenue) to private actors for doing what they might well have done anyway.

Tax Policy. Congress is also involved, albeit much more indirectly, in the realm of local borrowing through federal tax policy. Although such policy is not formulated with the municipal bond market particularly in mind, changes in federal tax laws significantly affect patterns of investment in that market: Investors buy municipals primarily because of the provisions of the tax code. For example, the profits of commercial banks are taxed at the full marginal corporate rate, whereas those of savings and loan institutions are not. Commercial banks are therefore important buyers of municipals, whereas thrift institutions are not. However, when tax policy was recently changed so as to increase by $25,000 the amount of commercial bank profit that would be taxed at low rates, it is estimated that commercial banks invested as much as $4 billion less in municipals than they would have invested without that relatively minor change in the tax code. Similarly, if savings and loan associations were to be taxed at the same rate as commercial banks, it is estimated that the former would buy roughly $40 billion worth of municipals.[61] Tax policy thus has an enormous impact on the size and characteristics of the tax-exempt market.

The process by which local governments borrow money, then, is one involving them as issuers of notes and bonds, rating agencies as calculators of risk, financial advisors and bankers as strategists, Congress as guardian of the public purpose and formulator of tax policy, and investors as weighers of risk, rate of return, and tax advantages. The market encompasses all of these actors—all with their own perspectives, needs, modes of operation, norms, and traditions. Their complex relationships, whether sporadic or continuous, whether direct or symbiotic, constitute the municipal bond market.

New Uses for the Market

As we already mentioned, the volume of borrowing for traditional purposes has declined and governments have increasingly become brokers, borrowing funds at tax-exempt rates, on the one hand, and relending them, on the other hand, at interest rates below "the going market rate" (that is, below the interest rate prevailing in the *taxable* financial markets). This brokerage function has grown as the tax-exempt market has increasingly been used to provide incentives and/or subsidies to quasi-public and private actors so that they will carry out a public purpose. For example, municipal bonds are used to provide funds at below the "going market rate" for hospitals' capital expenditures and for industries' air- and water-pollution equipment. In 1977 pollution control bonds for industry worth $2.9 billion were issued by special authorities, and tax-exempt bonds in 1978 financed roughly 75 percent of all hospital capital costs, to the tune of over $3 billion.[62]

Although the issuance of tax-exempt revenue bonds for hospitals and pollution control has not engendered controversy, their issuance for industrial development and for mortgage subsidy has. The provision of "cheap money" to private firms and homeowners has led to a debate that highlights some of the problematic relationships existing between the public and private sectors.

Industrial Revenue Bonds

Although Mississippi first issued industrial revenue bonds (IRBs) in 1936 to attract industry and was subsequently imitated by other southern states, the dollar volume of such bonds was small, and they did not attract much attention. In the 1960s, however, northeastern and midwestern states began to offer the bonds to attract employers; indeed, they drew much attention as they came to be used to provide funds at below-market rates for all sorts of enterprises—large corporations, in particular. Congress had not expected local governments to use their powers to borrow at tax-exempt rates for such purposes, and it was not pleased to be giving up federal tax revenue for the benefit of large corporations. In 1968 it restricted the issuance of IRBs intended for private industry to ensure that they primarily benefited smaller firms. These bonds came to be known as "small issue" industrial revenue bonds, because they could only be issued in relatively small amounts.

By 1981 forty-seven states allowed the issuance of small issue IRBs (hereafter referred to simply as IRBs), and their use had become widespread. In 1980, $8.4 billion worth were issued.[63] Whereas in 1975 IRBs accounted for only 4 percent of the total volume of long-term tax-exempt bonds, by 1980 they accounted for 15 percent.[64] Rather than being restricted to the industrial employers whom Congress had envisioned as the primary beneficiaries of the bonds, by 1981 they were being used to attract commercial and retail facilities as well: Roughly two-thirds of the states had passed legislation allowing IRBs to be issued for such purposes. In some states, such as Minnesota and Pennsylvania, commercial projects were actually the major beneficiaries of IRB funds.[65] The Congressional Budget Office found that by the beginning of the 1980s, IRBs were increasingly being issued for nonmanufacturing uses including fast-food outlets, bowling alleys, automobile dealerships, restaurants, and corporate headquarters.[66]

IRBs as Routine. Ironically, since so many states now allow the issuance of IRBs, local governments are no longer able to use them to gain a competitive edge in attracting employers. On the contrary, the offer by a "job-hunting" local government to lend tax-exempt funds has become quite standard: Local officials often have to make such an offer just to stay in the competition for new jobs.

Furthermore, many firms now routinely approach local government for IRB funds. In fact, by 1979 some officials were becoming overwhelmed by the number of requests. In Ohio, when Hamilton County Commissioners decided to issue IRBs for commercial as well as industrial projects, applications flooded in. *The Cincinnati Enquirer* reported "all but checkout-counter lines at the county commissioners' twice-a-week staff meetings."[67] Given that within roughly six months the commissioners agreed to issue a $7 million bond for a K-Mart–Kroger project, as well as bonds for "two car dealerships, one shopping center, two motels, and four franchise chicken restaurants,"[68] it is perhaps not surprising that concern began to develop over the Pandora's box they had opened.

The Debate. The so-called public purpose performed by the beneficiaries of IRB funds is not always self-evident. Is the mere provision of employment a public purpose? Is provision of employment at a franchise chicken restaurant as much a public purpose as employment at a small manufacturing firm? Would not many commercial and retail firms open such facilities even without "cheap money"? If they would do so anyway, why give them a subsidy? And if they would not, does this indicate that the project lacks economic viability and that IRBs are actually subsidizing businesses that could not make it on their own? In that case, should government be involved in such subsidizing in the fragmented, decentralized, and helter-skelter fashion currently characterizing the issuance of IRBs? Such questions indicate just how ambiguous the notion of public purpose is in relation to private sector employment. Given this ambiguity, the use of IRBs for commercial, retail, and other purposes has become highly controversial.[69]

Defenders of the status quo, however, contend that a job is a job regardless of whether the employer is a manufacturer or a retailer. They argue that commercial and retail firms provide the kinds of unskilled and semiskilled service-type jobs desperately needed to replace the unskilled manufacturing jobs that either have been replaced by automation or have moved overseas. Moreover, as interest rates skyrocketed and as the differential between tax-exempt and taxable rates widened, many businessmen argued that they simply could not afford to open a business if they had to pay "market rates" on their loans. They claimed that they needed some relief from the very high interest rates they would be forced to pay in the taxable financial markets.[70]

The controversy—as well as the concern over the federal tax revenue lost due to the growth in this sector of the tax-exempt market—has awakened the interest of Congress. In 1982 it limited the types of projects for which IRBs could be issued; in particular, the issuance of IRBs for food establishments and entertainment facilities was restricted.

The Public-Private Sector Relationship. IRBs are an indicator of the changed relationship between the private sector and local government discussed in Chapter 2. Because jobs are such a preoccupation of state and local officials, officials are often eager to offer IRB funds to prospective employers. From the point of view of local officials, the IRB is an excellent instrument with which to provide "cheap money" to the local economy. Insofar as the *federal* government loses tax revenue through the use of IRBs (given that investors who lend money to private firms in the tax-exempt market rather than the taxable market do not pay federal taxes on their interest), one Hamilton County Commissioner accurately described IRBs as "a neat way of using federal dollars at the local level."[71] Although the extensive use of IRBs may raise interest rates in the bond market as more investors have to be attracted, the increase in interest costs is largely invisible and abstract to many local officials as compared to the easily grasped employment associated with IRB-funded businesses.

Because it is Washington that is foregoing revenue and because local officials are competing against each other for private sector jobs, it is difficult for such officials voluntarily to restrict the issuance of IRBs. If one local government does become very conservative in its policy, it may find that the applicants it has refused then take their jobs elsewhere. Officials do not wish to give other local governments a competitive advantage, and because it costs them relatively little to maintain their own standing in the competition, the incentives for self-restraint are few. Restrictions on IRBs, therefore, will have to be nationally imposed so that all localities will enjoy the same competitive position.

It is up to Congress to grapple with the extremely complex question of what a public purpose is in the field of attracting, creating, and maintaining jobs, for local governments are too removed from the revenue losses and often too vulnerable to the threat of job losses to define public purpose narrowly. On the other hand, if an instrument that originally allowed local governments in depressed areas to attract industry has now become so widespread and generalized that it functions as a fairly general subsidy to the private sector in most of the United States, it may be time to face the deeper issue of which IRBs are a sign. That issue essentially involves this question: What is the nature and extent of the subsidy needed by the private sector to perform its task of production and employment?[72]

Mortgage Revenue Bonds

The issue of what properly constitutes a public purpose has also arisen in the household sector. Does it serve a public purpose to subsidize home ownership for the middle class in order to entice this group of people back into the central city? Even if it does and, further, even if the purpose is accomplished, will not suburban cities then also subsidize middle-class homebuyers in order to keep them in the suburbs?

This issue arose because local governments first entered a field of lending that had been the domain of state governments and then changed some of the ground rules. After 1978 city governments began to borrow at tax-exempt rates in order to relend on a large scale to middle-income single-family homebuyers. The local programs were often aimed at a higher-income group than were state programs, and they focused on homeownership rather than on rentals. Through the issuance of the mortgage revenue bond (MRB), cities were able to give mortgages for single-family homes at roughly 2 percent below the mortgage rates offered in the market.

The U.S. Treasury became extremely concerned about the implications and effects of this new use of the tax-exempt market, and the controversy over the mortgage subsidy bonds became extremely heated and often emotional. The Treasury strongly favored congressional action to remove tax exemption from state and local borrowing designed to assist homebuyers rather than renters;[73] local officials, on the other hand, were vehemently opposed to congressional action completely prohibiting tax-exempt MRBs.[74]

Congress largely sided with the Treasury. The final bill passed limited the amount of MRBs that could be issued annually within a state, put a limit on the price of homes that could be bought, required that all recipients be first-time buyers, and prohibited issuance of tax-exempt housing after December 31, 1983. Although bonds designed to assist deteriorating neighborhoods were treated a bit less restrictively than others, the regulations concerning them were not as generous as local officials had hoped they would be.

The debate that took place over the use of MRBs illustrated both how difficult it is, given current political and social structures, to revitalize central cities without in some way subsidizing the middle class and how politically and financially awkward it is to do this—especially when lower-income citizens need subsidized rentals. Although the Treasury argued that federal assistance should be restricted to lower-income groups, central city officials generally felt that helping only the neediest would not improve the city's tax base, renovate its neighborhoods, or help its budget. Rather, they claimed, homeowners as well as renters are needed for a healthy city.

The concerted use of MRBs by central city officials, however, had led suburban governments to begin issuing them as well. If all cities had been allowed to continue issuing them, the bond could easily have become, in a process similar to that which occurred with IRBs, a general subsidy for middle-income homebuyers. Of course, Congress could have chosen to allow only those cities suffering from some agreed-upon set of urban ills to use the bonds, but that action would have required the legislature to develop at least the rudiments of a national urban policy. Congress has failed to develop such a policy and probably will be unable to do so in the future.

Tax-Exempts as a Substitute for National Policy

The new uses of the tax-exempt market have largely been applied to those areas in which there is a national problem but no coherent national policy. The MRB was used to attract owner-occupiers to the central city in an effort to shore up both the city's property tax base as well as its "quality of life." By contrast, Congress, never having formulated a national urban policy, has been unwilling to provide the kinds of resources needed to make a serious and coordinated effort at attracting the middle class back to declining cities. Nor has it accepted the steady deterioration of many older cities as a natural consequence of the free-enterprise system, which permits firms and workers to move at will to more economically suitable locations. Rather, it has passed legislation in a piecemeal fashion and funded programs that have failed to reverse the trend of decline.

The small issue industrial revenue bond also addressed a problem toward which Congress had not formulated a coherent policy. Although by 1981 both Democrats and Republicans in Congress had become concerned with the health of the U.S. economy, local officials had some time earlier recognized the strong interdependence between the public and private sectors. The IRB, in fact, was an attempt at the local level to assist the private sector, resulting from the recognition that government depends on the private sector to provide employment. Local officials acknowledged the link between private employment and local finance in a crude, almost inarticulate, and implicit fashion—but they did at least take some action. Given the structure of local government, the result was often a subsidy of the private sector allocated in an uneconomic, haphazard, and necessarily uncoordinated fashion. But to be fair to local officials, the federal tax code itself deliberately provides incentives in a splintered way. Furthermore, the congressional debate in 1981 about how best to provide more generalized and coordinated federal tax incentives to business indicated that such fragmentation would triumph at the federal level—and that it would do so not because of the imperatives of government structure, but because Congress would choose to keep a structure of piecemeal incentives uninformed by any comprehensive standard of public purpose.

Local officials have used the tax-exempt market to address problems that are recognized (and the consequences of which are felt) first at the local level. Although the outcomes of such action often give grounds for criticism, it is important to note that local officials have tried to use the tools available to them to tackle problems that Congress has been unsuccessful in solving.

Politics, Local Government, and the Market

Analysis of the interdependence between local government, on the one hand, and the municipal bond market, on the other, is an excellent way to begin understanding the intersection between the various "systems"—economic, financial, intergovernmental, metropolitan, political, and administrative—to which a local government is related. The bond market represents one point at which these systems intersect. Moreover, because such analysis forces us to take a close look at special-purpose governments such as public authorities (which are often ignored in discussing, for example, urban politics or urban policymaking), it raises questions about the different types of governance that characterize the geographic area we call a city and the implications of such differences for policymaking.

A study of the market may not give us the details of what is normally considered the "stuff" of city politics, but it does indicate where and how that stuff fits into the larger picture. Although it is obvious that municipal government does not exist in isolation, it is nonetheless difficult to get a grip on the *multiple* relations in which city (as well as other local) officials are involved. Studies of intergovernmental relations, for example, necessarily focus on one set of relationships. Similarly, scholars examining the impact of capitalism on the city focus on the development of corporate capital, capital accumulation, and/or conflict and legitimacy.[75] In contrast, by focusing on the bond market, we are compelled to think about numerous intersecting relationships: those between the city government and the public authorities that operate within its boundaries, as well as those between city government and the larger economic world within which city government exists.

In the section to come, I shall very briefly consider four sets of relationships between the market and local borrowers. The discussion here is exploratory, but it will indicate the types of issues raised by an inquiry into the links between the municipal bond market and the major political and administrative processes characteristic of urban areas.

1. *The operations of the municipal bond market are shaped in three major ways by the intergovernmental system within which local, especially municipal, officials operate.*

First, the market, using risk as its criterion, must discriminate among local borrowers primarily because neither Washington nor the state capitols, with few exceptions, give any kind of guarantees to lenders. The lack of either state or federal loan guarantees leaves local governments without the kind of uniform protection that more central involvement often brings. That is, the market could conceivably lend to local governments *as a class* if all localities had some kind of "floor" provided by Washington or the state government. In Great Britain, for example, all local governments are generally considered credit-worthy, and they are therefore not judged on their individual fiscal vices and virtues. The reasons for such uniformity of treatment stem from the application of more standardized audit procedures than those used in the United States, and especially from the fact that borrowing has to be approved by the central government (which will also lend money to local governments if they cannot borrow in the market). British lenders are thus assured that if a borrower defaults, London will lend it funds to cover the deficit; further, the requirement that local authorities be rigorously audited reassures lenders that default is unlikely to happen in the first place.[76]

In the United States, by contrast, the federal government does not approve loans, require comprehensive audits, or guarantee that loans to local governments will be repaid (in the case of loan guarantees given to New York City, Congress made it very clear that it did not intend to establish a precedent). Washington, for the most part, stays out of local borrowing. State governments do impose limits, but they then dilute them: State audits are often sporadic and incomplete, whereas state legislatures pass legislation allowing constitutional limits and restrictions on debt to be circumvented. The lack of active federal and state oversight forces the market to use risk as the basis for its investment decisions and, therefore, to discriminate between local borrowers. Both the individual fiscal conditions of cities and their revenue-producing projects are exposed to the full force of market judgment. Local governments are, within certain limits, free to borrow without state or federal approval, but they pay for their discretionary powers by exposure to calculations based on risk.

Second, the market responds to a city's borrowing needs according, in part, to that city's treatment by the federal and state government. Monies from both sources are important in giving cities and other governments the financial capacity needed for borrowing purposes. Federal money has been particularly useful in this respect. In essence, the combination of aid for capital and operating expenditures that has come from Washington has helped maintain many Frostbelt cities as *viable risks.*[77]

To the extent that federal aid has maintained the solvency and the economic viability of local governments, the market has benefited. Lenders, after all, depend on borrowers for their profits. The market thus has a direct interest in Washington's urban policies: Cities that slip into such poor fiscal shape that they become an unacceptably bad risk represent lost "customers." The older securities of such cities also tend to plummet in value, resulting in severe loss to investors trying to sell them in the secondary market. Because it is not really in the market's interest to be forced to exercise frequently its ultimate weapon—namely, the refusal of further loans—cuts in federal aid that threaten the financial viability of cities are potentially damaging to investors as well.

Third, both lenders and borrowers will try to use the intergovernmental system to prevent default and/or bankruptcy by lobbying for various types of assistance from other levels of government. These efforts will be more successful for some cities than for others. New York City was able to get both state and federal help because of the huge amounts of money involved, the power of the banks holding city securities, and the symbolic value of New York City in the international markets as the seat of U.S. financial power. Cleveland was not so fortunate, however; although the state did exercise some powers of oversight and did offer some financial help, this city had to deal with its default largely on its own.

Although our sample of defaults is exceedingly small, it is probably safe to say that federal assistance will not be repeated, certainly not on the scale offered to New York City. It is more difficult, however, to say whether New York City will prove unique in winning sizable help from state authorities or whether Cleveland will subsequently appear exceptionally unfortunate in having been unable to mobilize more help from the state capitol. Nonetheless, the existence of the state-local intergovernmental system, characterized by the state's powers to regulate local finance, makes that system a possible actor in the relationship between a city and bondholders in the case of default. The importance of this system is perhaps best illustrated by the jitters caused on Wall Street over the possibility of a state government default, for a state in such a case could not turn to a higher level of government with expectations of the constitutionally clear-cut relationships that exist between state and local government. Certainly, the New York City case showed that bondholders—banks, in particular—will try to use the power of the state government both to protect their investments in municipal securities and to impose fiscal discipline on a city. But the case of Cleveland suggests that such a strategy is not always completely effective.

2. *The bond market's treatment of a city reflects that city's success in attracting federal money or private sector jobs, or both, and reinforces prospects for further success.*

As mentioned in Chapter 2, city governments compete for federal aid and for private sector jobs. Some of the federal aid has been used to help attract jobs, and, as earlier mentioned in this chapter, the bond market has also been used to attract jobs through the issuance of IRBs. The more successful cities are in getting federal money and private sector jobs, the better their relative position in the bond market. And the better they do in the market, the less money they have to pay for interest costs, the more attractive they seem to businessmen as places to move to or stay in, and (at least in the case of declining cities) the stronger become their claims on Washington for continued help in attracting jobs, insofar as they can argue that federal money is already being used effectively. Conversely, a city that is unable to attract private jobs and sufficient federal aid will do badly in the market, thereby increasing its interest costs and burdening its already overloaded budget.

Because risk is the determinant of investment behavior, the market does not serve as a redistributive or compensatory mechanism; rather, it penalizes the weak and rewards the strong. It also reinforces the process of economic decline and boom. It must be emphasized that this situation is not the result of a deliberate strategy on the part of investors; on the contrary, it is an imperative flowing from the logic of investment based on risk.

It has been suggested that a national public bank should be established that, by lending to local governments out of favor with the market, would compensate for the effects of the vicious cycle mentioned earlier and thus protect weak local governments from being further weakened by the financial market. The market, however, imposes a form of fiscal discipline that is seen by borrowers and lenders alike to be more impartial and therefore more authoritative than any exercised by government. Many officials are therefore reluctant to renounce a process that, while hurting weak governments, nevertheless forces them to live within their means at the risk of being cut off from credit.

3. *The process of circumventing state restrictions on municipal borrowing in order to obtain capital for urban development has involved a proliferation of authorities, and such proliferation inhibits the ability of city governments to control the provision of services within their boundaries.*

Students of urban politics used to spend much of their time arguing about who governed in cities, but this issue has now become much less relevant. Whoever does govern—through city-wide institutions, at least—is able to choose among relatively few options. The ability of special districts and public authorities to obtain credit separately from city or county government has fragmented power within the metropolitan area, and within city boundaries, to the point that merely understanding the distribution of formal authority, much less influence, has become a gigantic task.

It has been suggested that, even without the complications entailed by examining special-purpose authorities and districts, the fragmentation of power within city government *itself* has made many big cities ungovernable. That is, the cities' policymaking system is structurally incapable of providing "coherent policy-making and service delivery."[78] Big city governments have difficulty in making coherent policy even in those areas over which officials have control, but they obviously have even more difficulty affecting the many functions outside their jurisdiction. The problem of fragmentation is therefore more serious than the incapacity of city-wide institutions. Officials in many cities, large and small, suburbs as well as central cities (and those in rural as well as in urban areas), often have relatively little control over the capital infrastructure that shapes a city and the opportunities enjoyed by its residents. Even if a city does have a policymaking system capable of formulating and implementing coherent policy, it is generally unable to act in many policy areas that are vital to city life.

Special districts and public authorities crisscross almost all cities, except perhaps the very smallest. The power to control what happens within a city is thereby fragmented. As long as twenty-five years ago,

John Bollens recognized the problem, which has since grown far worse. He remarked that the "uncoordinated, splintered efforts" of special districts dispersed policymaking among many governmental bodies.[79] Bollens' analysis would apply even more strongly today, for special districts and public authorities[80] are the main contributors to the extreme fragmentation of formal power, not to mention influence, in urban areas. Insulated from the public (because their boards are usually appointed rather than elected) and autonomous in policy-making, these authorities shape the entire urban area; as a result, city officials are often unable to exercise even coordination, much less control, over their operations. Annmarie Hauck Walsh, after conducting the most exhaustive study to date of public authorities, concludes that "the primary question concerning public authorities today is how to direct their financial and management resources toward broad governmental goals." This question arises, she argues, because "government control . . . is weak and uneven."[81]

Especially because special-purpose governments usually deal with capital facilities, their actions may literally transform the landscape of both central and suburban cities. And the facilities built, as Walsh points out, are usually chosen on the basis of financial return, for the bond market more strongly emphasizes financial criteria for authorities than for general-purpose governments with the right to tax. Walsh finds, for example, that authorities favor "highways over rail transportation, water supply and power production over pollution abatement and recreational use of water resources, school building over expansion of student counseling, sports arenas over open spaces, industrial parks over small business assistance," and so on.[82]

In short, city officialdom does not control much of the capital infrastructure on which the city's most basic functions depend, and it therefore exercises much less control over the kinds of recreational, transportation, and even business opportunities that residents will have than most voters assume. Although city residents may be dissatisfied with the bus system, sewer problems, or airport noise, there is generally little that their elected officials can do about such complaints. Furthermore, the city government, when internally divided, is in a weak position even to negotiate with individual authority boards, each of which has a relatively clear idea of its mission, a fairly straightforward calculus for achieving it, and an insulation from the public that frees it from worrying about citizen input or hostile interest groups.

The distribution of power in the urban/metropolitan area, then, is directly affected by strategies for increasing access to the municipal bond market. Like the sorcerer's apprentice, city governments have employed a formula to help them in their tasks that has run out of their control; but there is no sorcerer in sight to end the chaos caused by this process.

4. *In times of "normal politics," the market serves as an outer boundary within which a city's political choices take place; in times of fiscal crisis, lenders occupy a central place in the municipal political process.*

The market generally acts as a de facto "outer boundary" for political choices made by city officials about service levels, tax rates, and economic development. I use the term "outer boundary" because lenders are not usually concerned with specific policies of borrowers— as long as the latter maintain credit-worthiness. Just as lenders have not been concerned per se with the working conditions offered by corporations that have borrowed funds in the taxable financial markets, so they are not concerned with the kinds of policies pursued by local officials—that is, as long as such policies do not stop officials from meeting debt payment deadlines.

Because lenders are mainly concerned with getting their money back, they evaluate a city's performance according to strictly financial criteria, rather than according to its politics or to the kinds of social goals it may (or may not) have chosen to pursue. Lenders are interested in cash flow, the match between revenue and expenditure, and the health of a city's economic base—not in whether the city government is providing for its poor, trying to reduce inequality, or providing avenues of political participation. The fact that New York City came by its fiscal problems through its generosity to the poor was irrelevant to the market. Once it became clear that New York City was living far beyond its means, lenders would not lend. The calculation of risk is paramount— but indifferent to "good intentions."

However, this indifference works both ways. As long as borrowers satisfy lenders' criteria, the market will not penalize them for also being generous to the poor. For example, although California has been a high-tax, high-service state, the state's credit rating has been excellent. Its booming economy has been able to support a high level of services without suffering erosion; lenders have therefore considered the state government a good risk.

The market—and the fears of those controlling it—forces cities to maintain a minimal level of solvency and to regain solvency once it has been lost. In the absence of such solvency, the risk of lending to cities will be too high, and the cities will be denied access to the market. Officials usually try to avoid, even at high political cost, any budgetary situation that might provoke a denial of credit. Indeed, they will avoid even approaching such a situation. The worried reactions of city officials to lowered ratings indicate that such officials recognize the tacit threat posed by the market.

Although the market sets the broad limits within which local officials operate and although it exerts various pressures, implicit and explicit, upon a city's management of its finances, it does not enter directly into the political arena unless there is a crisis. The representatives of the financial community—bankers, for example—do not usually take a public stance in clashes or publicly participate in coalitions between the various groups that engage in "city politics" as conventionally understood. Although bankers are often consulted by city officials about a wide range of financial matters, such bankers usually become newsworthy only when lenders show signs of refusing to support a city.

This is not to say that the principles of the market are absent from political debate. The logic used by lenders in assessing risk—and the criteria they deem important—is also often expressed by groups (business and taxpayer groups especially) that see a city more as a financial enterprise than as a dispenser of services. Such groups stress the same factors as do lenders: They want a city, above all, to live within its economic and financial means, and they generally desire enlargement of the tax base. Conversely, they do not wish that tax base to be unduly burdened, nor do they wish the city to spend more than it receives.[83]

When a city is declining economically, such an emphasis on defending (or expanding) the tax base and on balancing the budget nearly always results in a downgrading of those services used primarily by the poor. Such services, whatever their other virtues, do not enhance a city's credit-worthiness; instead, they represent a burden on the budget that does not, at least directly, enhance a city's tax base by helping economic development. Furthermore, services for the poor are primarily paid for by the nonpoor—those most likely to move out of the municipality, thereby weakening its tax base. The logic of the financial market thus discourages both redistributive policies in times of decline as well as the use of operating deficits to provide services beyond the city's budgetary capability.

The market actually dominates the making of political decisions when a city is on the brink of default or has actually defaulted. At that point, the interest of bondholders becomes an explicit and highly visible force; to the extent that this interest is harmed, penalties will be imposed by lenders on the city. Political leaders do not have the margins for maneuver otherwise available to them in times of routine politics; the conflicts are obvious, and clear-cut choices have to be made. The fundamental choice is not merely one between cutting services and having the city's rating dropped, but rather one between retrenchment and being cut off from the market altogether. In the cases of both New York City and Cleveland, officials cut services and increased taxes rather than cause the cities to be permanently cut off from the market.[84]

Even if those groups demanding fiscal prudence are not heeded prior to a crisis, the market itself will in the end, however crudely and with whatever mistakes of timing, force local officials to listen. If the local officials fail to "live within their means," however elastic and ambiguous the definition of that term might be, sooner or later they will be penalized. The arguments of the market are represented in all cities by at least a few groups. If they are heeded, a crisis is unlikely to occur; if they are not, the market will force city officials to listen.

Officials have, in fact, little choice but to listen to the counsels of lenders. Once a borrowing government has been perceived to be so high a risk that lenders will not lend at any interest rate, local officials either have to make their government a better risk or else give up borrowing—and the prospect of future borrowing—altogether. The latter option is, of course, a very difficult one, given that a city in crisis may be unable even to meet its current payroll without borrowing, and certainly will be incapable of providing further capital facilities from its own funds. Simply put, over the long term, a city government would find it nearly impossible to continue providing the services demanded by its citizens if it were cut off from credit.

Substantial power (although, as Leeds persuasively argues in Chapter 5, not complete power) is thus directly exercised by the financial community over cities in trouble and indirectly exercised over others wanting to stay out of trouble. Two features of such power make it extremely problematic for city governments. First, it is power exercised in such a way as to be unaccountable to voters. Voters cannot force lenders to lend to their city government, nor can they impose a lowering of the interest rate charged. The city is therefore subject to strong sanctions over which local voters have no control.

Second, it is power exercised in a way that is usually invisible or unintelligible to voters; even when its workings *are* seen, their effects are often unacceptable to significant elements of the population. This situation does not come as a great surprise. The burden of interest rates and their link to bond ratings, for example, do not usually play a major part in political debate. Furthermore, the ultimate sanction—long-term denial of credit—has never had to be exercised in the post-war period (Cleveland was in default for only twenty-two months), so there exists no dramatic case that can be used to illustrate the consequences. Citizens are therefore unlikely to understand why bond ratings are important or why access to the municipal bond market is necessary for city government. The specialized language of the investment banker is simply not a normal part of political debate in cities.

Considering the arcane nature of the financial world and the fact that the consequences of default or of declining ratings are not felt immediately, it is actually easy to see why citizens are sometimes baffled by their officials' fears of being cut off from credit. Liberals and the poor, especially, are apt to resent the priority given to keeping up a city's reputation on Wall Street, particularly when the cost of such respectability is a cutback in services. They tend to argue that even if a city cannot meet its debt payments, it should maintain services to the poor, rather than cut such services in order to repay debt. Robert Lekachman articulated this view most clearly during New York City's fiscal crisis. After analyzing the effects of budget cutbacks on hospitals, transit fares, schools, and parks, he put forth the following argument:

> In sum, we are experiencing a substantial redistribution of resources from families in average or worse circumstances to affluent investors, bank stockholders and other unneedy citizens. . . . I find it hard to believe the average resident of New York would be worse off now and in the near future if the city defaulted on some of its debt. Given a choice, I would rather go broke in good company than suffer the Egyptian captivity of Ma Bell, the banks and the life insurance companies. But nobody asked me or any of the other voters.[85]

Many city residents probably feel the same way, although it is worth noting that voters in Cleveland supported the raising of taxes to help balance the budget; in New York City, moreover, voters generally accepted Mayor Koch's argument that it was necessary to reduce services. Still, it is not immediately obvious to some that repayment of debt is so important as to justify the dismissal of city employees and substantial cutbacks in service. The importance of maintaining or regaining access to the market is another matter that remains unclear. As one resident of Cleveland put it on the day the city came to an agreement with the banks holding its notes, "I guess it's a good thing they did it, but I don't know that it's going to make much difference to me. Things have just been going along without it, you know."[86]

The views expressed by Lekachman and by this Cleveland resident are very different from those of most local officials. The latter generally attempt to anticipate the market's reaction and to fashion policies that will keep them in good standing or at least secure the minimum approval necessary for borrowing to continue. The market rarely has to deny credit, simply because local officials try so hard to keep their cities credit-worthy. As Raymond Owen points out in Chapter 7, "government" is concerned with continuity, stability, and predictability. The bond market is crucial to that kind of stability, since its monies are essential for the kinds of long-term capital projects and economic development that government has to undertake. Moreover, politicians depend on that stable presence, for it gives them the slack, the flexibility, to provide services that will help them politically.

At times, however, the gap between the perceptions of officials and those of voters makes it difficult for the former to convince the latter that a financial crisis will be as damaging to a city as officials fear. The peril of being denied credit is real for city officials, but it is often too ambiguous to be fully understood by many citizens. When the prospect of a crisis does occur, as in Cleveland, voters may be willing to approve a tax increase that they had previously rejected when it is proposed as a way to *prevent* the crisis. Officials may well feel caught between the demands of the market and those of their voters when they try to prevent a crisis, given that the voters may not see the market's relevance for the city. When a crisis does occur, however, many of the market's demands are almost bound to prevail, sooner or later.

The Director of Ohio's Budget and Management Office succinctly analyzed the relationship between voters, the bond market, and city government as follows: "What's important is not what the public thinks. It's what the people in the New York bond rating agencies think."[87] The leader of Cleveland's police union seemed to agree when he said, "You can only go so long without getting back into the bond market."[88] Finally, the finance director of Cleveland pointed out that the city will have to spend more than $400 million over six years to repair collapsing bridges and streets, with still more to be spent in the future to upgrade a rapidly deteriorating water and sewer system. Although the federal and state government contributed substantially to the initial $400 million expenditure, $60 million had to be found by the city itself. As the director ironically put it, "Sixty million dollars, when you don't even have a bond rating, is a lot of money."[89] His comment sums up the point of this chapter.

Notes

1. For giving me a sense of market dynamics, I am grateful to my interviewees: municipal finance officers, investment and commercial bankers, and officials at both the Treasury Department and the Office of the Comptroller of the Currency. I would also like to thank the Faculty of Arts and Sciences and the University Center for Urban Research of the University of Pittsburgh for the grants that funded this research.

2. George E. Peterson, "Capital Spending and Capital Obsolescence: The Outlook for Cities," in *The Fiscal Outlook for Cities: Implications of a National Urban Policy*, ed. Roy Bahl (Syracuse, N.Y.: Syracuse University Press, 1978), p. 53.

3. John E. Petersen, "The Municipal Bond Market: Recent Changes and Future Prospects," unpublished paper, Government Finance Research Center, Municipal Finance Officers Association, 13 February 1981, table 3, p. 11.

4. Ibid., p. 8.

5. Ibid.; see also Ralph C. Kimball, "States as Financial Intermediaries," *New England Economic Review*, January/February 1976, pp. 17–29.

6. Advisory Commission on Intergovernmental Relations, *City Financial Emergencies: The Intergovernmental Dimension* (Washington, D.C.: Government Printing Office, 1973), pp. 61–63.

7. Ronald W. Forbes and John E. Petersen, "Background Paper," in *Building a Broader Market: Report of the Twentieth Century Fund Task Force on the Municipal Bond Market* (New York: McGraw-Hill, 1976), p. 43.

8. U.S., Congress, Congressional Budget Office, *Small Issue Industrial Revenue Bonds* (Washington, D.C.: Government Printing Office, 1981), p. 47.

9. I am grateful to Professor Patric Hendershott of the School of Management at Purdue University for these data.

10. John E. Petersen, "Financial Roundup for State and Local Government," *Resources in Review* (Municipal Finance Officers Association) 3 (March 1981):4.

11. Forbes and Petersen, "Background Paper," p. 44.

12. U.S., Congress, Joint Economic Committee, *Financing Municipal Facilities, Hearings before the Sub-committee on Economic Progress*, vol. 1, statement of Roy M. Goodman, 90th Cong., 1st sess., 1967, p. 9.

13. Dan Moreau, "Delay is Sought in City Bond Sale," *Richmond Times-Dispatch* (Virginia), 2 December 1980.

14. Alan Eisner, "S & P Cuts Hub's Bond Rating," *Boston Herald American*, 3 December 1980.

15. Forbes and Petersen, "Background Paper," p. 56; for a general discussion of the relationship between local government borrowing and the provision of social services, see Alberta Sbragia, "Borrowing to Build: Private Money and Public Welfare," *International Journal of Health Services* 9 (May 1979):218–220.

16. "Cities Bet on Banks Short-term," *Business Week*, 24 March 1980, p. 98.

17. Annmarie Hauck Walsh, *The Public's Business: The Politics and Practices of Government Corporations—A Twentieth Century Fund Study* (Cambridge: MIT Press, 1978), p. 118.

18. Petersen, "The Municipal Bond Market," table 5, p. 14.

19. Advisory Commission on Intergovernmental Relations, *Understanding the Market for State and Local Debt* (Washington, D.C.: Government Printing Office, 1976), pp. 44–53.

20. However, as Walsh points out, many public authorities receive a significant amount of their revenue from governments that do levy taxes. (Walsh, *The Public's Business*, p. 57).

21. Ibid., p. 23.

22. Peterson, "Capital Spending and Capital Obsolescence," pp. 58–59.

23. Walsh, *The Public's Business*, p. 56.

24. Lennox L. Moak and Albert M. Hillhouse, *Concepts and Practices in Local Government Finance* (Chicago: Municipal Finance Officers Association, 1975), p. 316.

25. Robert Lamb and Stephen P. Rappaport, *Municipal Bonds: The Comprehensive Review of Tax-Exempt Securities and Public Finance* (New York: McGraw-Hill, 1980), p. 15; see also Walsh, *The Public's Business*, pp. 129–149.

26. Lynn E. Browne and Richard F. Syron, "The Municipal Market since the New York City Crisis," *New England Economic Review*, July/August 1979, p. 12; Petersen, "The Municipal Bond Market," table 1, p. 3.

27. *The Rating Game: Report of the Twentieth Century Fund Task Force on Municipal Bond Credit Ratings* (New York: The Twentieth Century Fund, 1974), p. 1.

28. The national bond market does not, however, provide *all* of the funds borrowed by state and local governments. Lamb and Rappaport point out that many municipal issues "are really small- to moderate-sized loans to municipalities for such things as a fire engine, school bus, or bridge. These bonds might not ever truly enter the national public bond market at all." These municipal issues are "tailor-made" for local banks and "will probably never be resold or leave the community, the state, or indeed the bank's vault" (Lamb and Rappaport, *Municipal Bonds*, p. 28). The aggregate dollar volume of "local bonds," however, is very small compared to that of bonds sold in the national market.

The federal government also loans some funds to local governments. In 1975, "federal loans to states and local governments for only six major functions totaled over $1.5 billion" (Deil S. Wright, *Understanding Intergovernmental Relations* [North Scituate, Mass.: Duxbury, 1978], p. 126).

29. For a more detailed account of the processes and technicalities involved in buying and selling municipal bonds in the national market, see Lamb and Rappaport, *Municipal Bonds*, pp. 40–50; Walsh, *The Public's Business*, pp. 55–80; Alan Walter Steiss, *Local Government Finance: Capital Facilities Planning and Debt Administration* (Lexington, Mass.: Lexington Books, 1975), pp. 103–151.

30. *Moody's Bond Record*, September 1981, p. 129.

31. Unrated bonds are usually "local" bonds and are bought by local banks.

32. Alan D. Mutter and Harry Golden, Jr., "Lower Rating Could Cost City $3.6 Million," *Chicago Sun-Times*, 20 September 1979.

33. Lamb and Rappaport, *Municipal Bonds*, pp. 58–72.

34. Wes Hills, "Dayton Fights Downgrading of Its Bond Rating," *Dayton Daily News*, 26 July 1979; Dave Allbaugh, "Dayton Plans to Issue Bonds Despite Rating, *Dayton Daily News*, 28 July 1979.

35. John Leach, "Top Bond Ratings Elude City and County Because of Growth Rate," *Phoenix, Arizona Republic*, 21 October 1979.

36. Jo Mannise and Phil Sutin, "Dispute May Affect City's Credit," *St. Louis Post-Dispatch*, 28 December 1979.

37. See, for example, Clyde Haberman, "Koch, in Miami, Makes Bond Pitch," *New York Times*, 17 March 1981, p. B6.

38. Financial advisors sometimes find themselves in awkward situations, for city officials who have been counseled to take out a bank loan rather than go to market may be irate upon learning that the same advisor has counseled another city they view as "inferior" to go ahead and borrow in the market. One advisor, working for a major bank with numerous municipalities as clients, recalls being tongue-lashed for having counseled one city to go to market while suggesting a bank loan to another. When the city officials who had taken out a bank loan learned of his advice to the other city—a city they believed, against all available evidence, to be in worse shape than their own—they were furious. The advisor said, "I was just stunned. Civic pride sometimes comes in and makes city officials blind."

39. George E. Peterson, "Finance," in *The Urban Predicament*, eds. William Gorham and Nathan Glazer (Washington, D.C.: The Urban Institute, 1976), p. 66.

40. John Leach, "County Blamed for Using 'Archaic' Accounting," *Phoenix, Arizona Republic*, 16 September 1979.

41. "Who's Watching the Books?" *Standard & Poor's Perspective*, 26 November 1980.

42. Ibid., p. 5.

43. *The City In Transition: Prospects and Policies for New York, The Final Report of the Temporary Commission on City Finances* (New York: Arno Press, 1978), p. 70.

44. For the classic study of "debt payment performance," see George H. Hempel, *The Postwar Quality of State and Local Debt* (New York: National Bureau of Economic Research, 1971), especially pp. 26–29.

45. See U.S., Congress, House, Committee on Banking, Finance and Urban Affairs, *Securities and Exchange Commission Staff Report on Transactions in Securities of the City of New York to the Subcommittee on Economic Stabilization*, 95th Cong., 1st sess., 1977.

46. U.S., Congress, House, Committee on Banking, Finance and Urban Affairs, *Role of Commercial Banks in the Financing of the Debt of the City of Cleveland, Hearing before the Subcommittee on Financial Institutions Supervision, Regulation and Insurance*, statement of Mayor Dennis Kucinich, 96th Cong., 1st sess., 1979.

47. Ibid., Federal Reserve Staff Memorandum of Review into Allegations of Cleveland Mayor Dennis J. Kucinich Concerning Cleveland Trust Company, p. 126.

48. Ibid., p. 568.

49. New York City's problems also temporarily changed the way certain cities' bonds were treated in the market. See Peterson, "Finance," p. 67; Lynn E. Browne and Richard F. Syron, "Big City Bonds after New York," *New England Economic Review*, July/August 1977, pp. 3–9.

50. Even more worrisome is the possibility that a state government *and* the major city government within the state might default simultaneously.

Although some analysts had been afraid that New York State might default in the mid-1970s, the state's fiscal problems were seen as having been caused by the massive aid it was giving to keep New York City out of default. The possibility that a state and a city government might default independently gives analysts a very bad case of the jitters.

51. *Building a Broader Market: Report of the Twentieth Century Fund Task Force on the Municipal Bond Market* (New York: McGraw-Hill, 1976), p. 6.

52. Forbes and Petersen, "Background Paper," pp. 77–89.

53. Ibid., p. 77.

54. However, the thesis that bank investment in municipals is determined primarily by the amount of residual funds available rather than by calculations of maximizing profit has been challenged. See John E. Petersen, "State and Local Government Debt Policy and Management," in *State and Local Government Finance and Financial Management: A Compendium of Current Research*, eds. John E. Petersen, Catherine Lavigne Spain, and Martharose F. Laffey (Washington, D.C.: Government Finance Research Center, Municipal Finance Officers Association, 1978), p. 64.

55. Peter Lewis, "The Case for the Urban Development Bank," *Financing State and Local Governments*, Federal Reserve Bank of Boston, Conference Series No. 3, 1970, p. 166; Browne and Syron, "The Municipal Market since the New York City Crisis," pp. 14–15; see also Ralph C. Kimball, "Commercial Banks, Tax Avoidance, and the Market for State and Local Debt since 1970," *New England Economic Review*, January/February 1977, pp. 3–21.

56. "New Era in Spread Management," *U.S. Banker*, December 1980, p. 48. In times of interest rate volatility, all investors may be reluctant to buy municipal bonds (as well as all other types of bonds) of any maturity. The reason is straightforward. If an investor buys a municipal bond paying 8 percent interest and then has to sell it in the secondary market when interest rates are 10 percent, he or she will have to sell the bond at a price lower than that at which he bought it and will therefore lose money. Investors, accordingly, are not eager to buy bonds if they expect interest rates to climb.

57. Forbes and Petersen, "Background Paper," p. 74.

58. Petersen, "State and Local Government Debt Policy and Management," p. 68.

59. Ibid., pp. 68–69; for a sampling of largely favorable responses to the idea of a national development bank, see U.S., Congress, Committee on Banking, Finance and Urban Affairs, *Summary of Requests for Comments on a Proposed National Development Bank*, Staff Study Prepared by the Subcommittee on Economic Stabilization, 96th Cong., 1st sess., 1979.

60. See, for example, Patrick Healy, "Further Comments on Proposed Capital Financing Alternatives," *Tax Policy* 37 (January–February 1970):8–9.

61. Data were received from Professor Patric Hendershott.

62. Lamb and Rappaport, *Municipal Bonds*, pp. 188, 225; for a critique concerning the use of tax-exempts to finance pollution control equipment, see George E. Peterson and Harvey Galper, "Tax Exempt Financing of Private Industry's Pollution Control Investment," *Public Policy* 23 (Winter 1975):81–103.

63. Congressional Budget Office, *Small Issue Industrial Revenue Bonds,* p. 3.

64. Ibid., p. 47

65. Ibid., p. 18.

66. Ibid., p. 19.

67. Mike Turmell, "County Wants to Stem Flood of Bond Requests," *Cincinnati Enquirer,* 17 October 1979.

68. Ibid.

69. For good journalistic summaries of the issues involved in the debate, see Gerald Tebben, "County Issues More Bonds than Ever," *Columbus Evening Dispatch* (Ohio), 1 June 1979, and the series of related articles in *Nation's Cities Weekly,* 23 March 1981.

70. On May 29, 1981, the average interest rate on new municipals was 10.38 percent and on corporate bonds it was 15.25 percent. The differential was nearly 5 percent. By comparison, in January of 1977 the differential between the average rate on new Aa municipal bonds and that on new Aa corporate bonds was only 2.44 percent. It is not surprising that as differentials widened, IRBs seemed increasingly attractive to businesses (Department of the Treasury, *Treasury Bulletin,* June 1981, pp. 69–70).

71. Turmell, "County Wants to Stem Flood of Bond Requests"; for a discussion of restrictions placed on IRBs in 1982, see Randy Hamilton, "The World Turned Upside Down: The Contemporary Revolution in State and Local Government Financing," *Public Administration Review,* January/February 1983, pp. 22–23.

72. For discussions of that question from various points of view, see Charles Lindblom, *Politics and Markets: The World's Political Economic Systems* (New York: Basic Books, 1977); James O'Connor, *The Fiscal Crisis of the State* (New York: St. Martin's Press, 1973); Richard Rose and B. Guy Peters, *Can Government Go Bankrupt?* (New York: Basic Books, 1978); Roger Friedland, Frances Fox Piven, and Robert Alford, "Political Conflict, Urban Structure, and the Fiscal Crisis," in *Comparing Public Policy: New Approaches and Methods,* ed. Douglas Ashford (Beverly Hills: Sage, 1977), pp. 197–226.

73. U.S., Congress, House, *Tax Treatment of Mortgage Subsidy Bonds, Hearings before the Committee on Ways and Means,* part I, 96th Cong., 1st sess., 1979, pp. 6–9.

74. Ibid. See, for example, pp. 177–180, 263–265; U.S., Congress, Senate, Committee on Governmental Affairs, *Intergovernmental Fiscal Impact of Mortgage Revenue Bonds, Hearing before the Subcommittee on Intergovernmental Relations,* 96th Cong., 1st sess., 1979, p. 128; U.S., Congress, House, *Tax Treatment of Mortgage Subsidy Bonds,* p. 620.

75. See, for example, O'Connor, *The Fiscal Crisis of the State;* David Harvey, *Social Justice and the City* (Baltimore: Johns Hopkins, 1973); Ira Katznelson, "The Crisis of the Capitalist City: Urban Politics and Social Control," in *Theoretical Perspectives on Urban Politics,* eds. Willis D. Hawley et al. (Englewood Cliffs, N.J.: Prentice-Hall, 1976), pp. 214–229; Manuel Castells, *City, Class, and Power* (New York: St. Martin's Press, 1978).

76. See Alberta Sbragia, "Cities, Capital, and Banks: The Politics of Debt in the U.S.A., U.K., and France," in *Urban Political Economy*, ed. Kenneth Newton (London: Frances Pinter, 1981), pp. 200–220, and "The Politics of Local Borrowing: A Comparative Analysis," *Studies In Public Policy*, no. 37, Centre for the Study of Public Policy, University of Strathclyde, Glasgow.

77. See Advisory Commission on Intergovernmental Relations, *Understanding the Market for State and Local Debt*, pp. 23–24; U.S., Congress, Senate, Committee on Finance, *Targeted Fiscal Assistance to State and Local Governments, Hearings before the Subcommittee on Revenue Sharing, Intergovernmental Revenue Impact, and Economic Problems*, 96th Cong., 1st sess., 1979, p. 131; John E. Petersen, "Big City Borrowing Costs," in *Cities Under Stress: The Fiscal Crises of Urban America*, eds. Robert W. Burchell and David Listokin (Piscataway, N.J.: The Center for Urban Policy Research, Rutgers, The State University of New Jersey, 1981), pp. 245–246.

78. Douglas Yates, *The Ungovernable City: The Politics of Urban Problems and Policy Making* (Cambridge: MIT Press, 1977), p. 30.

79. John C. Bollens, *Special District Governments in the United States* (Berkeley, Calif.: University of California Press, 1957), p. 255; see also Advisory Commission on Intergovernmental Relations, *The Problem of Special Districts in American Government* (Washington, D.C.: Government Printing Office, 1964).

80. There is some debate about which units should be called "public authorities" and which should be known as "special districts." The two terms are often used interchangeably.

81. Walsh, *The Public's Business*, p. 259.

82. Ibid., p. 338.

83. For a historical perspective on when and why business groups developed these views, see Martin Shefter, "The Emergence of the Political Machine: An Alternative View," in *Theoretical Perspectives on Urban Politics*, eds. Willis D. Hawley et al. (Englewood Cliffs, N.J.: Prentice-Hall, 1976).

84. For an excellent discussion of how the process of expansionary spending followed by retrenchment has historically worked in New York City, see Martin Shefter, "New York City's Fiscal Crisis: The Politics of Inflation and Retrenchment," in *Managing Fiscal Stress: The Crisis in the Public Sector*, ed. Charles H. Levine (Chatham, N.J.: Chatham House, 1980), pp. 71–94.

85. Robert Lekachman, "Swallowing Big Mac: Banks and Beggars in New York City," *The New Leader*, 1 September 1975, p. 9.

86. Iver Peterson, "Cleveland's Council Clears Pact Ending City's Default," *New York Times*, 9 October 1980, p. A22.

87. "Cleveland Striving To Polish Its Image," *New York Times*, 12 October 1980, p. 59.

88. Peterson, "Cleveland's Council Clears Pact Ending City's Default," p. A22.

89. Ibid.

5

City Politics and the Market: The Case of New York City's Financing Crisis

Patricia Giles Leeds

On March 17, 1975, the mayor of New York was advised by representatives of the local financial institutions that they would no longer purchase and underwrite city debt. The city's overreliance on borrowing, not only for capital improvements but also to meet current operating expenses and to redeem existing debt, had saturated the market with city paper and, consequently, eroded its financial credibility. The traditional source of capital for U.S. local governments—the financial market—was closed to New York City. By March 31 the outstanding indebtedness of the city exceeded $14 billion. Over $2.4 billion of this was due to mature before the end of the fiscal year on June 30, with $550 million due within two weeks of March 31. Combined with upcoming municipal payrolls, the city needed close to $1 billion just to meet operating expenses and debt payments through April. On April 4 Mayor Abraham Beame informed the governor that without immediate assistance the city would default within ten days.

To understand the significance of the market closing and to interpret subsequent developments, we must first understand what kind of crisis the city faced. Although numerous commentators have referred to this whole period as New York City's "fiscal crisis," that term fails to distinguish two relatively separate stages in the evolution of the city's budgetary problems. It is more helpful to view the events of March 1975 and after as a *financing crisis*, which, although the outcome of a continuing *fiscal crisis,* was distinctive in both its characteristics and consequences.

This chapter begins with a discussion of the different analytical models associated with fiscal and financing crises. It offers an explanation of the structural dynamics of the New York City crisis by focusing on the options and strategies available to the major actors in the crisis— namely, the city, the banks, the public employee unions, and the state and federal governments. It then turns to a review and assessment of the solution imposed and of the institutional and political changes that have resulted from it. The chapter concludes with an examination of how the controversial means used to resolve the New York City crisis may have affected the structure of municipal finance generally and the specific alternatives available to other cities facing similar fiscal distress.

Fiscal and Financing Crises: Two Models

Fiscal crisis, as the term is most appropriately employed, refers to a structural imbalance between revenues and expenditures, a persistent pattern whereby spending outpaces the taxation to support it. Fiscal crisis, then, refers to a general condition of U.S. cities, the most important indicators of which are budget deficits, rising taxes, and recurring efforts to enforce economies. The explanations for the emergence of fiscal crises vary according to the analytical and ideological predilections of the observer. Some observers perceive a systematic tendency on the part of contemporary U.S. cities to run budget deficits because they are compelled to carry out the contradictory functions of maintaining conditions favorable to capital accumulation (the generation of tax revenues) and ensuring legitimacy through the democratic political process (the creation of electoral majorities).[1] Others perceive fiscal crises to be periodic episodes that stem from the expansion of political demands as new groups (immigrants, the working class, blacks, welfare recipients, city employees) enter city politics and as political elites fail to organize and constrain these new forces into stable governing conditions.[2]

What these interpretations have in common is the premise that a fiscal crisis is a more or less prolonged pattern of decisions about taxing, spending, and borrowing. In this sense, the term "crisis" may not be completely accurate after all, insofar as the underlying conditions that yield a fiscal crisis can be quite stable. In elucidating the key features of a fiscal crisis and in contrasting it with a financing crisis, we may find it useful to consider the political process, the strategic positions and interests of the central actors, and the major policy options of each.

1. The politics of fiscal crisis are the incremental politics of coalition-building, bargaining, and logrolling by which politicians govern diverse cities. These are the politics of expansion and distribution.
2. The principal actors in a fiscal crisis perceive their strategic interests as the maximization of short-term gains. Politicians trade benefits for votes; city employees and have-not groups press for concessions by threatening noncooperation and disruption of city services and public order. The banks and financial institutions are willing partners to this process because they also stand to profit in the short run; that is, they have more opportunities to make loans when distributive politics drive the city into the red. For so long as any one of the central characters retains the possibility of making gains, they all have powerful incentives to engage in tacit collusion to sustain the conditions that perpetuate the fiscal crisis.
3. The options available to city officials in a fiscal crisis are not especially constricted, or at least they do not appear to be so. A fiscal crisis may actually broaden the options of politicians, in that it removes the balanced budget norm requiring that benefits be paid for at the time they are distributed. Thus opened up is a range of creative, if questionable, bookkeeping and budgetary techniques that have the effect of increasing the number of alternatives open to a city, at least in the short term.

The necessary condition for a fiscal crisis is borrowing, and for U.S. cities this means ready access to the municipal bond market. *A fiscal crisis is based on extensive borrowing in the bond market; whereas a financing crisis refers to the inability of a city to continue to market its debt.* A financing crisis has one immediate, unavoidable, and profound consequence: The city is unable to meet its financial obligations. That is, either the city's current operating expenses or its debt service remains unpaid. The fiscal crisis does not end when the financing crisis begins: The structural conditions that generated chronic budget deficits are still present, but the ability to cover up the fiscal crisis with borrowing is eliminated. Furthermore, the urgency of the financing crisis alters the city's politics, the strategic positions and interests of the major actors, and the policy options open to city officials. Finally, the short-term institutional arrangements created to deal with the financing crisis may have long-term consequences for the underlying political dynamics that had generated the fiscal crisis in the first place.

Fiscal crises do not necessarily turn into financing crises, but when they do, city budgetary politics are sharply altered as follows:

1.   The politics of a financing crisis are highly volatile and unstable. This type of crisis is a focused and abrupt emergency that must be dealt with carefully if default and bankruptcy are to be averted. Politics-as-usual are no longer possible in this situation.

2.   The strategic interests of the principal actors shift from maximizing short-run gains to minimizing losses. The calculation of their interests and of the costs attached to particular strategies and behaviors is more problematic because the financing crisis introduces a high degree of uncertainty and greatly enlarges the scope of conflict. *The politics of fiscal crisis are organized around the distribution of benefits; the politics of a financing crisis are concerned with the equitable distribution of losses and risk of losses.*

3.   The options available once a financing crisis has been allowed to develop are exceedingly narrow. Everything depends on finding new sources of capital or on reestablishing access to existing sources. In a fiscal crisis, groups can press their advantage with the city on the basis of such resources as electoral clout and the ability to engage in routine pressure group politics. In a financing crisis, these resources become subordinated to control over capital, and political cleavages and alignments are rearranged to take into account the ability of groups to provide access to capital that is intended to finance the city's debts and current operations. The politics of retrenchment, which may recur periodically during a fiscal crisis, are secondary to the politics of capital finance in a financing crisis.

The Dynamics of Fiscal Crisis in New York City

The fiscal crisis that afflicted New York City between 1969 and 1975 was the outcome of a variety of economic, social, and political forces. A long-run economic decline was punctuated by a severe recession beginning in 1969 that set off a rapid distintegration of the city's manufacturing and export base.[3] Socially, the period from the mid-1960s was marked by the rise of new groups to prominence in the city's politics. The increasing militancy of the black minority and of the powerfully organized city employee unions is reflected in sharply rising welfare costs and increasingly generous wage and pension settlements with the public employee unions.[4] These changes were mirrored in the city's political system as the older, stable party system of the Wagner years was replaced by weak political leadership under Lindsay, who was unable or unwilling to resist the pressures to increase spending. Sufficient in themselves to cause fiscal stress, these changes occurred within a structure of intergovernmental relations decidedly adverse to the city's ability to maintain a balanced budget.

The means available to the city to raise the revenues to meet these demands were strictly limited by political considerations and by state constitutional and legal provisions regulating the city's ability to raise taxes and incur debt. Taxes in New York City were already among the highest and most varied in the nation. Raising them would not only have involved considerable political costs but might also have further eroded the city's diminishing economic base. Moreover, these fiscal decisions and political tradeoffs did not rest entirely with local officials. The state legislature must generally consent to the creation and rapid increase of a variety of taxes not restricted by the constitution (i.e., personal and corporate income taxes, sales taxes, and a host of user taxes), but it could and did refuse to authorize such taxes when their political costs were too high.

In general, both the city's taxing capacity and its borrowing capacity are tied to its taxable real estate base. The state constitution limits revenues from the property tax to 2.5 percent of the five-year average full valuation of taxable property in the city and borrowing to 10 percent of the same figure.[5] Although the state permits the city to issue either long- or short-term debt, such borrowing must entail the general obligation of the city and be secured by its general taxing and revenue powers.[6] To ensure that borrowing is limited to legitimate purposes, the Local Finance Law and the City Charter require the city to maintain two separate budgets. The *expense budget* contains those items that constitute day-to-day operating costs; it is financed by the city's locally raised revenues as well as by intergovernmental transfers, and it must be balanced. To offset seasonal imbalances in these revenues, the city may issue short-term debt in anticipation of revenues from real estate taxes (TANS), from state and federal aid or other taxes (RANS), or from a long-term bond sale earmarked to repay the short-term notes (BANS). Short-term debt is excluded from the constitutional debt limitation but must be repaid within the year it is issued. Long-term debt can be issued only to finance the *capital budget*, which contains items considered to be physical improvements with "periods of probable usefulness" greater than one year. All long-term debt falls under the constitutional debt limit.[7] In sum, the debt limitation is aimed directly at curtailing the city's long-term indebtedness; the tax limitation is directed at restraining the city's operating costs and short-term debt.

It was clear by 1975 that these legal and constitutional restrictions were not effective in curtailing either the city's borrowing or its taxing. Through the mid-1960s and early 1970s, the city, with the assistance and approval of the state legislature, slowly and almost imperceptibly began to extend the boundaries of acceptable financial practice. Each individual innovation was undertaken for a specific, limited, and seemingly legitimate purpose, but cumulatively they led the city toward the closing of its financial options.

The city circumvented its constitutional debt limit in two ways: (1) Special districts or public authorities were created by the legislature to build, finance, and operate many services and programs that the city needed but was unable to finance within its debt limit or within its operating budget;[8] and (2) the city engaged in the systematic and deliberate overestimation of state and federal aid and its own tax revenues.[9] The overestimation of anticipated revenues allowed the city to borrow over the short term against revenues that often failed to materialize. The city did not, indeed could not, engage in these dubious practices without the assistance and authorization of the state. In 1963 the legislature amended the city's charter to permit it to issue short-term notes in anticipation of estimated revenues rather than actual revenues collected in the preceding year.[10] When these estimated revenues did not appear, the city simply rolled over the debt. From 1961 to 1975 the city increased its short-term indebtedness from $100 million to $4.5 billion.[11]

But it was the evasion of the tax limitation that proved the most slippery of the slopes down which the city tumbled into financial instability. The two principal ploys were the capitalization of operating expenses and the conscious and deliberate misrepresentation of the city's taxable real estate base.

The capitalization of operating expenses was based on a constitutional provision that automatically increased the real estate tax without limitation in order to meet the debt service on city bonds.[12] By shifting items normally considered to be operating expenses to the capital budget, the city could avoid the constitutional tax limit. Furthermore, these expenditures could be financed by a much smaller increase in the real estate tax than would have been necessary had they been included in the operating budget, as the debt servicing charges were only a small proportion of their total cost—a cost that was stretched out over many years. The state legislature cooperated in this charade. Over a period of ten years, it consistently approved amendments to the Local Finance Law designating as capital improvements many services and programs that clearly were not.[13] In addition, the legislature approved numerous extensions of the "periods of probable usefulness" of capital projects, thereby stretching out existing debt. By 1975 over half the items in the city's capital budget had formerly been in the operating budget; they belonged there, and they threatened the city's ability to maintain its true capital infrastructure. Furthermore, the debt service charges incurred on these capitalized operating expenses consumed a full 58.6 percent of the city's real estate tax levy.[14]

The second route used to bypass the tax limitation was the deliberate overestimation of the city's taxable real estate base. Because the expense budget rested on the simple premise that assessed taxes could actually be collected, any overestimation or misrepresentation of this base would lead to an immediate and cumulative deficit. Nonetheless, the city pursued this policy with vigor. Notes in anticipation of real taxes were inflated beyond reason through assessments on property that was not in fact taxable (i.e., city property, diplomatic holdings, and property involved in bankruptcy proceedings) and through taxes that were legitimately owed but in fact uncollectable.[15]

The Coming of the Financing Crisis

The combination of all these strategies eventually took its toll. The practice of issuing new debt to retire old debt reached its zenith in 1975 when the city incurred more than $9 billion in new debt, mostly short-term and all at higher than normal interest rates.[16] In the six years from 1970 to 1975, New York City doubled its total indebtedness from $5.8 billion to $12.3 billion. A full 36 percent of this, $4.5 billion, took the form of short-term notes.[17] The city's borrowing in itself accounted for more than 25 percent of all the debt issued on the national municipal market,[18] and interest payments on the debt consumed 14 percent of the city's entire budget.[19]

This increased borrowing took place at the same time that conditions on the municipal bond market prevented it from absorbing the city's debt. The national recession in the early 1970s set off a wave of short-term borrowing by cities that more than quadrupled between 1967 and 1975.[20] During the recession, furthermore, commercial banks and insurance companies—the traditional purchasers of municipals—suffered declining profits and, hence, lost much of their economic incentive to invest in tax-exempt, low-interest securities. The municipal bond market contracted, leaving only private individuals and households as major potential investors. In a contracting market, cities like New York, which was borrowing not only for expansion and development but also to pay for day-to-day survival, were particularly disadvantaged. New York City had to go to the market with over $4 billion in short-term securities between October 1974 and February 1975, and it had to pay interest rates nearly one-third above the market's average yield of 6.8 percent.[21]

The shaky condition of the national market for state and local securities was greatly weakened in the winter of 1975 by the default of the Urban Development Corporation, a New York State public authority.[22] The anxiety of investors that was caused by this failure triggered a series of self-protective moves on the part of the city's banks, which were already feeling the pressure of the contracting market. Ironically, because the banks occupied partly contradictory roles as both underwriters and investors in city securities, their actions had the unintended effect of placing them in an even more vulnerable position and led directly to the transformation of the fiscal crisis into a financing crisis.

As underwriters, the banks and financial institutions play a quasi-public role that is crucial to the operation of the U.S. system of municipal finance: They act as agents or salesmen for the city. When the banks underwrite city securities, either individually or as part of a syndicate, they purchase the entire issue with the intent of selling it to the public or "primary" market—namely, other banks, brokers, insurance companies, or private investors. The banks earn a profit by raising the cost of the issue to the public above their own costs, thus creating what is known as the "spread."

As "voluntary" investors, banks are comparable to other investors. They decide to buy a certain issue because it is economically attractive for their own accounts or for those of their trust clients. As long as their role as investor is voluntary, the banks retain an autonomous and potentially powerful leverage over the city's budgetary and social policies. For if the banks are free to buy or sell, to underwrite or refuse to do so, they can potentially dictate the conditions for the purchase of debt and thereby override other political interests in the city.

But there is a second kind of investor role: that of the "forced" or "involuntary" investor. Forced investment is, first of all, a consequence of the structure of underwriting. When a bank (or syndicate of banks or financial institutions) underwrites an issue, it is committed to retain the entire issue regardless of market response. If an issue "founders," the bank is liable for the "overhang" of unsold securities. It is compelled either to hold the issue in its own portfolios at a loss or to make additional attempts to sell to the public at a greater and greater discount. The size of the loss incurred is a function of (1) the market's reluctance, (2) the amount of the initial overhang, (3) the spread between the original price and the discounted price at which it is eventually sold to the public, and (4) whether the issue was competitively bid or negotiated. The underwriter absorbs the entire loss with a competitive issue but, with a negotiated issue, maintains the option to reset the purchase price and lessen the total loss.

Forced investment is most likely to occur in times of economic decline. Its extent is a function of both the volume of borrrowing and the degree of market acceptance. Throughout 1974–1975, the contracting and resistant market and the gigantic size of the new issues combined to increase the likelihood that the New York City banks would be left holding a sizeable portion of the new issues they were underwriting. In response, the banks moved to cut their losses by (1) forcing up interest rates through collusion to control the bidding process, often offering only one bid, (2) seeking to replace competitive bidding with negotiated purchases, and (3) increasing the size of the market by reducing the denomination of issues in order to spread the risk to smaller private investors rather than to institutional investors. But the most serious response was the decision of the major banks to quietly unload their holdings while continuing to underwrite new issues. This decision most clearly brings into relief the structural contradiction between the two roles of underwriter and investor in times of economic crisis.

From April 1974 to February 1975, the banks sold off $2.5 billion of their own holdings in city securities.[23] These sales were conducted on what is called the *secondary market*—the market for securities previously issued and bought. A hedge against the banks' growing fears about the city's solvency, this move came at a time when the city needed to borrow at least $750 million monthly. The banks were thus in the position of dumping their own holdings of city paper onto the secondary market at the same time that, as underwriters, they had come under more pressure than ever to accept and pass on large quantities of new securities in the *primary market*.[24]

To say the least, the banks found themselves in a questionable ethical posture. At the very moment that the banks had begun to doubt the wisdom of investing in city securities, they were finding it necessary to encourage other investors to buy huge new quantities. To the extent that the banks had access to information unavailable to potential investors, their dilemma became legal as well as ethical. To make matters worse, they had saturated an already badly contracted market by selling off their old city paper, thus making it much more difficult to find buyers of the new debt. Yet they had no choice but to go on underwriting new issues so that the city could avoid default, for default would undermine the value of the city securities remaining in their portfolios (estimated at over $2 billion) and in their trust accounts (another $2 billion).

To relieve pressure on the market, the mayor appealed directly to another source of investment capital: the pension funds of the city employees with accumulated assets of over $8 billion. Interest rates on city notes and bonds were outdistancing practically all other securities. On practical grounds alone, it seemed reasonable for the funds to invest in city paper. The argument made political sense, too. The large assets were a direct result of the previous decade of increasingly militant bargaining by the municipal employee unions, and the enormous growth of the pension funds was held by some to be a major factor in the city's fiscal difficulties. The use of these assets to fund the city debt seemed a just solution.

But there were equally compelling reasons against such purchases: (1) New York City bonds and notes—like all other municipal issues— are tax exempt, so the interest they bear is not equal to that of taxable bonds. Traditionally, pension funds have not invested in tax-exempt municipals because they do not require tax shelters and therefore find the relatively low interest rates unattractive. The peculiar circumstances of the New York City crisis, however, increased the interest rates on city securities to abnormally high levels. These rates seemed to make the bonds a lucrative investment, but such high yields on tax-exempts reflected the extremely high risk being incurred by investors. (2) That risk could not, of course, be ignored. But who would actually bear it? A reasonable argument could be made that it was currently retired workers who would absorb the risk of questionable investments in order to protect the jobs of those still in the work force. (3) Because the pension funds did not have sufficient floating capital, they would have to sell off extensive holdings at a loss in order to make the new purchases. Insofar as any loss was then amortized by the city and automatically increased its contributions to the funds, the actual benefits to the city of such a step were difficult to estimate.[25] (4) More complex was the question of increased dependence on the city if the purchases were made. Because the funds were already dependent on the city for continued contributions, purchases of city securities would only doubly bind the funds to the city's fiscal solvency. Given the city's shaky financial situation, this dependence created a structural contradiction for the pension funds comparable to that of the banks. (5) The pension funds are jointly trusteed with city officials and union representatives, who have equal votes on investment decisions. It was thus conceivable that the same union leaders who represented the municipal labor force across the bargaining table would now have the power to make investment decisions that would directly affect the city's financial survival while indirectly affecting the city's ability to fund contract settlements. What seemed, at first glance, to be a concession by labor might also be seen as a potential source of short-term leverage on city budgetary and fiscal policies.

The purchases could be described as being within the spirit if not the letter of the rules governing such investments. Insofar as they provided the city with the capital needed to make continued contributions to the funds, the investments were for the "exclusive benefit" of the retirees. And, insofar as the investments were made in fully secured general obligation notes, they were not considered prohibited.[26] Weighing all the factors in the situation, the trustees agreed, during the first quarter of 1975, to purchase over $500 million of the city's short-term debt.

Even with this additional financing, the city was unable to stabilize its borrowing. Amidst internal squabbling and incomprehensible bookkeeping, this unstable financial situation began to come apart. On February 19, 1975, an abortive sale of $290 million in tax anticipation notes (TANS) served as the prelude to the complete unraveling of this situation.[27] Unable to satisfy a bond counsel that it had sufficient tax receivables to cover $112 million of the proposed issue, the city was forced to withdraw the issue. The March 7 issue of $537 million in bond anticipation notes (BANS) and the March 13 issue of $375 million in revenue anticipation notes (RANS) met with an almost nonexistent market. On March 14, 1975, the banks were left with an overhang of 15 percent of the RANS and more than half of the BANS. They advised the comptroller that they were "scared." With the market growing more and more resistant, investment in city securities became increasingly illiquid. On March 17 the banks informed the city that they could no longer continue to underwrite city debt.

This decision formally ended the tacit collusion between the banks, the city, and the other players who benefited from the decade of deficit financing. On April 2, when Standard and Poor's downgraded the city's bond rating to "below investor quality," the market officially closed. Politics-as-usual were suspended.

Constrained Options

With the capital markets closed, the city was without sufficient cash to meet debt payments to its creditors, pay salaries to its employees, and provide services to its citizens. The burden of this debt was so crushing that even retrenchment severe enough to threaten delivery of the most basic services would not have generated enough cash to meet even current obligations. Bankruptcy, or at least default, seemed to hold out the only solution.

But the options of bankruptcy and/or default were illusory. Both were without the procedural guidelines necessary for their implementation. More importantly, both lacked the precedents necessary to estimate and evaluate their probable consequences. It was the onset of the financing crisis, therefore, that introduced a high degree of uncertainty into the situation and altered the ability of the major actors (the city, the banks, the unions, and the state and federal governments) to calculate accurately the costs attached to particular strategies and behaviors. The need to resolve the crisis in the context of these highly volatile and ambiguous options led each major interest to develop its own "worst-case scenario" concerned not with the maximization of gains but rather with the minimization of loss and the equitable distribution of risk.

Default and Bankruptcy

Default occurs when one is unable to meet payment on a legally committed debt—in the case of a city, either a general obligation note or bond. In a broader sense, it can also mean the failure to meet payrolls and provide services. Although default was an imminent possibility, and in fact occurred under the name of a debt moratorium, it did not provide a useful means of responding, even temporarily, to the crisis.

At the time, neither state nor federal law provided clear guidelines with which to help a city in default renegotiate its debt.[28] The most serious problem was the absence of priorities for the payment of the city's obligations. Hence, default might deteriorate into an unseemly scramble by the city's creditors, vendors, voters, and employees for first place in line. Bond- and noteholders of general obligation debt formally held first lien (claim) on the city's revenues and taxing power, but it remained an open question as to whether this lien would be honored when balanced against the capacity and the necessity of the city to maintain delivery of essential services.

Bankruptcy held out the illusion of a highly institutionalized and legally binding procedure that would not only allow the city to buy time to reorder its affairs but might actually result in a permanent reduction of its debt burden as well. Under default the city would remain liable for the repayment of all its debts, although possibly at lower interest rates and over an extended period. Under bankruptcy, on the other hand, the courts might relieve the city of a major part of its financial obligations. Furthermore, because such obligations were governed by federal law, it was generally argued that bankruptcy proceedings would supersede state prohibitions against the voiding of contracts with unions, pension funds, and creditors, as well as automatically sidestep the protections afforded under the contract clause of the federal constitution.[29] Yet, at the time of the crisis, municipal bankruptcy was an untried procedure: No city the size of New York had ever filed before. The actual powers of the bankruptcy court were unknown or, at least, untested. No precedents existed as guidelines with which to approximate the actual costs of bankruptcy for the major interests in the city's financial affairs.

As it turns out, bankruptcy was never a feasible alternative. Logistically and administratively, it would have been all but impossible for New York City to seek the protection of the bankruptcy court. Chapter IX of the federal bankruptcy statute required a municipality to have *prior approval* of more than 51 percent of its creditors and to provide the court with a list of their names and addresses.[30] Any plan developed for the restructuring of the city's debt, moreover, would need the consent of two-thirds of the creditors. These administrative and procedural requirements could not be met for the simple reason that New York City bonds and notes were in the form of *bearer* rather than *registered* obligations, and thus no one had an exact fix on who the city's creditors were. Even if such creditors had been located and polled, it is doubtful that two-thirds of them would have agreed to any specific settlement.

Bankruptcy would have remained an inadequate response to the city's problems in any case. When a private individual or firm goes bankrupt, assets are liquidated and the proceeds are distributed among the creditors. When the debtor is a governmental entity, however, priority must be given to the continuation of those services on which the health and safety of its residents depend. A city's property is held in trust for its residents and cannot be seized by its creditors. Likewise, as long as the city retains taxing powers and its citizens retain their taxable income and property, the city cannot be considered truly insolvent in the way that a private individual or firm might be. Municipal bankruptcy is a far more limited procedure than its private counterpart. To be sure, bankruptcy allows for a stay of proceedings against the city while its debt is renegotiated and a payment schedule is laid out, but it cannot lead to the dissolution of the corporate entity. In short, the city's political sovereignty is retained.

Perhaps more critically, it is not clear that bankruptcy would have provided relief from the city's most pressing financial problem—that of regaining access to borrowing. At the time of the crisis, there were no provisions in Chapter IX to ensure the city's ability to borrow; in all probability, then, bankruptcy proceedings would have made borrowing more difficult if not impossible. Legislation in at least thirty states prohibited financial institutions and the trustees of investment funds from buying the securities of a state or municipality that had failed to meet its debt obligations (in some cases these restrictions lasted ten to twenty years).

Perceived Costs of Bankruptcy

Bankruptcy threatened the traditional control of city officials over the budget, consequently affecting their discretion in responding to the demands of voters as well. This usurpation by the federal bankruptcy court of the city's political autonomy was a price the city was not willing to pay to regain its fiscal solvency. Even a total state takeover of the city's revenues and expenditures—the functional equivalent of the feared powers of the bankruptcy court—was the much preferred and eventually chosen option.

Any diminution of the city's powers directly threatened the ability of the municipal unions to influence the city's budgetary policies. Electoral pressure would have been irrelevant in a situation in which the city's affairs were being externally controlled. Equally irrelevant in the face of an externally mandated and enforced financial plan would have been collective bargaining, regarded by the union leadership as the structural underpinning of their institutional power. The unions recognized the need for major contract givebacks but also realized that control over the process by which these concessions were to be achieved was more critical than the substance of the concessions themselves. Unilateral imposition of such retrenchments by a bankruptcy court would have denied both the city and the unions any measure of discretion. Of course, it is far from certain that the bankruptcy court would have had these powers, or if they had, that such powers would have been used. Nonetheless, the unions would eventually cooperate in a strategy of voluntary negotiated settlements to bring about the necessary savings in order to ensure, to the limited extent possible, the city's autonomy as well as their own.

The banks held $2 billion of the $14.6 billion outstanding debt. Although this constituted only 25 percent of their equity capital and under 5 percent of their total assets, bankruptcy would nonetheless severely affect their liquidity. The banks' holdings in city securities would be marked down from book to market value, which, in turn, would decrease the estimate of their assets and curtail their lending activities. The banks were equally threatened, according to some commentators, by their potential legal liabilities under the Securities and Exchange rule that a seller of securities is responsible for any misrepresentations or fraud in connection with a sale. It has been suggested that the banks preferred continuing privately to finance the city rather than submitting to the public scrutiny of a bankruptcy proceeding. To date, the banks' vulnerability to such charges remains unsettled.[31]

As with the banks, the pension funds stood to lose financially if the city declared bankruptcy. In fact, the pension funds stood to lose even more than the banks, for the legal statute defining the funds was sufficiently ambiguous as to permit the possibility that, under bankruptcy proceedings, the funds' assets might be open to the claims of the city's general creditors. Not only would the funds lose the return on their investment in city securities, in addition to the city's continuing contributions, but the accumulated assets themselves might be lost as well.

A critical decision made by the union leaders was that, as trustees of these funds, they would cooperate with and indeed exert pressure on the city to use the funds to avert bankruptcy. The condition for their cooperation was that they be indemnified against any losses that resulted from these purchases.

Bankruptcy of New York City, the largest municipal issuer, threatened the national credit markets as well. It would have driven up the interest rates paid by municipalities, precipitating a string of financial failures by ailing cities unable to borrow to sustain themselves. These extensive city failures would most likely have generalized to the state markets—especially New York State, itself already overextended in the credit markets. To secure its own credit rating and market access, it was essential that New York State enter the negotiations early in order to resolve the crisis.

Finally, given New York City's unique position in the national as well as international economy, the consequences of bankruptcy transcended local and state boundaries.[32] It was estimated that due to the quantity of New York City securities held nationally, at least sixty-nine banks would have failed and innumerable others would have had their capital assets severely impaired. In turn, lending activity would have been curtailed nation-wide, and the gross national product (GNP) of the nation would have decreased by at least $20 billion. At a time when the nation was emerging from a debilitating recession, it was incumbent upon the federal government eventually to enter the negotiations, if for no other reason than to limit its own potential losses.

In order to contain the conflict, reduce the uncertainty, regain access to borrowing, and minimize their potential losses, the major parties to the crisis sought an accommodation. This is not to say that the participants acted in concert or out of a common definition of the public interest, but that the necessity of regaining access to capital eventually compelled each of them to make the maximum concessions possible in the interest of arriving at an overall settlement.

Responses and Solutions

The state responded to the mayor's initial pleas with cash advances totaling $800 million between April and late May of 1975.[33] By June it had become obvious that this amount was insufficient to meet the city's cash needs and ineffective in extracting from the city those budgetary and fiscal concessions required for reentry into the market. Because the city could not borrow, the state agreed to borrow for it. On June 20 the state legislature created a new public authority, The Municipal Assistance Corporation (MAC), to serve as the city's interim

borrowing agent and to oversee the implementation of a program of
fiscal retrenchment and discipline.[34] The statute authorized MAC to
exchange its long-term bonds for the city's maturing short-term notes
in order to restructure and stretch out the tidal wave of debts cascading
down upon the city. MAC was also given the authority to secure $3
billion in financing from July through September while the city attempted
to make structural changes necessary to restore investor confidence.
This strategy backfired, however, when MAC's initial offering on July
10 met with strong market resistance, even though it bore the extraordinarily high interest rate of 9.5 percent.

Faced with a reticent market, informed by representatives of the
federal government that no aid would be forthcoming from that quarter,
and promised by the banks that they would invest their own funds in
new MAC issues even at a loss if the city would institute a program
of fiscal retrenchment, MAC moved to exercise its oversight powers to
bring about dramatic reforms of the city's finances and thereby restore
investor confidence. In mid-July MAC proposed a plan of massive
budgetary and fiscal cutbacks that included freezes on wages, hiring,
and capital construction, major new service reductions, layoffs of at
least 31,000 employees, higher transit fares and tolls, and the imposition
of tuition at the City University.[35] But it was far from certain, early in
the crisis, that this program could be legally or politically implemented.

Wage costs, including payments to the employee pension funds,
constituted a high proportion of the operating budget, but such emergency
measures as a wage freeze, renegotiated contracts, and massive lay-offs
depended, in large part, on voluntary compliance by the unions for
their effectiveness. It could not be assumed that workers would stay
at their jobs if wages and benefits were drastically slashed. At the least,
a serious and potentially dangerous interruption of basic city services
might have resulted.

Any quick and substantial savings required the city to break existing
contractual agreements with its employees, vendors, and creditors, but
such action was prohibited by state and federal law. Under the state
constitution, for example, pension contracts with public employees could
not be impaired,[36] nor, under the City Labor Relations Law, could the
collectively bargained wage and benefit agreements with the municipal
unions be easily altered.[37] More generally, the contract clause of the
federal constitution appeared to give broad protection against any
unilateral action short of bankruptcy that the city might wish to take
to abrogate or defer any of its contractual obligations.[38]

Because the city and the unions were initially unwilling to cooperate
publicly in these retrenchments, the debate turned to whether the state
had the authority under its police power to impose them. At first, the

city and the unions argued that the home rule provision of the state constitution appeared to protect the city from state usurpation of its prerogatives.[39] More importantly, the contract clause of the federal constitution applied directly to state action that might seek to abrogate city obligations. Proponents of a forceful state role brushed these objections aside, contending that once a situation existed that threatened the health, safety, and welfare of the state's citizens, the protections of home rule as well as the contract clause could be superseded by a declaration of a "state of emergency" and the invocation of the state's police powers.[40] There was real concern, nevertheless, that because the state was a direct party to many of the contracts in question and would thus benefit financially from their impairment, it might not act with restraint and impartiality but, on the contrary, might use its police powers to achieve fiscal results otherwise unattainable through collective bargaining or the market.

Any resistance on the part of the city or the unions to MAC's plan would have created havoc with the market. A measure of the influence wielded by investor reaction in these strategies was the pressure exerted by MAC officials to implement the plan before they again went to the market with their August issue. The unions responded by forming a single coalition to bargain with the city. Under these unprecedented conditions, the various unions agreed to a deferral of wages promised under earlier contracts. To be sure, coalitional bargaining was, to some extent, evidence of the weakened condition of the unions. Yet the fact that the concessions were voluntarily made within the collective bargaining structure allowed the unions to (1) redefine the threatened wage freeze into a deferral; (2) negotiate the impact of the wage deferral on a sliding scale, thereby protecting the economic interests of the most vulnerable workers in each of the unions; (3) forestall the unilateral action by management outside of the bargaining structures; and (4) ensure that all losses attendant upon the negotiations were equally shared and distributed such that no single union could gain the upper hand.[41] All told, the negotiations resulted in major short-term losses for the unions, yet they also seemed to preserve those structures necessary to recoup these concessions in the long run.

However, even with this overt cooperation on the part of the unions and the city, MAC was hard pressed to raise the $840 million needed for the August financing. Aid from Washington, sought early in the crisis, was both legal and feasible and, depending on the form it took, still capable of resolving the city's major problem—access to capital. MAC officials again appealed to the federal government for some sort of federal guarantee for MAC bonds or city securities; either would automatically open the market by eliminating all investor risk.

But the ramifications of such a guarantee threatened to upset the existing credit hierarchy among federal, state, and local securities. If Congress were to guarantee the debt of New York City, while leaving the city's bonds tax exempt, Congress would create a "super" security even more attactive than its own taxable federal bond. The consequences of such action would reverberate throughout the national credit markets. Fear of setting a precedent that might be followed by dozens of other cities in similar financial distress, as well as a determination to force the local participants to make real sacrifices in order to solve their own problems, compelled President Ford to refuse, once again, any promise of aid. Instead, the president reiterated his earlier suggestion that the judiciary committees of the House and Senate move with greater speed on the pending revisions of the federal bankruptcy statute and, in particular, of Chapter IX to eliminate at least the administrative and logistical barriers to bankruptcy.[42]

Under pressure from the federal government, which had indicated that no support would be forthcoming without further state intervention, MAC, together with the governor, prepared a financial and legislative proposal that allowed for a virtual state takeover of the finances of New York City. On September 9, 1975, the state legislature enacted the Financial Emergency Act, which declared that a "financial emergency" existed in the city of New York that compelled the state to "undertake an extraordinary exercise of its police and emergency powers under the state constitution and exercise controls and supervision over the financial affairs of the City of New York."[43]

The act also established the Emergency Financial Control Board (EFCB), composed of the governor, the mayor, the comptrollers of the state and city, and three private citizens appointed by the governor. This board was given explicit powers not only to develop, in conjunction with the city, a financial plan for the next three years but to implement it, as well, through the virtual usurpation of the fiscal and budgetary powers of the city. To this end, the board was given legal title to all city revenues, the power to monitor and ultimately to veto any city expenditure, and the power to reject collectively bargained labor contracts not included in the financial plan. In effect, what the city and the unions feared from bankruptcy was imposed through the state's police powers.

Tied to these measures were two provisions ensuring financing for the city through November. The state was to advance the city an additional $700 million in funds, and the state comptroller was mandated to invest $750 million of the assets of the state retirement funds, conditioned on MAC's ability to obtain additional financing from the city pension funds, banks, and insurance funds. These financing arrangements were hardly on paper when the court of appeals ruled that the mandated investment of the state pension funds violated the protection of the state constitution against impairment of contracts.[44]

By early November, then, it was clear that MAC could not provide the city with financing through December. At this point, the city had done all it could and had promised to do: It had (1) reduced city services; (2) negotiated a wage deferral with its employees; (3) laid off a quarter of its work force; and (4) imposed new taxes and charges on a variety of city services. The state had extended itself financially through direct cash advances to the city and indirectly through its pledge of moral obligation on the repayment of the MAC debt. Politically, it had pushed its police powers to the limit with its takeover of the city's fiscal decisionmaking. What the city needed was a long-term source of capital to stabilize its borrowing and financial needs.

To this end, the governor, along with MAC officials, made a final appeal to President Ford and Treasury Secretary Simon. On November 11 the governor and MAC presented a financial plan for the city conditioned on the promise of federal assistance. Worked out in close and difficult negotiations with MAC, the banks, the unions, and the pension funds, the agreement called for a complete restructuring of the city's and MAC's outstanding indebtedness. More critically, it called for the creation of new sources of capital without first regaining market access.

To provide this new financing, the pension funds agreed to purchase over $2.5 billion in new city obligations over the three years of the plan. To lessen the pressure of the debt coming due, both the banks and the pensions agreed to roll over and hold at lower interest rates the short-term city notes in their portfolios. Moreover, to eliminate and extend the capacity of MAC to borrow for the city, the unions and the banks agreed to stretch out and hold at reduced rates their previously purchased MAC bonds. To reduce further the pressure of maturing debt, the plan called for the state legislature to impose a moratorium on the payment of short-term city notes coming due in December of 1975 and in the first six months of 1976 (excluding those voluntarily rolled over by the banks and pension funds). To distinguish this action from an outright default, the plan offered these noteholders the option of exchanging their city notes for longer-term and lower-yielding MAC issues. To disperse the costs further, the plan called for the imposition of $200 million in additional city taxes and $600 million in additional state taxes. There was little left for either the city or the state to do.

Although no assurances were publicly given that federal aid would be provided, the various components of the plan conditioned on federal assistance began immediately to fall into place. On November 15 the state legislature again met in extraordinary session and enacted the moratorium on the city's general obligation debt—an action that sent shock waves through the credit markets.[45] On November 26 a restructuring agreement was signed that formalized the agreement worked out among the city banks and pension funds.[46] On December 4 the state legislature (1) granted the funds permission to invest in city bonds without regard to the proportion of their total assets involved; (2) indemnified the trustees for any losses incurred as a result of the investments; (3) authorized the trustees to consider the extent to which the investment affected the ability of the city to make future payments to the pension system and helped it to meet its long-term obligations to pensioners; (4) defined pension benefits as essential city services; and (5) immunized the funds from claims of general creditors.[47] Legislation exempting the investments from the exclusive benefit and prohibited transaction provisions of the internal revenue code was promised in order to preserve the funds' tax-exempt status.[48] Satisfied that all possible concessions had been enacted, President Ford signed legislation granting the city seasonal loans of up to $1.3 billion in fiscal year 1976 and $2.3 billion in 1977 and 1978.[49] This step by the federal government ensured the city a second source of long-term capital.

These interlocking agreements among the city, the banks, the pension funds, and the state and federal governments appeared for a time to have brought the financing crisis to an end. In 1976, however, the New York State Court of Appeals declared the moratorium on debt repayment unconstitutional.[50] This decision placed the entire settlement in jeopardy, and it immediately began to crumble. The banks threatened to demand repayment of their own holdings in city and MAC securities, in that these commitments had been made on the assumption that the moratorium was constitutional. In exchange for any participation in the restructuring of the city's debt, the banks demanded an extension of the life of the outside fiscal monitors and an expansion of the powers of the monitoring agencies. The unions countered by threatening to withdraw their financial cooperation. On balance, the withdrawal of the unions from the previous agreement would have been far more costly to the city than the loss of the cooperation of the banks. Although such cooperation was needed to restore investor confidence in the city, the strategic position of the unions checked, if not overrode, the influence of the banks. From these complex negotiations during 1976 and 1977 emerged the recognition among banking leaders that the pension funds and union leaders occupied roles comparable to theirs as financiers to the city. This joint interest was institutionalized in the Municipal Union/ Financial Leadership Group (MUFLG), which began meeting monthly to discuss questions of debt financing in addition to more general issues of economic development and tax and welfare policy.

When New York City failed to balance its budget in 1978, it again returned to the federal government for assistance. The seasonal loans were turned into federal guarantees on city securities.[51] To bypass the problem of a tax-exempt but federally guaranteed security, Congress stipulated that any guaranteed security would be taxable, but because the purchase of such securities was limited to tax-exempt pension funds, the taxes so imposed could never be activated. These negotiations coincided with the 1978 contract talks with the municipal unions. At this time, the federal government exerted great pressure on the unions to settle for a "no-cost contract" and on the state legislature to extend further the powers of the Financial Control Board. Tied to these concessions extracted from the city and the state were commitments from local interests such as banks and insurance companies to purchase a certain share of the city's nonguaranteed securities.

The Implications of the New York City Case

The financing crisis substantially changed the strategic positions of the major local political forces and introduced state and federal officials directly into city decisionmaking. The most general consequence of the crisis was to create conditions that produced a worst-case scenario of the possible outcome for each actor. The officials, in turn, were compelled to alter their behavior, seeking no longer to maximize their gains, as they had done during the fiscal crisis, but to minimize their losses. The most obvious outward manifestation of this new attitude was the willingness of the banks, the unions, and the city to engage in overt cooperation to bring the crisis to a close. This was not an inevitable outcome. Crises can easily exacerbate conflict and deepen antagonisms between adversaries and competing parties. On the surface, this is what happened in New York City; the public rhetoric of city politics certainly became more inflammatory. But most remarkable is that despite such bitter antagonisms, the leaders of the major interests were ultimately able to engage in face-to-face bargaining to hammer out a relatively quick settlement. The overriding goals of reestablishing credit and creating new sources of capital, which were shared by all major participants, created a unique set of political and economic interdependencies that culminated in a shifting of the balance of forces in city politics.

Some simplistic accounts of the period have tended to attribute exceptional powers to the banks, charging that they single-handedly engineered the closing of the market and then enforced their own priorities on a helpless city. There is just enough truth to this view to give it appeal. Granted, the banks set the crisis in motion, but, as I have argued, they were not all-powerful actors pulling strings from on high. The banks avoided what would have been the enormous costs of a serious default or bankruptcy, but they did not emerge from the crisis unscathed. It is not so much that they were coerced into rolling over existing city debt or that they were induced to accept lower interest rates on the securities—for in these respects they lost far less than did the pension funds. More to the point, because the city's credit needs became so overextended, the banks were unable (or unwilling) to satisfy them and, as a consequence, lost their virtual monopoly over the city's access to capital. To be sure, because the city's eventual need to regain full access to the market guided the policies and actions of all of the existing oversight agencies—especially MAC—the banking community played an important role. But before the crisis had run its course, the pension funds, along with the federal government (rather than the traditional bond market), were the principal sources of city credit and capital. Evidence that this shift affected the banks' strategic influence over city affairs can be found in their unsuccessful efforts in 1977 and 1978 to dictate the extension and substance of the external monitoring agency. It might be argued that the banks waited too long to require the city to reorganize its financial arrangements and that once the financing crisis was at hand, they no longer had the power to impose reforms single-handedly.

Throughout the years leading up to the financing crisis, the municipal unions enjoyed the greatest successes in their history. In fact, the favorable contracts they were able to win for their members played a significant role in the city's fiscal difficulties. The financing crisis threatened to end an era of powerful unionism. In any case, it seemed inevitable that the spending cuts likely to follow in the wake of the market's closing would fall with devastating effect on the unions. To be sure, although the unions suffered significant cutbacks, a wage deferral, and a no-cost contract, they were not simply the objects of post-crisis retrenchment. First of all, through their pension funds they emerged as the major creditor of the city, an ambiguous situation that gave them at least some leeway to bargain over the character and intensity of the retrenchment. Second, and in part a response to the new importance of the pension funds, the unions were brought in as official members of a number of formal committees and informal decisionmaking groups set up to deal with the crisis. In sum, the unions took on a quasi-managerial role in addition to their traditional role as external pressure groups.

An important side effect of this enhanced participation, especially given the publicity that characterized the crisis years, is that the unions now have a much more extensive knowledge of city finances than ever before. This side effect is, of course, a two-sided coin. The unions are no longer free to charge that the city is lying when it claims that its coffers are empty, a situation that touches on the underlying contradiction of the unions' new role. They are more integrated into city decisionmaking and thus have more influence on those decisions before they are made. At the same time, because they now bear a measure of responsibility for city policy, they are less able to press the interests of their members with the same unrelenting energy as before.

Finally, the most basic change that the crisis brought about in the internal politics of the city was the transfer of a substantial portion of the municipality's autonomy to external monitoring agencies: The Municipal Assistance Corporation (MAC), the Financial Control Board (FCB), and the Office of New York Affairs in the Treasury Department. At the present writing, these institutions are still in place and the city has not fully regained the right to conduct its own business. The events in New York City appear to be a straightforward example of intervention by higher governmental authorities for the purpose of imposing fiscal discipline.

When we turn from the consequences of the crisis for New York City to its impact on the system of municipal finance as a whole, we become involved in a much more speculative enterprise. As of this writing, notwithstanding recent surpluses and a balanced budget, the city faces potential budget deficits of $1.2 billion in 1983 and $1.7 billion in 1984.[52] Combined with the expiration of the federal loan guarantees as well as the authorization for the pension fund purchases, the city will likely face, once again, the question of alternative methods of debt financing and capital creation.

When New York City faces these issues in 1982–1983, it will do so in an environment much different from that in 1975. In that year, the debate was almost entirely focused on the city's mismanagement and profligacy. The city's problems could, without much exaggeration, plausibly be laid at its own doorstep. But the current faltering economy and the continued fears of federal deficits have pushed up interest rates demanded by all lenders. Cities with the highest investment ratings are paying double-digit rates. Considering, in addition, the current contraction and secular changes in the municipal bond market, as well as the reductions in state and federal grants that seem likely because of budget-cutting in Washington, we can predict that a large number of cities will fall into precarious financial situations. It will no longer be possible, then, to dismiss New York City's problems as the idiosyncratic result of poor planning and fiscal irresponsibility.

A renewed consideration of New York City's plight could open a discussion of some of the more general alternatives advanced in 1975 and 1978: a general taxable bond option to broaden the market for municipals; the creation of a federal agency (as, for example, an URBANK) to provide low-cost financing for cities unable to meet their needs on the market; or the continued use of municipal pension funds for debt financing.

The issue of a taxable bond option strikes at the heart of the doctrine of intergovernmental immunity from taxation by other levels of government. To allow federally guaranteed bonds to be issued as taxable securities would be a first step, critics argue, toward a restructuring of the traditional relationship between municipal markets and the larger taxable markets.[53] It is likely that the federal government would reimburse states and localities for some percentage of the higher interest they would have to pay to compete with other taxable securities. These reimbursements would not be automatic, however, and they might have a series of conditions attached to them.

An URBANK would be the public sector analogue to the plan to reindustrialize the Northeast and Midwest through some kind of general "Reconstruction Finance Corporation" for private industry.[54] But this, too, would introduce unknown political criteria into the calculus of lending and borrowing. In any event, the adoption of either the taxable bond or the URBANK seems unlikely, not only because of the past reaction of Congress but also because the current president seems committed to reducing the obligations of the national government. Nevertheless, if the bond market remains in its depressed state, demands for some type of reform may prove difficult to turn down.

The events in New York City will also have an important effect on the future role of the massive pension funds that are now one of the most important sources of capital in our economy. The New York City case led to legislative and judicial rulings that provide a rationale for the use of pension funds to bail out financially strapped cities.[55] To the extent that such legislation and court rulings provide a legal basis for the claim that pension funds may be invested for the purpose of maintaining the city's capacity to contribute to the funds, this whole episode may be interpreted as the opening wedge leading to the expansion of those criteria considered proper for the investment of funds. As one legal scholar has noted, future courts may conclude that

> the trustee could consider the value of a more stable city economy to the
> trust beneficiaries as pensioners. . . . the trustee might consider the value

of preserving the jobs of future and currently vested beneficiaries, not because this maximizes their pensions but because it is clearly in their best interest to avoid demotions, lay-offs, and salary cuts. . . . the trustee might consider the value of a stable city economy to the beneficiaries as citizens of the city . . . who enjoy . . . services.[56]

The extremely diffident language of the legislature and the courts is clearly disingenuous. There can be little doubt that the primary purpose of the investments was to rescue the city from default, only one and arguably not the most serious consequence of which would have been threats to pensioners. Moreover, although the preservation of pensioners' rights is the sole justification endorsed by the courts, the events in New York City have probably created conditions under which pension funds will be less immune to risk than before. Ironically, it is precisely the situation that allows for no other conceivable purchasers of city securities, a situation that would make the investment extremely risky and unlikely to be undertaken under the traditional criteria, in which the courts would feel justified in allowing the investment to take place. For if there are no other customers for the city's debt, then the funds are themselves in jeopardy. In other words, it is only when the city faces imminent insolvency that the investments are likely to be sanctioned.

Conclusion

Many writers have described what they see as a permanent fiscal crisis in U.S. cities brought on by a structural gap between expenditures and revenues. Pressed to provide an increasing array of services but denied the tax revenues to support them, cities are driven by the perverse logic of the situation to break their budgets and to search for other sources of revenue to sustain services. Faced with economic decline and diminishing revenues from the federal and state governments, some cities have tried to finance their deficits through borrowing. But this, given the nature of things, is a short-term solution only, for it does not address the economic and political sources of the problem. In time, the solution collapses, due to shrinking bond markets, skyrocketing interest rates, and the skepticism of investors. When the financial markets close the door, the fiscal crisis of the city gives way to a financing crisis. Just as the 1960s and 1970s saw the development of a chronic urban fiscal crisis, so the 1980s will likely witness a chronic financing crisis. In this way, the financial emergency that occurred in New York City in 1975 may become the shared experience of many U.S. cities.

The politics of a financing crisis, if New York City is a reliable guide, will be characterized not only by budgetary austerity and service reductions but also by political alignments organized around the need to create new sources of capital and to regain access to old sources. The politics that created the fiscal crisis will be different from those that settle the financing crisis. Cooperation between traditional adversaries (the banks and the unions) may replace overt competition. Because the politics of a financing crisis are much less congenial than those of a fiscal crisis, such a situation is not likely to be stable. Renewed economic growth could reinvigorate the capital markets and pave the way for a renewal of expansionary politics. In the absence of economic growth, we can expect major reforms in the means by which cities are financed. Given, as I have argued, that financing is fundamental not only to the provision of city services but to their politics as well, such reforms will have profound implications for the future of urban politics in the United States.

Notes

This paper could not have been written without the financial support of the Jonathan Meigs Fund of Cornell University, and the cooperation and assistance of District Council 37 of The American Federation of State, County, and Municipal Employees. In particular, I wish to acknowledge the assistance of three members of the Council: Evelyn Seinfeld, Research Librarian, Carol O'Cleireacain, Chief Economist, and Norman Adler, Political Action Director. Helpful comments and criticisms on earlier drafts of the paper were provided by Gary Freeman of the University of Texas, Jim Adams of the Wall Street Journal, and Martin Shefter of Cornell University. Research support has been provided by the Sarah Scaife Charitable Trust. I am grateful to them all.

1. For a complete exposition of this argument, see James O'Connor, *The Fiscal Crisis of the State* (New York: St. Martin's Press, 1975).

2. See Martin Shefter, "New York City's Fiscal Crisis: The Politics of Inflation and Retrenchment," *The Public Interest* 48 (Summer 1977):98–127.

3. The most complete compilation of statistics on these economic trends can be found in the New York City Temporary Commission on City Finance, Final Report, *The City in Transition: Prospects and Policies for New York* (New York: Arno Press, 1978), hereinafter cited as TCCF, Final Report.

4. There is a long and complex debate concerning the actual extent to which these contracts were "unnecessarily generous" and the extent to which these settlements affected the city's deficits. See TCCF, Sixth Interim Report, *The Fiscal Impact of Retirement Benefits: Some Proposals for Reform*, May 1976, and Seventh Interim Report, *The Fiscal Impact of Fringe Benefits and Leave Benefits: Some Proposals for Reform*, June 1976. For the unions' reply, see Jack Bigel, *Analysis of the Report of the Permanent Commission on Public Employee Pensions and Retirement Systems* (New York: Program Planners, Inc., 1976) and

Jack Bigel, *An Analysis of Public Employee Compensation Levels* (New York: Program Planners, Inc., 1976).

5. N.Y., *Constitution*, art. VII, sec. 10 (a), (b), (f), and art. VIII, sec. 4.

6. Ibid., art. VIII, sec. 2.

7. N.Y., Local Finance Law (McKinney, 1968) and the 1976 New York City Charter.

8. It is important to note that New York State and New York City are not unique in their use of special districts and public authorities to bypass state debt limitations. For a discussion of the implications of excessive reliance on public authorities, see William J. Quirk and Leon E. Wein, "A Short Constitutional History of Entities Commonly Known as Public Authorities," *Cornell Law Review* 56 (1971):521–597.

9. For complete documentation, see U.S., Congress, House, Subcommittee on Economic Stabilization, Committee on Banking, Finance and Urban Affairs, *Securities and Exchange Commission Staff Report on Transactions in Securities of the City of New York*, 95th Congress, 1st sess., August 1977 (hereinafter cited as SEC Staff Report). See especially Chapter 2 on the accounting practices and financial reporting of the city.

10. N.Y., City Charter, ch. 6, sec. 128 (g) (1979), and the discussion in Nicholas P. Guiliano, Timothy J. Heine, and Tammy Elaine Tuller, "The Constitutional Debt Limit and New York City," *Fordham Law Journal* 8 (1979): 185–229.

11. TCCF, Final Report, p. 70.

12. N.Y., *Constitution*, art. VIII, sec. 10.

13. For example, in 1968 a thirty-year PPU was assigned to a program of job and business opportunities expansion; in 1964 a three-year PPU was assigned to the cost of conducting a special census, and in 1967 a three-year PPU was assigned to codify municipal laws. See N.Y., Local Finance Law, sec. 11.00 (a) (73) (McKinney Supp. 1978) and N.Y., Local Finance Law, sec. 11.00 (a) (71) (McKinney 1968), respectively.

14. See M. David Gelfand, "Seeking Local Government Financial Integrity Through Debt Ceilings, Tax Limitations, and Expenditure Limits: The New York City Fiscal Crisis, the Taxpayers Revolt, and Beyond," *Minnesota Law Review* 63 (1979):545–608.

15. SEC Staff Report, ch. 2, pp. 29–32.

16. Municipal Assistance Corporation for the City of New York, *Annual Report* (1976) (hereinafter cited as MAC *Report*), p. 4.

17. TCCF, Final Report, p. 70.

18. Thomas Boast and Eugene Keilin, "Debt and Capital Management," in *Setting Municipal Priorities 1980*, ed. Raymond D. Horton and Charles Brecher (New York: Universe Books, 1979), pp. 79–111.

19. SEC Staff Report, ch. 3, p. 19, table III.

20. "New York City's Fiscal Problems: Its Origins, Potential Repercussions, and Some Alternative Policy Responses," Background Paper No. 1, October 10, 1975, Congress of the United States, CBO, Washington, D.C.

21. SEC Staff Report, ch. 4.

22. For a detailed discussion of the political ramifications of the UDC default, see Peter D. McClelland and Allan L. Magdovitz, *Crisis in the Making: The Political Economy of New York State Since 1945* (Cambridge: Cambridge University Press, 1981).

23. This entire sequence of events is well documented in chronological order in Chapter 1 of the SEC Staff Report.

24. It is important to note that the same set of institutional and individual investors is likely to compose both markets.

25. Subsequent to the investments, legislation was passed stipulating that any interest in excess of 4 percent earned by the pension funds would automatically reduce by equal amounts the size of the city's contribution to the fund.

26. Section 401 (a) of the Internal Revenue Code holds that "a trust does not qualify [for tax exempt status] unless . . . it is impossible . . . for any part of the corpus or income to be used for, or diverted to, purposes other than for the exclusive benefit of his employees or their beneficiaries." Section 503 (a) (1) (B) of the Internal Revenue Code holds that any trust engaging in "prohibited transactions" will lose its tax-exempt status. Prohibited transactions are any transactions in which the trust lends any part of its income or corpus, with the receipt of adequate security and a reasonable rate of interest, to the creator of the trust, to a person who has made a substantial contribution to the trust, or to certain other persons. More generally, all pension investments are governed by what is called "the prudent man rule," which holds that "fiduciaries, including persons to whom named fiduciaries delegate certain fiduciary responsibilities, must discharge their duties . . . with the care, skill, prudence, and diligence under the circumstances then prevailing that a prudent man acting in a like capacity and familiar with such matters would use in the conduct of an enterprise of like character and with like aims." See Employee Retirement Income Security Act (ERISA), sec. 404 (a) (1) (B), 29 U.S.C., sec. 1104 (a) (1) (1976).

27. SEC Staff Report, ch. 1, pp. 96–120.

28. It was not until the enactment of the Financial Emergency Act in September of 1975 that amendments were made to the Local Finance Law to govern the procedures for default. See N.Y., Local Finance Law, sec. 85.00-90 (McKinney Supp. 1976).

29. There is an ongoing controversy concerning the constitutionality of Chapter IX of the Federal Bankruptcy Code. By definition, the federal code preempts state legislation. The issue is whether under certain conditions the federal code goes beyond the permissible scope of congressional regulation of areas directly affecting state interests—interests protected by the "reserve clause" of the Tenth Amendment to the Constitution providing that "the powers not delegated to the United States by the Constitution, nor prohibited by it to the States, are reserved to the States respectively, or to the people." See "Municipal Bankruptcy, the Tenth Amendment, and the New Federalism," *Harvard Law Review* 89 (1976):1871–1905.

30. For a complete discussion of the procedures in filing bankruptcy under the old Chapter IX of the Federal Bankruptcy Code (codified at 11 U.S.C. secs.

401–403 [1970]), see Lawrence P. King, "Municipal Insolvency: Chapter IX, Old and New, Chapter IX Rules," *American Bankruptcy Journal* 50 (1976):55–65.

31. James Ring Adams, "New York City's Legal Hangover," *Wall Street Journal*, March 24, 1980.

32. For a detailed discussion of the perceived consequences of default and bankruptcy and of the options open to federal and city officials, see U.S., Congress, House, Committee on the Budget, *Impact of the New York City Fiscal Crisis on the Federal Budget*, 94th Congress, 1st sess., October 23, 1975; U.S., Congress, Joint Economic Committee, *Impact of New York City's Economic Crisis on the National Economy*, 94th Congress, 1st sess., November 10, 1975; U.S., Congress, Joint Economic Committee, *New York City's Financial Crisis: An Evaluation of its Economic Impact and of Proposed Policy Solutions*, 94th Congress, 1st sess., November 3, 1975; and U.S., Congress, Senate, Committee on Banking, Housing, and Urban Affairs, *Voluntary Municipal Reorganization Act of 1975*, 94th Congress, 1st sess., November 4, 1975, pp. 17–24.

33. These payments were in the form of advances on the city's share of the state contribution to welfare costs. The first payment of $400 million was not due the city until June 1975, and the second payment of $400 million was not to be received until a full thirteen months later. Moreover, these advances merely enlarged the city's deficit, in that the city would eventually be liable for the sums to pay its welfare expenses. See MAC *Report*, 1976, for a summary of state actions.

34. The Municipal Assistance Corporation (MAC) is legally independent of both the city and the state. It issues nonguaranteed debt, which is binding on neither the state nor the city. Although secured by a special arrangement diverting the city's share of the state sales and stock transfer taxes, as well as state aid, and backed by the moral obligation of the state, it is not a legally enforceable debt. However unlikely, the state legislature could, at any time, choose not to advance to MAC the funds necessary to meet its obligations, or it could abolish the tax upon which the revenues accruing to MAC are drawn. In either event, the debtholder would be without clear legal recourse. A precursor to MAC was created by the state legislature in 1974. The Stability Reserve Corporation (SRC) was given similar statutory authority to "borrow for city." SRC, like MAC, issued nonguaranteed debt. When it was challenged on the grounds that it violated the state's full faith and credit provision, the Court ruled (*Wein v. City of New York*, 36 N.Y. 2nd at 617, 331 N.E. 2nd at 517, 370 N.Y.S. 2d at 555) that because neither the city nor the state was legally liable for its debt, the SRC could not be in violation of the Constitution. Ironically, this ruling, which saved the SRC from constitutional attack, had the simultaneous effect of so weakening investor confidence as to make it impossible for the SRC to market its securities—which activity was the sole reason for its existence.

35. Municipal Assistance Corporation, *Minutes of Special Meeting of the Board of Directors*, July 30, 1975.

36. N.Y., *Constitution*, art. V, sec. 7, provides that membership in a public retirement system is a contractual relationship and, therefore, that the benefits from such a system cannot be diminished or impaired. The funds are also

protected by the New York City Administrative Code, sec. B3-21.0 and by the New York *Laws,* 1975, ch. 890, sec. 3.

37. The collective bargaining law of the New York City Administrative Code, chapter 54, sec. 1173-1.0-13.0 (1975) covers employee negotiations with the city.

38. U.S., *Constitution,* art. I, sec. 10: "No state shall . . . pass any . . . law impairing the obligation of contracts. . . ." This contract clause was originally intended to protect private contracts, specifically against the mass of debtor relief legislation passed by state legislatures during the period that preceded the ratification of the Constitution. Its application to the protection of contracts between governmental entities (states and their legal subdivisions) and private parties has been a matter of legal controversy. See, especially, "The Constitutionality of the New York Municipal Wage Freeze and Debt Moratorium: Resurrection of the Contract Clause," *University of Pennsylvania Law Review* 125 (1976):167–214.

39. The New York Home Rule provision is contained in N.Y., *Constitution,* art. IX, sec. 1 (b) and (c). It holds that "all officers of every local government whose election or appointment is not provided for by this constitution shall be elected by the people of the local government, or of some division thereof, or appointed by such officers of the local government as may be provided by law . . . and that property, affairs, or government" of the municipality are exclusively local and subject to the municipality's control.

40. The doctrine of the state's police power, which was developed in a series of Supreme Court decisions beginning in the Depression, has severely weakened the protection of contracts afforded by the federal constitution's contract clause. The seminal case for the development of the police power doctrine as a justification for the direct impairment of contracts is *Home Building & Loan Association v. Blaisdell,* 290 U.S. 398 (1934). The court held that if the legislative judgment arrived at by the state was addressed to a "legitimate end" and if the measures taken were "reasonable," then the police powers of the state would not be contrary to the contract clause. The state was justified in the exercise of its police power to preserve the economic interests of the state and to "safeguard the economic structure upon which the good of all depends. . . . the preservation of essential stuctures of sovereign power (must be) read into contracts as a postulate of the legal order. . . . while emergency does not create power, emergency may furnish the occasion for the exercise of power." Generally, the police powers of the state may be activated to "protect the health, safety, or welfare of their citizens."

41. For a complete discussion of these negotiations, see David Lewin and Mary McCormick, "Coalition Bargaining in Municipal Government: The New York City Experience," *Industrial and Labor Relations Review* 34 (January 1981).

42. For a fairly accurate account of the federal government's position, see statements by Secretary of the Treasury William Simon in U.S., Congress, House, Subcommittee on Government, Committee on Government Operations, *Federal Response to Financial Emergencies of Cities,* 94th Congress, 1st sess., June 23, 25, and 26, 1975, pp. 79–111; and in U.S., Congress, Joint Economic Committee,

New York City's Economic Crisis, 94th Congress, 1st sess., September 24 and October 8, 1975, pp. 47–100.

43. New York State Financial Emergency Act for the City of New York, N.Y. Unconsol. Laws, ch. 868 (McKinney Supp. 1975).

44. The Court of Appeals held this provision of the Financial Emergency Act in violation of the state constitution, art. V, sec. 7, which provided for the protection that "membership in any pension or retirement system of the state or of a civil division thereof shall be a contractual relationship, the benefits of which shall not be diminished or impaired." It is important to note that it was not in the investment of the funds into MAC bonds (which at the time were not being bought by the public) that the court found fault, but in the elimination of discretion of the trustees. There was no stipulation that the trustees could not voluntarily make this purchase. See *Sgaglione v. Levitt*, 37 N.Y. 2nd 507, 337 N.E. 2d 592, 375 N.Y.S. 2d (1975).

45. New York State Emergency Moratorium Act for the City of New York, N.Y. Unconsol. Laws, ch. 874 (McKinney Supp. 1975), as amended; N.Y. Unconsol. Laws, ch. 875 (McKinney Supp. 1975). For a discussion of the impact of the moratorium on the rights of bondholders, see William J. Quirk, "N.Y. Moratorium Act Seen Altering Essential Premises of Bond Investment," *Bond Buyer*, May 24, 1975, p. 1.

46. The agreement is referred to as the "Amended and Restated Agreement," November 26, 1975.

47. Investment of Funds by Pension and Retirement Systems Act, N.Y. Laws, 1975, ch. 890 (enacted on December 4, 1975).

48. See U.S., Congress, House, Committee on Ways and Means, Hearings on H.R. 11700, New York City Pension Fund Legislation, 94th Congress, 2nd sess., February 23, 1976. This bill became P.L. 94-236 on March 19, 1976.

49. See H.R. 1048, P.L. 94-143.

50. The law was challenged on the grounds that the moratorium violated the state constitution's full faith and credit clause as well as the federal constitution's prohibition against the impairment of contracts. The trial court upheld the moratorium and the appellate division confirmed it on the ground that the city faced a "grave public emergency" that constituted a threat to its "citizens and its viability and resources." The moratorium was held to be a "limited and conditional solution" (*Flushing National Bank v. Municipal Assistance Corporation*, 84 Misc. 2d 976, 379 N.Y.S. 2d 978 [1975]).

One year later, the New York Court of Appeals (the state's highest court) reversed the decision on the limited grounds that the moratorium violated the "full faith and credit clause of the State Constitution." The court did not proceed to rule on the question of the State's police power versus the federal constitution's contract clause. This issue remains unresolved (id., at 40 N.Y. 2d 731, 358 N.E. 2d 847, 390 N.Y.S. 2d 22 [1976].

51. See H.R. 12426 (P.L. 95-339). See also U.S., Congress, House, Subcommittee on Economic Stabilization, Committee on Banking, Finance and Urban Affairs, *New York City's Fiscal and Financial Situation*, 95th Congress, 2nd sess., February 21, 22, and March 2, 1978; and U.S., Congress, Senate, Committee

on Banking, Housing, and Urban Affairs, *New York City Financial Aid, Hearings on S. 2892 and H.R. 12426,* 95th Congress, 2nd sess., June 6, 7, 12, 13, 1978.

52. See FCB Report, July 1, 1981, and Office of the Special Deputy Comptroller for the City of New York, "Review of the Proposed New York City Four-Year Financial Plan for Fiscal Years 1982 Through 1985," Report 25-82, June 10, 1981 (hereinafter cited as OSDC Report, June 10, 1981).

53. See James Ring Adams, "The New York City Crisis: Centralization by Default," *Publius* 9 (Winter 1979):97–104. For a more extended discussion of this and other options, see Marvin W. Bagwell, Michael W. Evans, and Mark F. Nielsen, "Statute: The Municipal Bond Market, An Analysis and Suggested Reform," *Harvard Journal of Legislation* 16 (1979):211–267.

54. Felix Rohatyn, "Reconstructing America," *New York Review of Books,* February 5, 1981, pp. 16–20. See also Bagwell et al., op. cit.

55. See, for example, the court ruling in *Withers v. Teachers Retirement System of the City of New York,* 447 F. Supp. 1248 (S.D.N.Y. 1978), upholding the investments made by the Teachers Fund.

56. "Public Employee Pensions in Times of Fiscal Distress," *Harvard Law Review* 90 (1977):1007–1008.

6

State Government: The Overseer of Municipal Finance

Susan A. MacManus

State governments supervise the financial activities of their municipalities. States determine where cities get their money, how cities borrow money, how cities spend money, and how cities manage their financial affairs. States have the legal power to regulate municipal finance by virtue of their superior constitutional position.

According to state constitutions, states also have the power to authorize the formation (incorporation) of a new city. Likewise, states possess the power to abolish or dissolve an already existing city. (Rarely does a state abolish a city, but when it does, the reason is usually that the city cannot meet its financial obligations.) Because municipalities are legally "creatures of the state," state governments regulate their taxing, borrowing, spending, and financial administration.

Widespread state regulation of municipal finance began in the late 1800s and early 1900s in reaction to the default by a number of cities on their outstanding municipal bonds.[1] A new wave of state regulations began in the late 1970s, after New York City's fiscal crisis. The goals of state regulation of municipal finance today are the same as they were in the 1800s: *detection* of financial difficulties, *correction* of deficiencies causing the difficulties, and *prevention* of future fiscal crises.

In this chapter, I shall describe primarily how states regulate the taxing, borrowing, spending, and financial administration of their municipalities. I shall briefly discuss the effect such regulations have on the financial conditions of cities. And finally, I shall identify some of the new forms of state assistance designed to strengthen the financial condition of municipalities and to prevent future fiscal crises.

State Regulation of Municipal Revenue Sources

Cities obtain money from three primary sources: intergovernmental revenues, tax revenues, and nontax revenues.

Intergovernmental revenues come from either the federal or state government in the form of grants-in-aid or shared revenue. For example, a city may receive federal money to revamp a slum or build a highway. Some revenues may come from other local governments in the form of interlocal transfers. By the end of 1978, as indicated in Table 6.1, cities received 39.1 percent of their revenue from intergovernmental sources (15.6 percent from the federal government; 22.1 percent from state government; and 1.7 percent from other local governments). Intergovernmental revenues are generally referred to as "external" sources of municipal revenue.

Tax revenues come from property taxes and from nonproperty taxes (sales and income taxes). Referring again to Table 6.1, we see that by the end of 1978, cities were getting 42.5 percent of their revenue from tax sources (24.9 percent from property tax and 17.6 percent from nonproperty taxes).

Nontax revenues are of two types: current charges and miscellaneous general revenues. Current charges are amounts received from the public for specific services and from sales of commodities and services. They are also referred to as "user fees" or "user charges." Common examples are charges for collection and disposal of garbage; admission fees for the use of city swimming pools, golf courses, or stadiums; parking fees at meters or municipally operated garages; fees for occupational licenses; and court fines. Miscellaneous general revenues, on the other hand, come from interest earnings, receipts from the sale of city property, and special assessments. A special assessment is what property owners are charged for the construction of street lights, sidewalks, or other public improvements, so as to defray the costs of those improvements. By the end of 1978, cities were collecting 18.1 percent of their revenues from various nontax sources (see Table 6.1).

Tax and nontax revenues are referred to as locally raised or *"own-source" revenues*. As indicated by the figures in Table 6.1, cities raise a little more than 60 percent of their revenues locally. This percentage will probably increase in the near future as federal funds to cities are cut in an effort to balance the federal budget (see Table 6.2). The primary concern in this chapter is the contraints on the options open

TABLE 6.1
General Revenue of Municipal Governments, by Source and by State,
1977-78 Total, Per Capita and Percentage Distribution

State and Region	General Revenue		Intergov. Rev.[1]		Own Source Revenue						
	Total (millions)	Per Capita	From Federal	From State	Total Own Source	Total Taxes	Taxes Property	General Sales	Income	All Other	Nontax Charges & Misc.
United States	$65,486.5	$ 300.02	15.6%	22.1%	60.6%	42.5%	24.9%	6.1%	5.1%	6.4%	18.1%
New England	4,452.1	362.93	14.7	21.0	63.6	54.4	54.0	-	-	0.5	9.2
Connecticut	1,044.9	335.33	12.3	24.3	63.2	53.9	53.4	-	-	0.5	9.3
Maine	212.6	194.69	13.2	24.3	60.8	49.0	48.5	-	-	0.4	11.8
Massachusetts	2,602.1	450.89	15.5	19.6	64.1	54.9	54.5	-	-	0.3	9.2
New Hampshire	196.0	255.55	14.3	15.7	67.9	55.4	54.1	-	-	1.3	12.6
Rhode Island	356.3	382.30	15.3	24.3	60.1	56.2	55.7	-	-	0.6	3.9
Vermont	40.2	82.55	30.3	4.7	64.2	46.5	45.3	-	-	1.2	17.7
Mideast	23,607.1	559.05	12.9	31.3	54.6	43.9	24.1	5.0	9.8	5.0	10.8
Delaware	110.4	189.04	32.2	15.4	51.4	32.6	19.9	-	9.3	3.3	18.8
Dist. of Col.	1,681.7	2,506.26	41.4	-	56.9	50.3	11.8	9.4	17.2	12.0	6.5
Maryland	1,313.0	316.54	16.9	45.1	36.5	27.7	19.6	-	4.4	3.7	8.8
New Jersey	1,914.8	261.76	8.2	25.7	65.6	58.2	45.8	-	-	12.4	7.5
New York	16,383.3	923.21	8.9	36.9	53.2	42.2	24.0	6.3	8.5	3.4	11.0
Pennsylvania	2,203.9	187.36	21.9	11.5	65.1	49.3	18.3	-	25.2	5.8	15.8

TABLE 6.1 (continued)

Great Lakes	10,169.5	246.71	17.4	19.5	61.5	40.9	23.7	4.0	8.2	5.0	20.6
Illinois	2,729.0	242.84	16.1	12.5	70.1	53.3	24.7	15.0	-	13.6	16.8
Indiana	957.9	177.85	20.8	21.9	55.2	34.2	33.5	-	-	0.7	21.0
Michigan	2,670.3	290.85	19.9	22.1	55.9	32.7	23.1	-	7.6	2.0	23.2
Ohio	2,283.5	212.77	20.3	10.2	67.6	41.6	11.8	-	27.4	2.4	26.0
Wisconsin	1,528.8	326.46	8.8	39.8	50.7	35.9	34.6	-	-	1.3	14.7
Plains	3,849.3	225.95	18.7	14.6	64.8	35.6	21.5	4.4	2.4	7.3	29.2
Iowa	645.7	222.20	20.2	19.2	59.5	30.6	28.8	-	-	1.8	28.8
Kansas	515.6	219.68	16.5	7.5	73.1	34.2	28.1	1.0	-	5.0	38.8
Minnesota	1,042.4	259.05	14.2	23.3	60.3	26.9	22.7	0.3	-	3.9	33.3
Missouri	1,096.7	226.26	22.4	7.5	68.5	48.0	11.6	11.3	8.5	16.7	20.5
Nebraska	328.9	209.62	19.9	16.0	61.6	36.3	24.9	7.5	-	3.8	25.3
North Dakota	108.2	165.70	17.4	15.8	66.3	21.4	17.7	-	-	3.8	44.8
South Dakota	111.8	162.03	24.3	5.4	69.4	40.6	26.3	11.7	-	2.5	28.8
Southeast	9,139.1	185.02	19.1	16.0	60.4	36.4	20.3	4.3	1.3	10.6	24.0
Alabama	699.7	187.69	17.1	6.0	74.5	39.3	6.3	16.3	3.3	13.4	35.2
Arkansas	287.5	132.67	22.4	20.9	56.3	17.1	7.9	0.2	-	9.0	39.2
Florida	1,666.6	192.43	16.9	14.0	67.3	38.7	21.9	0.1	-	16.7	28.6
Georgia	695.6	135.91	18.7	9.8	66.5	39.9	22.2	1.7	-	16.0	26.6
Kentucky	504.8	144.64	24.7	4.0	65.4	35.6	12.8	-	18.6	4.2	29.8
Louisiana	756.8	189.86	25.9	10.0	60.9	39.2	12.9	18.5	-	7.8	21.7
Mississippi	327.0	136.25	22.1	24.7	50.8	22.4	18.8	-	-	3.5	28.4
North Carolina	766.9	137.66	27.0	15.0	50.4	32.7	31.3	-	-	1.4	17.7
South Carolina	215.6	74.29	26.3	13.2	59.5	41.1	30.7	-	-	10.4	18.3
Tennessee	1,443.1	333.05	15.5	22.8	48.4	27.3	19.2	2.6	-	5.5	21.1
Virginia	1,570.1	303.28	14.6	25.7	58.8	46.2	28.0	5.3	-	12.8	12.6
West Virginia	205.4	110.37	19.6	3.5	76.2	35.7	10.9	-	-	24.9	40.5

TABLE 6.1 (continued)

State and Region	General Revenue		Intergov. Rev.[1]		Total Own Source	Taxes				All Other	Nontax Charges & Misc.
	Total (millions)	Per Capita	From Federal	From State		Total Taxes	Property	General Sales	Income		
Southwest	3,995.1	205.09	19.3	7.3	72.6	44.6	22.4	16.1	-	6.1	28.1
Arizona	614.7	259.04	21.2	22.6	54.4	35.5	10.8	18.9	-	5.9	18.9
New Mexico	258.3	212.59	23.5	32.9	42.8	20.6	10.1	4.7	-	5.9	22.1
Oklahoma	648.8	223.29	23.0	4.1	72.8	37.8	7.7	25.6	-	4.5	35.0
Texas	2,473.3	189.52	17.4	1.6	80.3	51.1	30.5	14.1	-	6.6	29.2
Rocky Mountain	1,321.6	216.34	17.0	13.4	67.3	40.2	16.4	17.3	-	6.5	27.2
Colorado	782.2	289.06	15.0	11.7	71.3	44.8	13.2	24.5	-	7.1	26.5
Idaho	116.0	131.52	26.8	14.1	56.8	31.8	28.4	-	-	3.4	25.0
Montana	125.9	161.41	19.1	11.7	68.3	38.4	34.2	-	-	4.2	29.9
Utah	199.6	151.67	18.4	7.3	73.7	43.3	16.4	18.5	-	8.4	30.4
Wyoming	97.9	230.35	15.9	40.7	34.2	9.1	5.1	-	-	4.0	25.1
Far West	8,952.7	293.17	14.5	18.7	65.6	43.4	22.3	10.8	-	10.2	22.2
Alaska	437.5	1,064.48	9.1	30.4	60.3	29.1	23.1	5.3	-	0.7	31.2
California	6,847.1	306.85	12.9	19.7	66.6	45.2	22.1	12.8	-	10.3	21.4
Hawaii	287.9	319.18	31.6	4.9	63.5	52.1	41.9	-	-	10.1	11.4
Nevada	160.5	240.99	14.1	11.6	58.1	30.9	16.3	0.7	-	13.9	27.2
Oregon	473.3	193.03	24.6	9.6	62.9	36.4	27.6	-	-	8.9	26.5
Washington	746.4	196.78	19.1	15.9	63.4	38.5	14.4	8.9	-	15.2	24.9

Source: Advisory Commission on Intergovernmental Relations, Significant Features of Fiscal Federalism 1979-80 Edition (Washington, D.C.: Government Printing Office, Report No. M-123, October 1980), Table 61, p. 82.

[1] Percentage distribution does not add to 100 percent due to the exclusion of interlocal revenue (1.7%) from Intergovernmental Revenue total.

TABLE 6.2
Municipal Revenues--The Changing Mix (Dollar Amounts in Millions)

Revenue Source	1962	1967	1972	1978	1979-1984 Projections
Total Revenue	$13,127	$19,283	$34,998	$65,379	
			PERCENT DISTRIBUTION[1]		
Intergovernmental Revenue					
Direct Federal Aid	2.5%	4.2%	7.3%	15.6%	Little or no real increase. Due to growing fiscal austerity and Reagan Administration budget cuts, the growth in federal aid flows will probably lag behind the rate of inflation.
State Aid	16.3	20.7	24.1	22.1	Some increase to offset federal aid slowdown and due also to the relatively strong revenue position of most states.
Tax Revenue					
Property Tax	44.2	38.1	31.3	24.9	Continued decline. High inflation rates will increase public discontent with property tax.
Nonproperty Tax	16.2	16.4	17.3	17.7	Real growth. Local income and sales tax revenue will increase at a faster rate than inflation.
Nontax Revenue					
Charges & Miscellaneous Revenue	19.2	19.2	18.5	18.1	Probable increase especially in localities with tight property tax lids.

Source: Adapted from Advisory Commission on Intergovernmental Relations, Significant Features of Fiscal Federalism, 1979-80 Edition (Washington, D.C.: Government Printing Office, Report No. M-123, October 1980), Table 62, p. 83.

[1] Will not total 100 percent due to the fact that interlocal transfers are included in total revenue and not shown separately.

to municipal governments in their efforts to raise revenue, as revealed in a discussion of how states regulate, or restrict, their municipalities' ability to generate own-source revenues. As we shall see, states regulate municipal use of tax revenue sources to a much greater extent than they regulate nontax revenue sources.

State Restrictions on Municipal Property Taxing Powers

Types of Property Taxes. A state may authorize the taxation of two types of property: real property and personal property. In 1979 87 percent of all property tax revenues were collected from real property taxes. Ony 13 percent came from taxes on personal property.[2]

Real property refers to land and improvements, including structures on the land. For taxation purposes, real property is usually broken down into several categories, which often parallel the zoning classifications of the municipality in question. For example, real property might be classified as residential (single-family or multi-family), industrial, commercial, or agricultural. Often the property tax rate will differ among these classifications even within the same municipality. In general, residential property yields the greatest amount of revenue. All fifty states allow their municipalities to tax real property, and the funds thus obtained constitute the only revenue source that all states allow their local governments to tap. However, as we shall see, the states vary considerably in terms of how much and under what conditions they allow their municipalities to use the real property tax.

Personal property taxes are of two types: tangible and intangible. Tangible personal property has substance and worth, and it can be touched. Examples are cars, boats, machinery, animals, furs, artwork, jewelry, clothes, and equipment. Tangible personal property can be classified into five categories: business inventory, commercial and industrial, agricultural, household, and motor vehicle properties. The states vary in authorizing local governments to tax these categories: In 1979, forty-six states authorized their local governments to tax commercial or industrial property; thirty-eight, agricultural property; thirty-three, business inventory property; twenty-two, household property; and twenty, motor vehicles.[3]

Intangible personal property has value but no physical substance; it is representative of value. Examples are stocks, bonds, notes, mortgages, savings accounts, and franchises. Only fifteen states allow for local taxation of intangible personal property. Such taxes, when they are imposed, generally represent only an insignificant part of the total assessed personal property.[4]

Restrictions on Property Taxes. The states differ markedly in the legal restrictions they impose on property (real and personal) taxing powers. They also vary widely in the degree of difficulty involved in altering these restrictions. For example, as Pfiffner points out in Chapter 3, a tax rate limit set in a state constitution is much more difficult to change than one set in a state statute: Alteration of the state constitution requires a state-wide vote of the citizenry, whereas alteration of a state statute requires only a majority vote of the state legislature.

State limitations on municipal property taxing powers are of five types: (1) tax rate limits, (2) tax levy limits, (3) full disclosure requirements, (4) assessment limits or constraints, and (5) removal of property from the tax base through exemptions. Most of these limitations have been applied to real property rather than to personal property. However, it is important to keep in mind that real property is the single largest source of revenue to municipalities (see Table 6.1).

Property tax rate limits are also referred to as *"millage rate limits,"* in that they limit the number of mills per dollar of assessed valuation that can be taxed. (One mill is the equivalent of $1 per $1000, or 10¢ per $100, of assessed valuation.) In some states, millage rates vary according to city size. For example, for cities over 500,000 in population the millage rate limit may be 20 mills, but for cities under 500,000 the limit may be set at 10 mills. In many states, millage rate limits do not apply to the costs of municipal debt service (bonding) or insurance premiums.

Initially, tax rate limits were imposed to control the rate of increase in property tax levels. The first states to establish such limits were Rhode Island (1870), Nevada (1895), Oklahoma (1907), and Ohio (1911);[5] by 1970 a total of forty states had imposed some type of tax rate limit. According to a recent report of the Advisory Commission on Intergovernmental Relations (ACIR), however, during the 1970s such limits lost most of their effectiveness as tax control mechanisms because of rapidly rising property values.[6]

Levy limits, in effect, restrain the "increase in revenue from one year to the next, either by some specified percentage mentioned in law or else according to the rate of increase of some measure such as inflation or income."[7] Examples of such levy limits are Massachusetts's 4 percent tax limit on local tax levies and Michigan's constitutional amendment, which limits the growth of local tax revenue to the growth of the U.S. Consumer Price Index (CPI).

Levy limits became popular in the 1970s. Before 1970 only three states (Arizona, Colorado, Oregon) had such limits, but by the end of 1979 the number of states had grown to twenty (Alaska, Arizona, Colorado, Delaware, Indiana, Iowa, Kansas, Kentucky, Louisiana, Michigan, Minnesota, Ohio, Oregon, South Carolina, Utah, Washington, Wisconsin, Florida, Massachusetts, and New Mexico).[8]

Full disclosure, or *truth in taxation,* requirements also became popular during the 1970s. Where such requirements are in effect, "a property tax rate is established that will provide a levy equal to the previous year's when applied to some percentage of the current year's tax base. In order to increase the levy above the amount derived by using the established rate, the local governing board must *advertise its intent to set a higher rate, hold public hearings,* and then approve the higher rate by vote of the board."[9] Before 1970 none of the states had such a requirement, but by the end of 1979, ten states did. These states were Arizona, Florida, Hawaii, Maryland, Montana, Texas, Virginia, Tennessee, Kentucky, and Rhode Island.[10]

Assessment limits control the rate of increase in property assessment (valuation or revaluation). For example, Proposition 13 in California restricts assessment increases (based on revaluation) to 2 percent a year (unless the property is sold, in which case it can be put on the tax roll at its current market value). Like levy limits and full disclosure requirements, assessment limits first appeared in the 1970s. By the end of 1979, six states (California, Idaho, Minnesota, Iowa, Maryland, and Oregon) had imposed such limits.[11]

Property tax exemptions are a fifth, but somewhat different, type of state restriction on municipal property taxing powers. State legislatures can totally exempt certain types of property from taxation. Many states, in fact, exclude the following from taxation:

1. Government-owned property, that is, property held by federal, state or local governments;
2. Property used for "publicly beneficial" purposes, such as that owned by religious, charitable, or educational institutions;
3. Property used exclusively for publicly encouraged activities, such as pollution control and abatement;
4. New industrial property, which is usually exempted for a limited amount of time but initially exempted for the purpose of attracting new industry into an area; and
5. Property that is already taxed by another taxing mechanism, such as public utilities, which are subject to a utility tax.

Some states, although not exempting totally, may give tax breaks to farmers in an effort to prevent them from selling precious agricultural land to commercial developers. Other states may require that commercial property be taxed at lower rates than other types of property, for the same reason that they exempt new industrial property—to encourage business and industry to move into an area.

States can also exempt totally, or partially, certain groups of individuals from payment of property taxes (e.g., elderly people, disabled people, homeowners, and veterans). Exemptions benefiting senior citizens and handicapped people, in particular, represent an attempt to introduce progressivity into a tax that is typically criticized as being highly regressive. By giving breaks to those least able to pay, such exemptions shift the burden to those most capable of paying—and thus the tax itself becomes more progressive.

Regardless of whether certain types of property or certain classes of individuals are exempted from paying the property tax, however, the result is the same—reduction of a municipality's tax base. One recent study estimates that "approximately one-third of $800 billion of America's real estate is tax-exempt [and] that American taxpayers pay $15 billion a year in extra property taxes because other citizens pay none."[12] The problem of lost property tax revenue as a result of state exemptions is more acute in some states than in others. In 1978, for example, exemptions effectively removed over 12 percent of the gross assessed property value from taxation in Louisiana (20 percent), Florida (19 percent), Alabama (18 percent), and Oklahoma (12 percent). By contrast, state exemptions in Arizona, Maine, North Dakota, Washington, and Wyoming resulted in a loss of less than 1 percent.

Tax Restriction Index. As previously noted, states vary considerably in the restrictions they place on their municipalities' ability to raise revenue through imposition of real and personal property taxes. The Real Property Tax Restriction index shown in Table 6.3, which was constructed by adding together these restrictions, reveals that ten states impose heavy restrictions on their municipalities' use of the real property tax; sixteen, moderate restrictions; nineteen, minimal restrictions; and five, no restrictions. In the next column is the Personal Property Tax Restriction index, which indicates that seven states impose very heavy restrictions on municipal use of the tangible personal property tax; twelve, heavy restrictions; twenty-one, moderate restrictions; and ten, only minimal restrictions. These restrictions affect the financial condition of municipalities, as we shall see later in the chapter.

State Restrictions on Municipal Use of Nonproperty Taxes

Nonproperty taxes include taxes on *income* (individual and corporate), on *sales* (general and selective), and on *privileges* (motor vehicle registration, operators' licenses). In fiscal year 1978, 6.1 percent of all municipal revenue came from the local general sales tax, 5.1 percent from the local income tax, and 6.4 percent from selective sales taxes (i.e., taxes on alcoholic beverages, tobacco products, hotel rooms, restaurant meals, gasoline, public utilities, and so on) and privilege taxes (see Table 6.1).

Municipal use of nonproperty taxes first began during the Depression of the 1930s in reaction to the financial crises in a number of large cities. New York City was the first city to impose a retail sales tax (1934); Philadelphia was the first to levy an income tax (1939). However, municipal use of sales and income taxes expanded most in the 1960s. Between 1963 and 1970, for example, the number of states authorizing local sales taxes doubled.[13] Then, during the 1970s, the number of states authorizing local sales and income taxes declined, primarily because of "an increased perception that they discouraged business investment within a city."[14] It has been predicted that, in the 1980s, the use of such taxes will expand once again as states loosen their restrictions in an attempt to help municipalities make up lost intergovernmental (federal aid) and property tax revenues (see Table 6.2).

State regulations restrict municipal use of nonproperty taxes to a greater degree than that of property taxes. In fact, a large number of states do not allow their municipalities to levy either a sales or an income tax. State restrictions on nonproperty taxes generally take four forms: (1) outright prohibition, (2) tax rate limits, (3) levy limits, and (4) restrictions on the type of municipality that can levy the taxes.

Outright Prohibition. The figures in Table 6.1 indicate that, as of 1978, only twenty-four states authorized their municipal governments to impose a general sales tax, and only nine authorized use of the income tax. Twenty states prohibited their municipalities from using either general sales or income taxes. States are more inclined to let their municipalities use sales taxes (general and selective) than income taxes.

Tax Rate Limits. These limits are similar in principle to the property tax rate (millage rate) limits. Nonproperty tax rate limits are established either in the state constitution or in state statutes. The most common municipal sales tax rate is 1 percent (1¢ on each dollar of sales); overall, however, the limits range from 0.5 percent to 4 percent.[15] The most common municipal income tax rate is also 1 percent (1¢ on each dollar of income earned). These rates range from 0.25 percent in certain Pennsylvania cities to 4.3 percent in New York City.[16]

Levy Limits. Nonproperty tax levy limits are relatively new and have generally accompanied state imposition of property tax levy limits. For example, California's constitutional amendment known as Proposition 13 stated that once the proposition went into effect (July 1, 1978), *no tax* (including nonproperty taxes) could be raised above its previous level unless a two-thirds popular vote approved the increase.[17]

TABLE 6.3
State Restrictions on Municipal Revenue-Raising and Borrowing Powers, 1980

State	Real Property Tax Restrictions[1]	Personal Property Tax Restrictions[2]	Nonproperty Tax Restrictions[3]	Borrowing Constraints[4]
Alabama	Moderate	Moderate	Minimal	Heavy
Alaska	Moderate	Heavy	Moderate	Minimal
Arizona	Heavy	Heavy	Moderate	Heavy
Arkansas	Moderate	Minimal	Moderate	Minimal
California	Heavy	Moderate	Moderate	Minimal
Colorado	Minimal	Moderate	Moderate	Minimal
Connecticut	None	Moderate	Heavy	Minimal
Delaware	Minimal	Very Heavy	Moderate	Minimal
Florida	Heavy	Moderate	Heavy	Minimal
Georgia	Minimal	Minimal	Moderate	Heavy
Hawaii	Minimal	Very Heavy	Heavy	Minimal
Idaho	Moderate	Heavy	Heavy	Heavy
Illinois	Minimal	Moderate	Moderate	Heavy
Indiana	Moderate	Moderate	Heavy	Moderate
Iowa	Heavy	Moderate	Heavy	Moderate
Kansas	Moderate	Minimal	Moderate	Minimal
Kentucky	Heavy	Moderate	Moderate	Moderate
Louisiana	Heavy	Heavy	Moderate	Minimal

TABLE 6.3 (continued)

Maine	None	Heavy	Heavy	Heavy
Maryland	Moderate	Moderate	Moderate	Minimal
Massachusetts	Minimal	Moderate	Heavy	Minimal
Michigan	Moderate	Heavy	Moderate	Minimal
Minnesota	Heavy	Heavy	Moderate	Minimal
Mississippi	Minimal	Moderate	Heavy	Minimal
Missouri	Moderate	Minimal	Minimal	Heavy
Montana	Moderate	Moderate	Heavy	Moderate
Nebraska	Minimal	Moderate	Moderate	Minimal
Nevada	Moderate	Minimal	Moderate	Minimal
New Hampshire	None	Heavy	Heavy	Minimal
New Jersey	None	Very Heavy	Heavy	Minimal
New Mexico	Moderate	Moderate	Moderate	Moderate
New York	Minimal	Very Heavy	Minimal	Moderate
North Carolina	Minimal	Minimal	Heavy	Moderate
North Dakota	Minimal	Heavy	Heavy	Heavy
Ohio	Heavy	Heavy	Moderate	Minimal
Oklahoma	Minimal	Minimal	Moderate	Moderate
Oregon	Heavy	Moderate	Moderate	Minimal
Pennsylvania	Minimal	Very Heavy	Heavy	Moderate
Rhode Island	Minimal	Minimal	Moderate	Heavy
South Carolina	Minimal	Moderate	Heavy	Moderate
South Dakota	Minimal	Very Heavy	Moderate	Heavy

TABLE 6.3 (continued)

State	Real Property Tax Restrictions[1]	Personal Property Tax Restrictions[2]	Nonproperty Tax Restrictions[3]	Borrowing Constraints[4]
Tennessee	Minimal	Moderate	Moderate	Minimal
Texas	Moderate	Minimal	Moderate	Minimal
Utah	Heavy	Moderate	Moderate	Moderate
Vermont	None	Very Heavy	Heavy	Minimal
Virginia	Minimal	Moderate	Moderate	Heavy
Washington	Moderate	Moderate	Moderate	Heavy
West Virginia	Minimal	Minimal	Heavy	Heavy
Wisconsin	Moderate	Heavy	Heavy	Heavy
Wyoming	Moderate	Heavy	Heavy	Moderate

[1]The Real Property Tax Restriction Index was constructed by determining: (a) the sources of legal constraints (0=None; 1=Statutory; 2=Constitutional); (b) the millage rate limitations (0=No limits; 1=Over 10 Mills; 2=1-10 Mills); (c) property tax levy limits (0=No; 2=Yes); (d) full disclosure law requirement (0=No; 2=Yes); and (e) assessment constraints (0=No; 2=Yes). No Restrictions=0 points; Minimal Restrictions=2-3 points; Moderate Restrictions=4-5 points; Heavy Restrictions=6-10 points. Source of the legal constraint and millage rate data was the Advisory Commission on Intergovernmental Relations, State Limitations on Local Taxes and Expenditures (Washington, D.C.: Government Printing Office, Report No. A-64, February 1977), Appendix B, pp. 49-65. The property tax levy limit, full disclosure law, and assessment constraint data were collected from Advisory Commission on Intergovernmental Relations, Significant Features of Fiscal Federalism, 1979-80 Edition (Washington, D.C.: Government Printing Office, Report No. M-123, October 1980), Table 127, p. 185.

TABLE 6.3 (continued)

[2]The Tangible Personal Property Tax Restriction Index was constructed by determining whether a state allowed its municipalities to tax: (a) Business Inventories (0=Taxable; 1=Taxable but subject to partial exemptions; 2=Taxable but only if used in production of income; 3=Local option, but generally exempt; 4=Nontaxable--exempt); (b) Other Commercial and Industrial Personal Property (same scale); (c) Agricultural Personal Property (same scale); (d) Household Personal Property (same scale); and (e) Motor Vehicles (same scale). Minimal Restrictions=0-5 points; Moderate Restrictions=6-10 points; Heavy Restrictions=11-15 points; Very Heavy Restrictions=over 15 points. Data were collected from U.S. Department of Commerce, Bureau of the Census, State and Local Government Special Studies No. 98: Property Values Subject to Local General Property Taxation in the United States: 1979 (Washington, D.C.: Government Printing Office, August 1980), Table E, p. 6.

[3]The Nonproperty Tax Restriction Index was constructed by determining whether a state allowed its municipalities to impose: (a) a local sales tax (0=No; 1=Yes); and (b) a local general sales tax (0=No; 1=Yes). Minimal Restrictions= 2 points; Moderate Restrictions=1 point; Heavy Restrictions=0 points. The data were collected from Advisory Commission on Intergovernmental Relations, Significant Features of Fiscal Federalism, 1979-80 Edition (Washington, D.C.: Government Printing Office, Report No. M-123, October 1980), Table 88, pp. 127-133 (income tax) and Table 78, pp. 101-103 (general sales tax).

[4]The Borrowing Constraints Index was constructed by determining: (a) the existence of rate limits (0=No; 1=Yes); (b) the source of legal constraints (0=None; 1=Statutory; 2=Constitutional; 3=Both); and (c) the power to exceed debt limits (0=Unlimited; 1=Moderate--restricted by vote requirement; 2=None). Minimal Restrictions=0-2 points; Moderate Restrictions=3 points; Heavy Restrictions=4-6 points. Data were collected from Advisory Commission on Intergovernmental Relations, Significant Features of Fiscal Federalism, 1976-77 Edition, Vol. II--Revenue & Debt (Washington, D.C.: U.S. Government Printing Office, Report No. M-110, March 1977), Table 61, pp. 83-91.

Restrictions on Type of Municipality Permitted to Use Tax. Legal access to sales and income taxes is not uniform, even within a given state. In those states that authorize an income or sales tax, typically only the largest cities will be allowed to impose such a tax. For example, Michigan and Missouri restrict use of the municipal income tax to their largest cities.[18] One study found that "among the forty-five largest cities in the country, twenty-four levied a general sales tax and twelve an income tax in 1977"[19]—a rate higher than that characterizing smaller cities. One of the primary justifications for such taxes is that a city can collect revenues from nonresidents (suburban commuters, traveling business people, and tourists) who use city services while residing outside of the city and who thus do not pay property taxes.

Some states also limit use of nonproperty taxes to home-rule cities—cities that have been authorized by the state to exercise all legislative powers not prohibited by law or by charter. In each such state, if the state constitution or state statutes do not *expressly* prohibit municipal use of either sales or income taxes, cities with home-rule charters can impose nonproperty taxes. Actually, granting home-rule cities the right to impose nonproperty taxes is a way of getting around Dillon's Rule—a restrictive interpretation of local government power maintaining that unless the power to do something (e.g., impose a tax) is specifically granted in the state constitution or state statutes, a city cannot do it.[20]

As of 1979, twenty-one states placed heavy restrictions on municipal use of nonproperty taxes; twenty-six, moderate restrictions; and three, minimal restrictions (see Table 6.3). The impact of such restrictions on municipal financial condition will be examined later in the chapter.

State Restrictions on Municipal Use of Nontax Revenues

Next to the real property tax, nontax revenues—especially user charges—have been the revenue source made most available to municipalities by states. Traditionally, states have imposed almost no restrictions on municipal use of nontax revenues (i.e., current charges and miscellaneous general revenues).

Of the few state restrictions, however, the most common holds that user fees can be no more than the "actual cost of providing the service in question."[21] This restriction is intended to meet certain legal requirements related to Dillon's Rule. If a fee is higher than the actual cost of a service, technically it is no longer a fee, but a tax. And, as previously noted, municipal governments (other than some of those with home-rule charters) are "prohibited from levying any tax which has not been specifically authorized by the state government."[22]

Nontax revenues such as user charges have become increasingly important, especially in those states in which tax revolt fever has confined the municipalities' use of the property tax. In short, user charges have helped cities in such states compensate for revenue lost from property tax limitations. Thus far, few states have imposed any limitations on the amount of money that can be raised from such revenues or on the amount of the fees themselves. In California, for example, Proposition 13 limited increases in existing nontax revenues and prohibited imposition of new nontax revenue sources without the approval of two-thirds of the voters. In general, however, states do not heavily regulate municipal use of nontax revenues.

State Regulation of Municipal Borrowing

Governments borrow money for many of the same reasons that individuals do: to finance the purchase of land, to make a capital improvement on land (e.g., construction of a building), to purchase expensive equipment (e.g., fire trucks, police helicopters, computers), or to meet a financial emergency (e.g., a shortfall in revenue). In one sense, borrowed money can be viewed by a city as a *revenue* source. In another sense, borrowed money can be viewed as an *expenditure*, in that the city must budget for repayment of the borrowed funds. In recent years, the tendency of cities has been to view debt as primarily a revenue source; in the short term, borrowed funds bring money into the city treasury. Indeed, borrowing has become a politically popular way to raise money and to balance budgets, essentially because the cost of borrowing (repayment) is shifted forward in time. The public is far less hostile in its reaction to a city's selling of bonds or notes to raise revenues than to an increase in taxes, particularly property taxes.

To reiterate some of the points made in Chapter 3, municipalities can go into two types of debt: long-term or short-term. *Long-term debt* is payable more than one year after the date of issue. In fiscal year (FY) 1979, long-term debt accounted for 96 percent of all outstanding municipal debt.[23] *Short-term debt*, on the other hand, is payable within one year from the date of issue. As of FY 1979, short-term debt accounted for 4 percent of all municipal debt outstanding.[24] Typically, states regulate municipal use of long-term debt more extensively than that of short-term debt.

Long-term debt can take two forms: full-faith-and-credit debt (general obligation bonds) or nonguaranteed debt (revenue bonds). *Full-faith-and-credit debt* is "long-term debt for which the credit of the city, implying the power of taxation, is unconditionally pledged."[25] In other words, it is backed by the taxing power of the issuing municipality.

Such debt is financed by the sale of "full-faith-and-credit" or "general obligation" bonds. Interest rates are generally lower on these bonds than on nonguaranteed bonds due to the reduced risk associated with the former.

Nonguaranteed debt is "long-term debt payable solely from pledged specific sources—e.g., from earnings of revenue-producing activities (utilities, sewage disposal plants, toll bridges, etc.), from special assessment, or from specific nonproperty taxes."[26] This form of debt, then, must be repaid from the revenues produced by the service or facility for which the debt is issued, and it is financed through the sale of revenue bonds. Interest rates are higher on revenue bonds than on general obligation bonds because of the greater risk involved. The cost of revenue bonds to the issuing municipality is thus greater than that of general obligation bonds. However, one of the more attractive aspects of revenue bonds is the fact that they generally are *not* covered by the state debt-ceiling restrictions that apply to the issuance of general obligation bonds.

In FY 1979, full-faith-and-credit debt accounted for 50 percent of all municipal debt outstanding, whereas nonguaranteed debt accounted for 46 percent.[27] However, municipal reliance on full-faith-and-credit debt declined 4.4 percent between FY 1978 and FY 1979, whereas reliance on nonguaranteed debt increased 5.2 percent during the same period.[28] Economic reasons, more so than state restrictions, explain the growth of nonguaranteed debt. Developing Sunbelt cities rely more heavily on revenue bonds to meet their substantial capital expenditure needs than do other cities; but they are in a better position to use revenue bonds in the first place, because their healthy financial conditions permit them to utilize nonguaranteed debt with no fear of default.[29]

Short-term debt, payable within one year from date of issue, is financed by *tax anticipation notes* (TANs), *revenue anticipation notes* (RANs), *bond anticipation notes* (BANs), or *bank loans.* Municipalities use short-term debt to close the revenue-expenditure gap in three situations: (1) when anticipating receipt of revenues such as property taxes, a share of the state sales tax, or a federal grant (TANs, RANs); (2) when anticipating the sale of bonds (BANS); or (3) when emergencies arise (requiring bank loans). State regulation of short-term debt is minimal, although state monitoring of such debt has increased considerably in recent years.

The legal restrictions placed upon municipal borrowing are set down in the state constitution, state statutes, or both. These restrictions take four basic forms: (1) ceilings on the proportion of a municipality's property tax base that can be used to finance full-faith-and-credit debt; (2) ceilings on interest rates that can be paid on long-term debt and on short-term bonds, notes, and loans; (3) restrictions on a municipality's power to exceed the debt ceiling and/or interest rate ceiling; and (4) requirement of prior state approval before debt (long-term or short-term) can be issued. Such restrictions on local government borrowing are "designed to protect the solvency of local governments (as well as that of the state), and to protect bondholders."[30] Examples of variations in state restrictions on municipal borrowing are shown in Table 6.4.

Looking at all fifty states (Table 6.3), we find that fourteen place heavy constraints on the borrowing powers of their municipalities; twelve, moderate constraints; and twenty-four, only minimal constraints. The effect of such constraints on municipal fiscal condition will be examined later in the chapter.

State Regulation of Municipal Spending

State governments have the legal power to determine the quantity of money that cities can spend, as well as the functions, programs, and services to be bought. They can regulate such municipal expenditures by (1) imposing expenditure lids, (2) earmarking certain revenues for expenditure on specific functions, (3) dictating the services that must be provided by a given municipality, and (4) mandating that cities meet certain procedural requirements or performance standards or that they provide minimal levels of service.

Expenditure Lids

Expenditure lids typically limit the rate of increase in expenditures or appropriations from one year to the next. Such rates may be either set percentages or figures representing such measures as inflation, income, or the CPI. In New Jersey, for example, expenditure rates can rise only as rapidly as rates of increase in state per capita personal income.[31] In California, "total annual appropriations cannot exceed the previous year's appropriation limit, adjusted for changes in cost of living and population."[32] Expenditure lids are "most often expressed in terms of a maximum allowed percentage increase in annual *operating* [as opposed to capital] expenses."[33]

Spending lids became popular during the 1970s as a way to control the growth of government. Before 1970, only Arizona had such limits. By November of 1979, seven other states—Iowa, Kansas, New Jersey, Massachusetts, Nebraska, Nevada, and California—had put spending lids into effect in their municipalities.[34]

Some financial experts argue that those states with expenditure lids should exclude (exempt) certain costs from their budgetary calculations. According to one such expert, "relatively uncontrollable cost

TABLE 6.4
Examples of State Regulation of Municipal Borrowing

State	Debt Management
California	Local governments are permitted to issue short-term debt. Procedures to follow in issuing debt and a debt limit are imposed but not enforced.
Minnesota	State law establishes procedures for issuing debt, sets limits and requires a referendum for general obligation issues by statutory cities.
Montana	State law does not permit the issuance of short-term tax anticipation notes, revenue anticipation notes or bank loans. The total amount of general obligation debt is limited and bond issues are reviewed prior to issuance by the State Attorney General to verify compliance with laws.
New Jersey	Many practices and procedures are required by law and a debt limit exists. The state reviews issues prior to sale to ensure compliance with laws.
Pennsylvania	There is a long-term debt limit on general obligation issues not approved by referendum. The Department of Community Affairs must approve the issues to ensure that the limit is not violated.
Rhode Island	A nominal debt limit applies to local government borrowing, and public sales of general obligation bonds are required.
Tennessee	All proposed short-term borrowing must be approved in advance by the State Director of Local Finance. Public sales are required.
Texas	The State Attorney General must approve all local bond issues. An administrative limit on the amount of debt outstanding has been set by the Attorney General, defined as a percentage of the statutory millage limits on local property taxes.
Washington	The state limits the amount of general obligation and special purpose debt outstanding.

Source: John E. Petersen, Catherine L. Spain, and C. Wayne Stallings. ."From Monitoring to Mandating: State Roles in Local Government Finance," Governmental Finance 8 (December 1979), Exhibit 1, p. 9.

such as pensions and medical insurance may go up so much as to consume a large share of the permitted increase in spending, leaving little money for wage increases and other increases in costs."[35] Thus far, however, not a single state has exempted spending for pensions and medical insurance from expenditure-lid calculations.

Earmarking Revenues

Earmarking is "a restriction imposed on the use to which a governmental revenue may be put."[36] States can effectively limit the ability of a municipality to determine what it will spend its money for by requiring that certain grants-in-aid or shared revenues be spent for specific services, functions, or purposes. A common example over the years has been the requirement that state gasoline taxes shared with (i.e., returned to) municipalities be spent on streets. Although the percentage of earmarked local revenues has steadily declined since the 1930s, a number of states still occasionally use earmarking to influence the expenditure priorities of their municipalities.

Functional Assignment

Municipalities in the United States vary considerably in the functions they perform. For example, nearly all municipalities provide police protection, fire protection, streets, parks and recreation, sanitation, and some sewerage functions. However, less than one-third of the total number have responsibility for welfare, hospitals, or education.[37] (Most of the states that assign these latter functions to their municipalities are in the Northeast.) In many states, these "least common" functions are performed by county governments, special district governments, or by the state itself (e.g., education in Hawaii). State governments in general have the power to determine which level of government will perform a particular function.

The functional assignments given to municipalities greatly affect their expenditure patterns. Cities that have to provide welfare, education, and/or hospitals (all tremendously expensive services) must spend large proportions of their budgets on these functions. An example is provided in Table 6.5, which compares the expenditure patterns of two cities over 500,000 in population—one with responsibility for welfare, hospitals, and education (City A) and one without responsibility for these functions (City B).

This comparison indicates that City A commits almost half (41.6 percent) of its expenditures to the three functions mentioned above. Obviously, the expenditure priorities (as measured by the percentage of a city's total expenditures that are allocated to a certain function) of City A and City B differ considerably. In City A, the five functions

TABLE 6.5
A Comparison of the Expenditure Patterns of Two Cities with Different
Functional Assignments: 1979

City A[1] (Responsibility for Education, Welfare, and Hospitals)		City B[2] (No Responsibility for Education, Welfare, Hospitals)	
Function	% of General Expenditures	Function	% of General Expenditures
Education	19.5%	Police Protection	12.8%
Welfare	15.7	Sewerage	12.2
Police Protection	8.7	Streets	8.9
Housing & Urban Renewal	6.7	Parks & Recreation	8.6
Hospitals	6.4	Fire Protection	8.0
Interest on Debt	6.0	Housing & Urban Renewal	6.4
Corrections	4.2	Sanitation other than	
Streets	3.6	Sewerage	4.6
Fire Protection	3.1	Interest on Debt	4.1
Health	2.7	Airport	3.2
Sewerage	2.7	Health	2.8
General Control	2.3	General Control	2.7
Financial Administration	2.0	General Public Buildings	2.2
General Public Buildings	1.9	Financial Administration	1.9
Sanitation other than		Corrections	0.6
Sewerage	1.3	Protective Inspections	
Parks & Recreation	0.9	& Regulation	0.3
Libraries	0.6	Parking Facilities	0.1
Protective Inspections		Education	-
& Regulation	0.3	Public Welfare	-
Parking Facilities	0.2	Hospitals	-
Airports	-	Libraries	-
Water Transport &		Water Transport &	
Facilities	-	Facilities	-
Natural Resources	-	Natural Resources	-
Other Expenditures	11.4	Other Expenditures	20.7
	100.2%*		100.1%*

Source: Calculated from U.S. Department of Commerce, Bureau of the
Census, City Government Finances in 1978-79 (Washington, D.C.:
Government Printing Office, September 1980), Table 8.
[1]Population = 684,891; Total general expenditures = $1,843,715,000.
[2]Population = 532,399; Total general expenditures = $ 278,055,000.
-Function not assigned to the city.
*Figures do not add to 100 percent because of rounding.

with the highest expenditure priority are, in order, *education, welfare,*
police protection, housing and urban renewal, and *hospitals.* In City B,
which takes no responsibility for education, welfare, or hospitals, the
five highest expenditure priorities are police protection, sewerage, streets,
parks and recreation, and fire protection. Clearly, state assignment of

functional responsibilities affects both the expenditure level (i.e., total dollars spent) and the expenditure priorities of a municipality.

Mandated Procedures, Performance Standards, and Minimum Levels of Service

A state mandate is "any constitutional, statutory, or administrative action that either limits or places requirements on local governments."[38] The number of mandates imposed by various states on their municipalities increased sharply in the 1970s (increasing by 615 from 1961 to 1970, and by 1,665 from 1971 to 1978[39]) and continues to increase in the 1980s. New York, California, Minnesota, and Wisconsin have been identified as those states that have imposed the greatest number of mandates. Each of these states has, in fact, imposed over 66 percent of the 77 different types of mandates identified by the Advisory Commission on Intergovernmental Relations in its study *State Mandating of Local Expenditures*.[40] By contrast, southern states have imposed the fewest (less than 15 percent).

State mandates have several justifications: (1) The state may decide that the particular activity or service is of sufficient state-wide importance that it cannot be left to the option of local governments; (2) state-wide uniformity in the provision of a service may be deemed essential by the state legislature, the courts, or a state agency; and (3) mandates may promote achievement of a desirable economic or social goal.[41] Regardless of the justification, however, such mandates have significantly affected the finances of the municipalities involved, as will be shown later in the chapter.

The bulk of all state mandates are personnel related, their purpose being to establish training, licensing, and certification standards; procedures for determining wage and salary levels (e.g., collective bargaining, compulsory binding arbitration); actual salary and wage levels for certain categories of employees; hours of employment; working conditions; disability benefit levels and procedures; and retirement benefit levels and procedures. Significantly few southern states have ever imposed mandates pertaining to collective bargaining, compulsory arbitration, or working conditions. It is clearly for this reason that southern states rank lowest, overall, in terms of the number of mandates imposed on their local governments; whereas personnel mandates are elsewhere the most numerous variety, they surface only relatively rarely in the South.

Various other types of mandates establish certain state-wide minimum standards that local governments must meet (e.g., jail standards; ambulance operating standards; air-, water-, and wastewater-quality standards; and solid-waste disposal standards). Likewise, a number of mandates require that certain minimum levels of service be provided by local governments to their citizens (e.g., bilingual education, preschool programs, and police and fire protection). Obviously, the implementation of these mandates costs money. And thus it follows that state mandates can affect municipal expenditure levels and priorities to much the same degree as can state assignment of functional responsibilities.

State Regulation of Municipal Financial Administration

States take an active role in overseeing the financial management activities of their municipalities for four primary reasons:[42] (1) to foster local fiscal control, (2) to ensure fiscal solvency, (3) to promote efficient and effective resource management by local governments, and (4) to oversee local performance of programs mandated or financed by the state. State governments have taken a more active role in overseeing financial administration since New York City's financial crisis in the mid-1970s. According to one expert, this crisis brought home the fact that the budgeting, accounting, payroll, purchasing, and program-evaluation systems and procedures of many cities had become antiquated and thus ineffective as management, or fiscal control, tools.[43] Indeed, New York City's difficulties clearly illustrated that "inefficient, outmoded or nonexistent financial management systems help create or contribute to [municipal] fiscal crises."[44]

The power to upgrade the quality and effectiveness of municipal financial administration lies with state government. In fact, as Donna E. Shalala notes, "through regulation, supervision, and technical assistance, [states] influence the whole spectrum of financial management, including budgeting, accounting, auditing, reporting . . . and cash management."[45] However, a recent study analyzing state involvement in local financial management in nine states reveals considerable variation in the means by which states attempt to supervise or regulate such activities and in the types of penalties, or sanctions, they impose on cities that fall short of state-imposed standards (see Table 6.6).

State Regulation of Municipal Accounting

State regulation of municipal accounting typically involves the following requirements: (1) a uniform system of accounting (i.e., uniform terminology, uniform principles of accounting, uniform classifications of balance sheet and operating statement accounts), and (2) the adoption by municipalities of accounting standards developed by such groups as the National Committee on Governmental Accounting or the Municipal

TABLE 6.6
Examples of State Regulation of Municipal Financial Administration

State	Accounting, Auditing, Financial Reporting	Budgeting	Cash Management
California	Annual financial reports must be submitted to the state comptroller, who publishes them in various compendia for statewide distribution but exercises no quality control over their preparation.	An annual budget is required of counties but voluntary compliance is considered sufficient.	The state restricts the investment instruments local governments may purchase but performs no enforcement.
Minnesota	State law prescribes reporting requirements for all local governments, but differentiates between small and large governments. The state has the authority to obtain reports if cities fail to submit them. Local governments are audited by independent or state auditors.	Most municipalities are not bound by state budget laws. Counties must submit a budget.	Laws regulate permissible investments and require depositories to pledge collateral if deposits are uninsured. Regulation is limited to a post-audit review.
Montana	All cities and counties must adopt a uniform statewide accounting and reporting system. State auditors are responsible for auditing local government.	Annual balanced budgets are required and must be prepared using a standard set of budget classifications.	Selection of depositories and investments are regulated and enforced through the annual post-audit.

TABLE 6.6 (continued)

New Jersey	Accounting procedure requirements are set forth by law. All local governments must be audited by Registered Municipal Accountants. Annual financial reports must be filed on standard forms.	State law sets forth extensive and detailed requirements governing preparation, adoption and execution. The budget must be approved by the state before it can go into effect.	State law sets forth detailed standards with regard to selection of depositories and investments. All cash must be deposited 48 hours after receipt. A post-audit checks for compliance.
Pennsylvania	Local governments must file annual reports on standard forms but there are no common accounting standards or auditing controls.	Local governments are required to file a balanced budget on a standard form.	Local governments have wide latitude in selecting depositories and investing funds.
Rhode Island	Local governments must submit annual financial reports to the Department of Community Affairs which have been audited by a CPA or the State Bureau of Audits.	Local governments must publish a budget summary on a standard form. A new law limits the size of the operating deficits cities and towns can accumulate.	There are few restrictions on local cash management practices.
Tennessee	The State Comptroller is authorized to establish accounting and reporting standards for all local governments. The state audits counties and oversees the municipal audits performed by professional accountants.	All local governments must prepare and publish balanced annual budgets. The state must approve a local budget if the jurisdiction has short-term debt outstanding.	State law specifies permissible investments and requires collateral from depository banks for funds not insured.

TABLE 6.6 (continued)

State	Accounting, Auditing, Financial Reporting	Budgeting	Cash Management
Texas	Cities must issue an annual financial report that has been audited by a CPA or a public accountant.	Local governments must submit their annual budgets, in any form they choose, to the State Comptroller. This is not vigorously enforced.	A new law requires local government to adopt a cash management program but there is no way to enforce this provision. There are many laws affecting the investment of idle funds and selection of depositories. Local governments lack flexibility.
Washington	Local governments must adopt a prescribed, uniform budgeting, accounting and reporting system. Annual financial reports must be submitted to the state and the state auditor is required to audit all local governments.	State law requires local governments to prepare an annual budget and submit it to the state.	There is wide latitude in selection of depositories and investments to encourage good practices.

Source: John E. Petersen, Catherine L. Spain, and C. Wayne Stallings. "From Monitoring to Mandating: State Roles in Local Government Finance," Governmental Finance 8 (December 1979), Exhibit 1, pp. 8 -10.

Finance Officers Association.[46] States may also dictate the method of accounting that must be used (e.g., cash, modified accrual, or accrual).

According to the Municipal Finance Officers Association, a uniform accounting requirement is adopted by a state because such standardization (1) helps to ensure municipalities' accountability for state funds, (2) greatly eases the accurate publication of comparable financial statistics for municipalities within a state, (3) aids state supervision of local budgeting, and (4) expedites the auditing of municipal accounts.[47] Even so, not all states have chosen to impose such a requirement on their municipalities (see Table 6.6).

State Regulation of Municipal Auditing

State regulation of municipal auditing generally establishes the type of auditor (state auditor, certified public accountant chosen by the city, or city auditor), the schedule by which audits are performed (annually or biennially), the source of payment for the audit (city, state, or both), the form of the audit report, and selection of the state agency to be responsible for collecting and reviewing the audits. The primary purpose of state auditing of local accounts is "to ensure compliance with state laws and to enforce fiscal accountability."[48] States vary considerably in their supervision of municipal auditing (see Table 6.6).

State Regulation of Municipal Financial Reporting

Certain states require that all municipalities annually report financial data to a state supervisory agency (see Table 6.6). Several states often publish such information. One-third of the states prepare an annual volume of local government financial statistics.[49] In the states that require such annual reports, state regulations determine the reporting format to be used, the date the reports are due, and the state agency responsible for the collection and analysis of the reports. In addition, state laws often require that municipalities publish a certain number of copies for distribution to citizens, local public officials, public libraries, and educational institutions.

Annual financial reports aid states (and municipalities) in the detection of situations requiring technical assistance or remedial action. They also aid in state supervision of municipal auditing and budgeting activities, help identify local financial trends within the state, and offer important data to state policymakers (the governor, legislators, agency heads), taxpayers' groups, large institutional investors, and researchers.

State Regulation of Municipal Budgeting

The variation among states with regard to regulation of municipal budgeting is even more pronounced than that pertaining to regulation of accounting, auditing, and financial reporting (see Table 6.6). State regulations often dictate (1) which local official will be held responsible for compliance (typically a budget officer), (2) whether a standard budget form will be used by all cities within the state, (3) whether the budget must be balanced or deficit spending will be allowed, (4) whether the budgetary (fiscal) year will conform to the calendar year (January 1–December 31) or to some other schedule (e.g., October 1–September 30), (5) whether a given city will have two separate budgets—one for operating purposes, one for capital—or only one budget combining the two types of expenditures, and (6) whether the state must review and approve a budget before it can be formally adopted by the municipality involved. State regulation of local budgets has been justified on the grounds that it "results in timely preventive or curative action either at the beginning of, or during, the budget year."[50]

State Regulation of Municipal Cash Management

During the fiscal year, the day-to-day flow of revenue is almost never equal to the expenditure flow. In other words, during certain periods cash balances build up and greatly exceed expenditure needs. Many municipalities, for example, receive lump-sum, scheduled payments from major revenue sources (such as property taxes or income taxes) at the beginning of the fiscal year or at quarterly intervals. However, normal operating expenditure demands tend to be spread more evenly throughout the year. Depending on the flow pattern, some cities may have excess cash available for short-term investment. Good management of such cash can greatly aid the financial condition of a city; and investment of otherwise idle funds can earn the city more revenue.

A recent report of the Advisory Commission on Intergovernmental Relations examined cash management at the state and local levels. It found that state laws can (1) influence or determine the types of eligible securities for the placement of surplus cash (e.g., certificates of deposit, U.S. Treasury securities, commercial paper, federal agency securities, corporate stocks); (2) set rules for depository selection (e.g., requirements that public funds be placed on deposit with institutions located within a city's boundaries, or requirements that deposits be placed in several banks, instead of just one); (3) set rules governing the amount that can be held by any one depository; and (4) determine the interest rates that depositories can pay to cities on their time deposits (such rates are often tied to U.S. Treasury Bill rates).[51]

In some states, statutory guidelines are sufficiently general as to allow each municipality a great deal of discretion in managing its cash. In other states, constitutional and/or statutory provisions are quite stringent, thus effectively limiting the municipality's ability to determine its own cash-management strategies (see Table 6.6).

This completes our look at how state governments supervise the taxing, borrowing, spending, and financial administration of their municipalities. We turn now to a discussion of the effects of state oversight on municipal financial condition.

The Relationship Between State Regulation and Municipal Financial Condition

A number of studies have identified taxing, borrowing, spending, and financial management patterns associated with municipal fiscal distress.[52] The most commonly cited signs of fiscal distress are (1) continued shortfalls of revenues relative to expenditures, (2) continued use of short-term debt to meet operating expenses, (3) a substantial amount of short-term debt outstanding at the end of a fiscal year, (4) a drop in the financial rating of a city's general obligation bonds as assessed by either Moody's Investors Service or Standard and Poor's, (5) large unfunded pension liabilities, (6) a declining tax base, (7) increases in delinquent property taxes, (8) big pay increases due to collective bargaining or compulsory binding arbitration activities, (9) high municipal tax burdens, (10) growing dependency on federal and state aid, (11) high per capita debt service costs, and (12) unsound budgeting and accounting practices. In short, the studies on this subject primarily contrast the taxing, spending, and borrowing patterns of fiscally distressed cities with those of fiscally healthy cities; most of them, however, do not fully examine the impact of state regulations on municipal fiscal condition.

In fact, only a few studies have focused on the fiscal effects of state legal constraints on municipal taxing and borrowing powers.[53] It is difficult to determine just how much of a city's financial condition is the result of state regulations on its finances and how much is attributable to a city's population growth or decline, ability to expand (or annex) its boundaries, land-use patterns (economic base), socioeconomic makeup, or quality of local financial administrators and public officials.

One study examining the impact of state legal constraints on the fiscal conditions of cities concluded that such restrictions did significantly affect financial condition.[54] The author, using fiscal data from 1974, 1975, and 1976 on 243 U.S. central cities, found that certain state restrictions were beneficial whereas others were not. Ironically, the states that imposed the *heaviest* restrictions on municipal property taxing powers before 1974 had contributed most effectively, although perhaps unknowingly, to the fiscal health of their cities. By imposing heavy restrictions on the property tax, for instance, certain states effectively mandated diversification of revenue structures. The result was a more balanced revenue structure—one that was less susceptible to the property tax revolt fever of the late 1970s and early 1980s.

As for nonproperty taxes (i.e., sales, income, and privilege taxes), the states that imposed the *fewest* restrictions effectively decreased the dependency of their cities on externally raised revenues (federal and state aid), on the unpopular property tax, and on the debt backed by that tax (full-faith-and-credit debt).

State restrictions on municipal borrowing—specifically, full-faith-and-credit (general obligation) borrowing—also affected the fiscal health of municipalities, though less significantly than did taxing regulations. In the same way that imposition of heavy restrictions on property taxes stimulated diversification of municipal revenue sources, heavy restrictions on long-term debt produced more balanced debt structures. The heavier the borrowing restrictions, the more balanced was a municipality's reliance upon both guaranteed and nonguaranteed long-term debt.

Another factor affecting the fiscal health of cities was state assignment of heavy functional responsibility to cities (rather than to special district, county, or state governments). Cities assigned responsibility for costly functions such as education, public welfare, and hospitals relied more on external aid, property taxes, and short-term debt than did cities without such responsibilities.

A more recent study reexamined the relationship between state constraints and a city's ability to improve its financial condition—in this case, focusing on the years between 1975 and 1979 and, again, using 243 U.S. central cities as the units of analysis.[55] The results were similar to those of the earlier study. Municipalities in states that imposed heavy restrictions on their use of property taxes (both real and personal) were more likely to have *improved* their financial conditions than those in states without such restrictions. On the other hand, the financial conditions of municipalities in states that imposed heavy restrictions on nonproperty taxes, assigned burdensome functional responsibilities, and imposed expenditure lids were more likely to have *worsened*.

Other studies have examined the impact of state programmatic and procedural mandates on municipal finance. One study of five cities in five different states focused on the impact of such mandates on municipal expenditure priorities.[56] The conclusion reached in this case was that programmatic and procedural mandates essentially forced local governments to increase their policy dependency on the state, particularly when the state did *not* pay for the implementation or provision of the mandated programs or procedures. According to the author, "If the mandating government [the state] pays for the activity, then the local government is not forced to reorder its priorities. If the mandated-upon government [the city] must pay, clearly the mandate acts as a constraint on the local government's policy freedom."[57] The findings also indicate that states paid for mandate costs in less than 20 percent of the cases.

Another study, referred to earlier, examined the extent to which eighty-eight specific state mandates helped or hindered the ability of 243 U.S. central cities to improve their fiscal conditions between 1975 and 1979.[58] This study found that one-third (32 percent) of the mandates imposed by states were significantly related to changes in municipal fiscal condition. Of this third, nineteen (68 percent) were associated with worsening financial conditions and nine (32 percent) were associated with improving financial conditions.

Personnel mandates related to collective bargaining, compulsory binding arbitration, disability, and retirement, particularly of public safety personnel (police and fire department employees), are most strongly associated with worsening conditions. For example, cities in which compulsory binding arbitration mandates had been imposed were generally seven times more likely to experience a worsening of their bond ratings between 1975 and 1979 than were cities without such mandates, and five times more likely under collective bargaining mandates. In support of these findings, Detroit's mayor, Coleman Young, recently urged the Michigan legislature to repeal the state's compulsory arbitration law (which, ironically, he had cosponsored in 1969). According to Young, "We know that compulsory arbitration has been a failure. Slowly, inexorably, compulsory arbitration destroys sensible fiscal management."[59]

Some types of state procedural and programmatic mandates improved the financial condition of affected municipalities. Mandates most strongly associated with improving municipal financial conditions are of two types: (1) those that force local governments to expand their planning and management capacities (e.g., comprehensive land-use planning requirements and property tax constraints or cutbacks forcing revenue diversification and/or cutback management), and (2) those that standardize service or program requirements, thus effectively putting a cap on local costs (e.g., medicaid payment level limits and limits on overtime).[60]

These studies do clearly illustrate the impact of state regulations on the financial condition of their municipalities. Some regulations have a positive effect; others have a negative effect. In response to these findings, many states have begun to reevaluate their regulations governing the taxing, borrowing, spending, and financial management activities of their municipalities. In the last part of this chapter, we shall examine some of the new approaches that states are taking to relieve the pressures on their cities' finances.

New Approaches to State Regulation of Municipal Finance

States are the principal architects of municipal finance. And, according to Alan G. Billingsley and Paul D. Moore, "as the architect of the financial framework within which local governments function, the state has a major responsibility to ensure that the system operates in an efficient and effective manner."[61] The state must "produce legislation that will identify and contain local fiscal problems before they reach crisis proportions."[62] A number of states took this route in earnest following New York City's fiscal crisis in the mid-1970s. Their new approaches to crisis prevention have generally fallen into three categories: (1) those that expand the revenue-raising capacity of cities, (2) those that transfer, or authorize transfer of, costly functions to other levels of government, and (3) those that place financial responsibility for state-mandated programs and procedures on the state.

Expansion of Revenue-Raising Capacity

One method by which states have expanded revenue-raising capacity has involved the *removal of restrictions from municipal use of income and sales taxes* (nonproperty taxes). In doing so, states have allowed cities to diversify their revenue bases and to become less dependent on property taxes and federal aid. Another approach has been to *increase the amount of shared tax (piggybacked) revenue* (from general and selective sales) that is returned to municipalities and to *treat it as general purpose aid* (no strings attached).

In line with the recommendations of the Advisory Commission on Intergovernmental Relations (ACIR), some states have also begun to reevaluate their policies regarding compensation to local governments for tax-exempt, state-owned property lying within city boundaries. The ACIR has recommended that states establish an inventory of all such property and develop mechanisms for *state payment in-lieu-of-taxes.*[63] Other states have adopted *tax equivalency plans.* Under such plans, states "set millage rates or levies for the land they own and then cooperate with local officials in assessing and calculating the total levy applied to each piece of property."[64] In addition, a number of states with property-tax-relief programs (circuit-breakers)—which grant exemptions on the basis of homeownership, age, disability, and/or military service—

have legislated that *states must reimburse the affected local government to cover the losses of these exempted revenues.*[65]

The newest approach to expanding the revenue-raising capacity of cities is *regional tax-base sharing*. First adopted by Minnesota, this approach spread to other states, specifically, New Jersey and Maryland.[66] The goal of tax-base sharing plans is to regionally equalize the benefits from property-tax-base increases and to reduce fiscal disparities among local governments within a given metropolitan area. For example, under the Minnesota plan, "forty percent of the revenues generated from the growth in the property-tax base in the seven-county area of metropolitan Minneapolis-St. Paul is put in a pool and distributed to the affected localities based on indicators of 'need,' measured by population and per capita wealth."[67]

Functional Transfers (Reassignments)

Another popular approach to municipal fiscal relief involves state mandates that transfer responsibility for certain functions (especially costly functions) to other levels of government with broader tax bases (see Table 6.7). A 1976 ACIR study of functional transfers revealed that of the more than 3,000 cities surveyed, one-third had transferred responsibility for one or more functions during the previous ten years to either another municipality, the county, special districts, regional councils of governments, or the state.[68] Thus, according to the ACIR, "the achievement of economies of scale, more even service provision throughout an entire area, and a more equitable system of financing the service are the principal arguments advanced in favor of an upward shift of functional responsibility."[69]

State Assumption of Financial Responsibility for Mandated Programs and Procedures

The tremendous increase in the number of state mandates in the 1970s and their impact on municipal expenditure levels and priorities resulted in a series of recommendations by the ACIR. These recommendations are based on the principle that "those who mandate new programs (or procedures) should share in the responsibilities of the costs that these programs (or procedures) impose on local government."[70] Specifically, the ACIR study recommended (1) full state reimbursement for state mandates if state-imposed tax lids seriously constrict local revenue-raising ability, (2) partial reimbursement for state mandates that prescribe expansion or improvement of already existing programs, (3) full state reimbursement for mandates affecting local employee retirement benefits, and (4) full state reimbursement for mandates covering "more properly local" matters, such as employee compensation, working hours,

TABLE 6.7
State-Mandated Functional Transfers (From Municipality to Higher Level of Government)*

Function	States	Function	States
Administrative and Legal	Florida, Georgia, Illinois, Michigan, New Hampshire, Oregon, and Virginia	Sewage Collection and Treatment	Connecticut, Kansas, Minnesota, Ohio, and Texas
Taxation and Assessment	California, Florida, Georgia, Missouri, New Jersey, New Mexico, Oklahoma, Pennsylvania, Tennessee, and Wisconsin	Solid Waste Collection and Disposal	California, Delaware, Florida, Idaho, Iowa, Kansas, Minnesota, New Jersey, New York, Ohio, Oregon, Pennsylvania, South Carolina, Tennessee, and Texas
Elections	Florida, Iowa, Kansas, Minnesota, North Carolina, North Dakota, and Washington	Water Supply	Michigan
		Transportation	New York, Ohio, and Wisconsin
Social Services	California, Delaware, Hawaii, Massachusetts, Michigan, Minnesota, New York, Ohio, Rhode Island, and Vermont	Education	Connecticut, Hawaii, and Wisconsin
		Public Health	California, Connecticut, Florida, Hawaii, Illinois, Kansas, Pennsylvania, and Rhode Island
Planning	Iowa, Minnesota, and Oregon		
Law Enforcement	California, Florida, Hawaii, Illinois, Minnesota, Nebraska, Nevada, South Dakota, and Virginia	Housing and Community Renewal	Connecticut
		Building and Safety Inspection	Iowa, Kansas, Michigan, Ohio, Oregon, Texas, Virginia, and Washington
Fire Protection and Civil Defense	Florida and Iowa	Environmental Protection	Michigan, Minnesota, New Hampshire, Ohio, Pennsylvania, and Virginia

Source: Advisory Commission on Intergovernmental Relations. State Mandating of Local Expenditures (Washington, D.C.: Government Printing Office, Report No. A-67, July 1978), Figure II-1, p. 20.

*From municipalities to counties, regional special districts, or state governments.

and working conditions.[71] Relatively few states have adopted policies calling for state reimbursement. Only four states (California, Montana, Louisiana, and Pennsylvania)[72] require state compensation for either mandated local costs or revenue losses, or both. However, a number of proposals related to state reimbursement are currently before other state legislatures.

Even more popular among the states has been the adoption of a *fiscal note requirement*. This requirement mandates that an estimate of the cost to *local* governments of any proposed state legislation be attached to the legislation. Local officials see this as a way to curb state mandating by forcing state legislators to realize the financial burden imposed on localities by mandates. Fiscal note requirements appear to be effective. Cities in those states that did *not* require fiscal notes were three-and-a-half times more likely to experience a worsening of their financial condition between 1975 and 1979 than were cities in states that did require such notes.[73] (As of 1978, twenty-two states had adopted the fiscal note requirement in both houses of their legislatures.)

The development of innovative approaches is going to become even more critical to the fiscal health of municipalities in the next few years, particularly as federal aid declines. It will be the task of state governments, the overseers of municipal finance, to ensure that their cities do not go bankrupt.

Notes

1. Jon A. Baer, "Municipal Debt and Tax Limits: Constraints on Home Rule," *National Civic Review* 70 (April 1981):204–205.

2. U.S., Department of Commerce, Bureau of the Census, *Property Values Subject to Local General Property Taxation in the United States: 1979* (Washington, D.C.: Government Printing Office, August 1980), table C, p. 3.

3. Ibid., table E. p. 6.

4. James A. Maxwell and J. Richard Aronson, *Financing State and Local Government*, 3rd ed. (Washington, D.C.: The Brookings Institution, 1977), p. 144.

5. Patricia S. Florestano, "Revenue-Raising Limitations on Local Government: A Focus on Alternative Responses," *Public Administration Review* 41 (January 1981):122.

6. Advisory Commission on Intergovernmental Relations, *Significant Features of Fiscal Federalism, 1979–80* (Washington, D.C.: Government Printing Office, Report No. M-123, October 1980), p. 185.

7. Steven David Gold, *Property Tax Relief* (Lexington; Mass.: Lexington Books, D.C. Heath and Company, 1979), p. 157.

8. Advisory Commission, *Significant Features*, p. 185.

9. Gold, *Property Tax Relief*, p. 162.

10. Advisory Commission, *Significant Features*, p. 185.

11. Ibid.

12. Florestano, "Revenue-Raising Limitations," p. 124.

13. Gold, *Property Tax Relief*, p. 196.

14. Ibid., p. 197.

15. Advisory Commission, *Significant Features*, table 78, pp. 100–102.

16. Ibid., table 87, p. 126.

17. Florestano, "Revenue-Raising Limitations," p. 126.

18. John H. Bowman, "Urban Revenue Structures: An Overview of Patterns, Trends, and Issues," *Public Administration Review* 41 (January 1981):138.

19. Gold, *Property Tax Relief*, p. 199.

20. Florestano, "Revenue-Raising Limitations," p. 122.

21. Gold, *Property Tax Relief*, p. 227.

22. Ibid.

23. U.S., Department of Commerce, Bureau of the Census, *City Government Finances in 1978–79* (Washington, D.C.: Government Printing Office, September 1980), table 1, p. 8.

24. Ibid.

25. U.S., Department of Commerce, Bureau of the Census, *City Government Finances in 1974–75* (Washington, D.C.: Government Printing Office, October 1976), p. 116.

26. Ibid., p. 117.

27. Department of Commerce, *City Government Finances in 1978–79*, table 1, p. 8.

28. Ibid.

29. Susan A. MacManus, "The Impact of Functional Responsibility and State Legal Constraints on the 'Revenue-Debt' Packages of U.S. Central Cities," *International Journal of Public Administration* 3 (1981):78.

30. Maxwell and Aronson, *Financing*, p. 208.

31. Coalition of American Public Employees, *Limiting Government: Ties That Bind* (Washington, D.C.: CAPE, March 1980), p. B-2.

32. Ibid., p. B-1.

33. Advisory Commission on Intergovernmental Relations, *State Limitations on Local Taxes and Expenditures* (Washington, D.C.: Government Printing Office, Report No. A-64, February 1977), p. 14.

34. Advisory Commission, *Significant Features*, p. 185.

35. Gold, *Property Tax Relief*, p. 165.

36. Maxwell and Aronson, *Financing*, p. 220.

37. Susan A. MacManus, *Revenue Patterns in U.S. Cities and Suburbs: A Comparative Analysis* (New York: Praeger, 1978), p. 45.

38. Advisory Commission on Intergovernmental Relations, *State Mandating of Local Expenditures* (Washington, D.C.: Government Printing Office, Report No. A-67, July 1978), p. 16.

39. Calculated from data presented in table 8 of Catherine H. Lovell, "Evolving Local Government Dependency," *Public Administration Review* 41 (January 1981):197.

40. Advisory Commission on Intergovernmental Relations, *State Mandating of Local Expenditures* (Washington, D.C.: Government Printing Office, Report No. A-67, July 1978), Table III-4, pp. 44–45.

41. Richard T. Moore and Robert J. Morin, "The Massachusetts Response to the Mandate Issue," *The Urban Interest* 2 (Spring 1980):59.

42. John E. Petersen, Catherine L. Spain, and C. Mayne Stallings, "From Monitoring to Mandating: State Roles in Local Government Finance," *Governmental Finance* 8 (December 1979):4.

43. Donna E. Shalala, "Using Financial Management to Avert Financial Crisis," *Governmental Finance* 8 (December 1979):17.

44. Maurice E. White, "ACIR's Model State Legislation for Strengthening Local Government Financial Management," *Governmental Finance* 8 (December 1979):22.

45. Shalala, "Using Financial Management," p. 18.

46. Lennox L. Moak and Albert M. Hillhouse, *Concepts and Practices in Local Government Finance* (Chicago: Municipal Finance Officers Association of the United States and Canada, 1975), p. 411.

47. Ibid., p. 412.

48. Ibid., p. 415.

49. Ibid., p. 414.

50. Ibid., p. 410.

51. Advisory Commission on Intergovernmental Relations, *Understanding State and Local Cash Management* (Washington, D.C.: Government Printing Office, Report No. M-112, May 1977).

52. See, for example, Advisory Commission on Intergovernmental Relations, *City Financial Emergencies: The Intergovernmental Dimension* (Washington, D.C.: Government Printing Office, Report A-42, 1973); Terry Nichols Clark et al., *How Many New Yorks? The New York Fiscal Crisis in Comparative Perspective* (Chicago: University of Chicago, Report No. 72 of Comparative Study of Community Decision Making, April 1976); Thomas Muller, *Growing and Declining Urban Areas: A Fiscal Comparison* (Washington, D.C.: The Urban Institute, 1975); George E. Peterson et al., *Urban Fiscal Monitoring* (Washington, D.C.: The Urban Institute, 1978); David T. Stanley, *Cities in Trouble* (Columbus, Ohio: Academy for Contemporary Problems, 1976); Charles H. Levine, ed., *Managing Fiscal Stress: The Crisis in the Public Sector* (Chatham, N.J.: Chatham House, 1980); Robert W. Burchell and David Listokin, eds., *Cities Under Stress: The Fiscal Crisis of Urban America* (Piscataway, N.J.: The Center for Urban Policy Research, Rutgers University, 1981).

53. Helen F. Ladd, "An Economic Evaluation of State Limitations on Local Taxing and Spending Powers," *National Tax Journal* 31 (1978):1–18; Florestano, "Revenue-Raising Limitations"; David Greytak and Donald Shephard, "Tax Limits and Local Expenditure Levels," in Robert W. Burchell and David Listokin, eds., *Cities Under Stress*, pp. 333–350; Richard A. Eribes and John S. Hall, "Revolt of the Affluent: Fiscal Controls in Three States," *Public Administration Review* 41 (January 1981):107–121; and Harold Wolman and George Peterson, "Policy Consequences of Local Expenditure Constraints," *The Urban Interest* 2 (Fall 1980):75–82.

54. MacManus, "The Impact of Functional Responsibility."

55. Susan A. MacManus, "State Mandates: Do They Help or Hinder Improvement in Municipal Financial Condition?" (Paper presented at the annual meeting of the American Society for Public Administration, April 12–15, 1981).

56. Lovell, "Evolving," p. 199.

57. Ibid.

58. MacManus, "State Mandates."

59. Neil R. Pierce and Jerry Hagstrom, "Federal Spending Cuts Could Worsen Older Cities' Ability to Borrow Money," *National Journal* 13 (February 7, 1981):219.

60. MacManus, "State Mandates."

61. Alan G. Billingsley and Paul D. Moore, "Defining New York State's Role in Monitoring Local Fiscal Affairs," *Governmental Finance* 8 (December 1979):13.

62. Ibid., p. 12.

63. White, "ACIR's Model," p. 24.

64. Florestano, "Revenue-Raising Limitations," p. 124.

65. Advisory Commission on Intergovernmental Relations, *Property Tax Circuit-Breakers: Current Status and Policy Issues* (Washington, D.C.: Government Printing Office, Report No. M-87, February, 1975).

66. Katharine C. Lyall, "Regional Tax Base Sharing: Nature and Potential for Success," and W. Patrick Beaton, "Regional Tax Base Sharing: Problems in the Distribution Function," in Burchell and Listokin, *Cities Under Stress*, pp. 493–528.

67. Florestano, "Revenue-Raising Limitations," p. 125.

68. Advisory Commission on Intergovernmental Relations, *Pragmatic Federalism: The Reassignment of Functional Responsibility* (Washington, D.C.: Government Printing Office, Report No. M-105, July 1976), p. 4.

69. Ibid.

70. Advisory Commission, *State Mandating*, p. 7.

71. Ibid., pp. 6–7.

72. Ibid., p. 22.

73. MacManus, "State Mandates," p. 12.

7
Managers and Politicians: The Politics of Spending Federal Money

Raymond E. Owen

Some Distinctions
Between Management and Politics

There are important distinctions between the management of money and the politics of spending federal money. Management can be thought of as a congeries of procedures and operating principles designed to make rational use of resources. Management has to do with careful recordkeeping, with close monitoring and evaluations of the impacts or effects of policies and programs, and with attempts to "maximize." Maximizing can be measured in the private sector by profits; in the public sector, government managers in specialized bureaucracies attempt to manage money so as to accomplish certain objectives. Politics, on the other hand, has to do with the relatively nonsystematic struggle for advantage among individuals, groups, political parties and factions, and governments. The results of that struggle determine the objectives that government tries to achieve. One of the recurring fascinations of democratic politics is the attempt to find the linkages and correspondences between government (management) on the one hand and politics on the other.

In the arena of public policy, these two styles of activity and decisionmaking operate simultaneously, intersecting with and often conflicting with and disrupting one another. The distinction between "managerial" and "political" styles does not precisely correspond to categories of individual actors, but in general one can think of bureaucrats, especially those in the large domestic departments of the federal government, as managers, and similarly one can identify elected officials at all levels—the president, members of Congress, governors, mayors, and members of city councils—as politicians. Of course, when politicians compose the minority in a legislature, or are engaged in campaigns to unseat the incumbent president, governor, or mayor, the substance of their criticisms is likely to be couched in terms that promise better management. Ronald Reagan's 1980 election campaign fussed over extensive waste in the federal government, hinted at abuses, and promised a more "business-like" approach. Although no bureaucrat or politician can be said to be a pure case of either the managerial or the political style—there are times and tasks that require a bit from both—it is probably the case that Republicans lean more toward the managerial style.

Government managers search for precision and efficiency, adopting techniques and procedures for dealing with sets and series of decisions in a routine fashion (thus protecting such decisions against "political" interference). By contrast, politicians generally like to ensure a bit of slack in the system; they prefer flexibility to efficiency and require that decisions never be seen as so routine or insulated that they cannot be reopened and adjusted. Managers tend to think in terms of systems or fairly long-term projects, whereas politicians usually have shorter-term worries. Politicians in a democratic system have to be ready to react to major and minor crises as they occur, and they have to be attentive to opportunities that serve the interests of their constituents. Certainly they find it helpful to be able to spread a bit of program money around to solidify a coalition for an upcoming election.

Another distinction to be kept in mind when thinking about the politics of spending federal money is that between what is sometimes called "targeting" of funds and/or programs and "spreading" the effects of funds and/or programs.[1] As the name implies, targeting refers to the process by which a particular policy or program distributes funds to help a particular area, group, or class. Redistribution policies intend to target their benefits to the poor (and their burdens to the nonpoor); programs for the elderly intend to target their benefits to a particular age group; and strip-mining regulations intend to target their benefits to a particular economic activity. Spreading, on the other hand, refers to policies or programs that provide benefits nonselectively. In democratic polities, in which elected representatives must approve both the shape and funding of government programs, there is a natural and powerful tendency for political officials to try to spread the benefits of any program in such a way that their own constituents benefit. Common language is full of terms that imply this natural inclination of representatives, "pork-barrel politics" being perhaps the one most often used.

To those of managerial orientation, the natural inclination of representative politicians to engage in pork barrel distributions of government benefits may seem short-sighted and wasteful, selfish at the expense of the public interest, and destructive of the implementation of national purpose. And so it is. Politicians, on the other hand, play out their roles in the democratic and pluralistic game of politics perplexed by the self-righteousness of those managers and bureaucrats who presume to define "national purpose," "the public interest," and "policy goals." Although politicians may not be able to articulate their puzzled discontent, they are justifiably suspicious of policy designers who claim to be able to discern "what the nation needs."

The idea of democratic government and free polities rests on the recognition that there can never be an indisputable single definition of the public interest, and that there will always be factions contending with one another, each completely convinced of the wisdom of its position and of the folly of its opponents' position. From an analytic perspective, we see sufficient disagreement concerning the "proper policies" for any given substantive area that it is probably safer to be only partially right than to be completely wrong. Certainly, the framers of the Constitution felt that way. They established a governmental system purposely designed to safeguard its citizens from those who might wish to eliminate flexible public responses to changing conditions. Our federal system is a hedge against certainty, a guarantee of ambiguity and imprecision. Engineers, business people, and others who prize lean and efficient systems, hierarchical organizations, and clear lines of authority with inescapable responsibility for "the bottom line" find our government's "politicized" ways of doing the public's business maddening. It was meant to be so.

Equally frustrating to those who yearn for precision and predictability in governmental operations are the imperfect connections between the national government and state and local governments. Federalism, or intergovernmental relations, consists of several different kinds of relationships, the most important of which involve money. Federal government funding for services and programs carried out by states and cities is the foundation upon which other connections are built.

Except for certain narrowly defined areas of constitutionally protected rights for citizens, the government in Washington cannot direct or order any action on the part of states or local governments. Although local officials and governors are often heard to complain about the unfair mandates placed on them by federal officials, it should be noted that these mandates do not exist apart from the accompanying largesse. Put another way, when state and city governments ask for and accept federal money for the services they want to provide, federal officials supply the money subject to certain conditions—for instance, that buildings will be made accessible to the handicapped. "Mandates" are simply part of the strings attached to receipt of the money. Complaints by state and local officials are political in nature, a way of attempting to curb federal tendencies toward increasing the number of strings it places on aid packages.

Policy by Indirection

Given the nature of federalism, with its division of sovereignty between the states and the central government, national policy in the United States must usually be carried out by indirection. National purposes can be perceived at any given time as awaiting just the right mix of incentives to local governments. Given that local governments in any sizeable community suffer from the same schizophrenia that afflicts all democratic government—namely, the tension between the urge to set priorities and solve problems on the one hand, and the representative's need to respond to crises and to spread benefits around in an equalizing way on the other—local implementation of national programs is unlikely to be uniform across all jurisdictions. The relative strength of managers versus politicians, and vice versa, in any given community is likely to affect the way in which national policy gets carried out as well as the ways in which federal money gets spent. In Chapter 8, these contingencies are illustrated by means of a study of congressional clout and the attendant disproportionate funding of urban renewal programs.

In addition to the tensions between government (i.e., management) and politics and the nonauthoritative relationships among governments under federalism, historical changes in national programming through time have affected the ways in which federal money gets spent. Because financial support follows national priorities, changes in Washington's definitions of problems often alter the mechanisms used to entice local officials to implement programs thought to be in the national interest. Although critics often claim that the governmental system is insufficiently responsive, the post–World War II changes in national policy have been extensive and have reflected Washington's reactions to events and exigencies of the moment. As policy shifted from one definition to another and programs to meet newly perceived needs were added on to existing arrangements, local governments wrestled with the constraints and opportunities implicit in each new wave of federal support. Politics played an important role in influencing the ways in which different local governments spent the money.

Historical Periods in National-Local Relations

There have been four reasonably coherent periods in the history of national-local relations since World War II, and the unfolding of these periods serves to illustrate the kinds of discontinuities in public policy that provide both constraints and opportunities for local officials and politicians. Presented in Table 7.1 is an outline of these periods.

Bricks and Mortar

Following World War II, U.S. cities found themselves in great need of capital (or physical) development. The Great Depression had disrupted and curtailed maintenance and replacement programs for public buildings, jails, roads, and bridges, and the war effort had further delayed such work.[2] The infrastructures of all large cities were in bad repair, and the large numbers of returning veterans put heavy pressure on private housing markets. In response to these needs, Congress initiated the Housing and Urban Renewal program and the Veterans' Administration (VA) home mortgage programs.[3] Because most of the money supplied to urban governments during this time was given for constructing buildings and water systems, the period has come to be known as the "bricks and mortar" period in intergovernmental relations.

These programs exemplify the ways in which government policies are usually carried out in the United States, for they involved the government in arrangements with companies and/or individuals from the private sector. Of course, businesses and contractors cannot be ordered to perform for the government; rather, they must be enticed to do so through the expectation of making a profit. There are many reasons underlying this arrangement, but the main ones have to do with the capitalist state in which we live and the constitutional federal system to which we adhere. The upshot is that many national policies are implemented by indirect, rather than direct, means. Of course, such policy implementation produces some rather unwieldy chains of linked participants or "necessary actors." The trick for national policymakers is to find mechanisms likely to entice businesses and individuals to do the required work while making certain that the individual interest of each enticed actor does not work against the national purpose. The "contract" mechanism is the means most often used toward this end.

Policy by Contract. The urban renewal program, described in more detail in the next chapter, was the first large-scale venture in "policy by indirection" undertaken after World War II. It operated on the basis

TABLE 7.1
Four Periods of Intergovernmental Funding with Attendant Styles of Administration and Citizen Participation, 1946-1981

Era's Name and Years	Characteristic Physical Projects	Characteristic Social Programs	Characteristic Citizen Participation	Characteristic Administrative Style
I. "Bricks and Mortar" 1946-1962	Urban renewal, airports, highways and water treatment systems	"Welfare," Social Security, surplus foods	None	"Picket fence" federalism, vertical fragmentation, categorical grants, some central lobbying

Intervening historical events: (1) Election of John F. Kennedy (2) "Discovery" of poverty (3) Security Act amendments of 1962 (4) Social Civil rights movement

| II. "Social Unrest, Social Change" 1962-1968 | Housing, community centers, health centers, recreation | "Welfare rights," Medicare, Medicaid, "War on Poverty," Model Cities | Riots, demonstrations, "Boardroom Power," Direct participation, Special elections | Vertical fragmentation, categorical grants, heavy lobbying |

Intervening historical events: (1) Vietnam (2) Election of Richard M. Nixon (3) Discontent with social programs and the "posturing" that accompanied direct participation

TABLE 7.1 (continued)

III. "New Federalism" 1969-1976	Housing, community development - fewer "strings"	"Entitlement" programs-- Food stamps, Indexed Social Security, formula-based categoricals	Public hearings, local government lobbying	General revenue sharing and block grants, central lobbying focused on formula

Intervening historical events: (1) Watergate (2) OPEC and the energy crisis (3) Inflation

IV. "Post New Federalism" 1977-1981	Housing, economic development, re-introduction of "strings"	Entitlement programs distributed automatically, by formula	Local public hearings, local politics	General revenue sharing and block grants (5- and 6-year plans)

Intervening historical events: (1) Election of Ronald Reagan (2) Election of a conservative Congress and a Republican Senate of subsidies designed to provide incentives for three different sets of actors to get involved. First, local governments were presented with a system of plans, procedures, and money subsidies that would enable them to entice local developers and businesses to participate in replacing slums and a generally worn-out infrastructure with economically self-sustaining businesses and residences. The new structures were attractive to local officials, in part because they refurbished the city, but also because they were likely to yield real estate taxes to the city—something slums and vacant lots cannot do. Second, because the federal government agreed to underwrite a high percentage (up to 75 percent) of the costs involved in buying and clearing urban land designated for urban renewal, the "assembled package" could be resold to a private developer at a cost much lower than market value. Thus an incentive was provided for developers to go to the trouble of planning, designing, and constructing commercial and residential buildings on the properties slated for renewal. Finally, the developer could offer individual businesses—including those interested in owning and managing residential (apartment) buildings—newly built structures at attractive prices. The whole of the process, from initial purchase of the land through approval of the contract conveying the new buildings to private ownership, was overseen and facilitated by special separate units of local government: the urban renewal authorities (URAs).

The URAs were analogous to small firms whose business it was to act entrepreneurially, to attract developers to the inner city. Developers are business people who seek to profit by organizing builders, land, and plans around the production of completed projects, which may then be sold to retail businesses, who in turn seek to make a profit. Upon the successful completion and sale of each development, developers then turn to new ventures. The URAs and the developers continued, often in renewed joint ventures, performing the specialized functions of subsidized entrepreneurship.

Urban renewal programs were the principal mechanism by which U.S. cities undertook their physical rejuvenation in the postwar period. Several cities, notably Pittsburgh, Minneapolis, and Philadelphia, named the combined renewal efforts their "Renaissance," and Pittsburgh's famed Golden Triangle stood as elegant testimony to the positive changes made possible through this public-private sector partnership. Physical reconstruction took place primarily because each of the sets of necessary actors followed its own interests. Local governments developed expertise in the planning and development "games," and official and personal alliances were forged between companies, individual entrepreneurs (developers), and government and political officials. These projects were overseen by federal urban renewal officials in Washington, who passed upon plans and supervised contract compliance in the individual city programs. As the urban renewal program developed through time, Congress repeatedly had to reauthorize it. The various reauthorizations provided opportunities for altering procedures and adding requirements in the "national interest." These "strings" became the cost paid by cities for participation. In return for the cash needed to set the process in motion, local governments agreed to live by federal rules and standards; and so began the era of the categorical grant-in-aid.

During the 1940s and 1950s, interest in physical redevelopment outweighed interest either in the social effects of such development or in social programming itself. Families living in tenements marked for slum clearance were summarily evicted and sent on their way—with no assistance and little concern for their welfare. Blacks, in particular, were driven from their homes; they quickly tagged the urban renewal program one of "Negro removal." Studies of families displaced by renewal programs clearly show that the unrecognized costs of the program included much grief and suffering by the poor.[4]

Loan Guarantees. The housing programs developed by the Federal Housing Authority (FHA) and the VA to cope with the demand for shelter (produced when returning World War II veterans rushed to marry and start families) were different in substance from urban renewal, but they likewise made use of "policy by indirection." The FHA and VA programs used government guarantees to entice mortgage bankers to lend money to veterans so that they could buy housing. This government-supported demand elicited a tremendous spurt of housing construction as builders rushed to provide and sell houses. Again, the key to getting the private sector actors moving was the federal promise to pay back any losses the banks might have incurred in the event of default by a veteran. By removing the element of risk from the investment, the government made the profit margin larger and hence more attractive to banks. Because the banks were willing to lend money for housing, builders could build with the confidence that their houses would sell. The great engine of profitseeking produced rapid expansion of the housing stock in the United States, mainly in the new suburbs—a largely unplanned consequence of setting in motion the forces of the free market. The social dysfunctions of this rapid growth of largely uncontrolled suburban sprawl are well known. The central cities lost working-class and middle-class populations to the suburbs, and with them went the cities' tax bases, public school populations, and consumers.

Summary: Politics and the "Picket Fence." Social programs were not high-priority concerns during the Bricks and Mortar period. There were income maintenance programs for the "deserving poor," the blind, the physically disabled, and the aged. Welfare, or "relief," programs varied widely from state to state, and the federal government provided some cash support for "families with dependent children," if the father was not present, as well as some assistance in the form of surplus farm products—dried milk, beans, and peanut butter—left over from purchases made to shore up farm prices. Toward the end of the Eisenhower years, some concern began to develop over what appeared to be a limited problem of social disintegration—juvenile delinquency;[5] but no real national attention was focused on these matters, and the presidential campaign of 1960 was argued primarily in the field of foreign policy. Quemoy, Matsu, and the "missile gap" were the main issues of interest, once Kennedy's Catholicism had been set aside.

The Bricks and Mortar period provided a beginning in the use of the categorical grant-in-aid as a prime channel for carrying out national purposes in local governments' jurisdictions. The contract mechanism provided the means by which local governments could hire others to do the actual work required; when the object was to build buildings, the whole system of linkages, supervised and managed by bureaucrats and planners, got the job done. The vertical relationships between the national government and the local governments obtained within functionally specific areas: Housing officials in the VA and the FHA understood housing finance and spoke the special language of mortgage bankers. Similarly, federal urban renewal officials communicated in the language of local planners and developers.

Unfortunately, the vertical system of housing officials, who were underwriting the middle-class flight to the suburbs, neither understood nor spoke the language of the vertical system of urban renewal officials, who were attempting to revitalize the central cities. The functionally specific vertical systems tended to operate in isolation from one another and, to make matters worse, they tended to be treated separately by the general government officials at both levels—that is, Congress at the national level, and mayors and city councils at local levels. Without coordination, the vertical systems tended to work at cross-purposes, all the while carrying out what each system took to be justifiable policies. The upshot was an intergovernmental system of policies, programs, and interactional patterns that many call "picket-fence" federalism.[6]

In picket-fence federalism, the "pickets," or vertical slats, are the systems of funding that connect the federal agencies to the state and local agencies, along with the formal and informal interactions that characterize such systems. In addition to the bureaucrats at the federal, state, and local levels, the pickets included contractors, developers, bankers, and business people, all interested in pressing their particular advantage. The analogy used by political scientists holds that the horizontal boards on the picket fence stand for the general elected governments at each level. It is critically important to recognize that elected officials at all levels—members of council, state legislators, members of Congress—tend to react to situations rather than to create them. That is, if governmental matters are proceeding smoothly, elected officials generally prefer not to stir up controversy. If no scandals are occurring and no constituents are demanding attention or investigation, elected officials prefer to let sleeping dogs and established bureaucracies lie.

During the Bricks and Mortar period, those whose interests were served through continued funding of the vertical systems of subsidies for capital programs—bankers, builders, developers, and local urban renewal officials—focused their lobbying attentions on the specialized subcommittees in Congress and maintained continuing informal relationships with federal administrators. Few elected city or national officials bothered to step back and take a broad view of this process. Had they done so, they would have seen the urban renewal system investing millions of dollars in central city buildings and physical structures, at the same time that the VA and FHA were spending millions of dollars underwriting the movement of veterans and others out of the central cities. This fragmentation of government into functions was further institutionalized as the special interests connected with each function lobbied to insulate their authorizations and flows of funds from political attention. Elected officials, normally reactive rather than creative and quite content with the smoothly functioning bureaucracies that so pleased the powerful interests in the home districts, grew accustomed to, and comfortable with, picket-fence federalism.

Social Unrest and Social Change

It is impossible to identify the exact time at which one period of history ends and another begins. As for intergovernmental money policies, changes in national administrations frequently involve changes in programs and policies. A change in administrations is often followed by a period of adjustment to power and by development of proposals. Such was the case at the end of the Bricks and Mortar period and the beginning of the "Social Unrest–Social Change" period.

The national election of 1960 brought the Democrats back to power, following eight years of relative somnolence under Eisenhower. John Kennedy staffed his government with major figures from the national Democratic party and with intellectuals from several top-quality universities. Both the party luminaries and the intellectuals were impatient to "get the country moving again." As it turned out, the country got moving so quickly that it outran the ability of Kennedy's staff to handle it.

The two great historical events that influenced the shape and nature of intergovernmental relations in the 1960s were the "discovery" of poverty in the United States and the civil rights revolution. At the same time, the vast network of instant information provided by the maturing of television news reporting accelerated the pace of national politics and changed the locus of decisionmaking.

From the New Frontier to the Great Society. John Kennedy's 1960 drive for the Democratic nomination took him into the primary election in West Virginia. The national press fixed its attention on the contrast between the rich and sophisticated eastern candidate and the desperate poverty of unemployed coal miners' families and hard-scrabble hill farmers. The significance of Kennedy's first-hand experience with these scenes of poverty is considerable, but the traditional Democratic party concern for domestic programs and the welfare of the poor and of the working class was probably more instrumental in shaping the policies later associated with President Johnson's "Great Society."

Kennedy's policy response to poverty, however, was hammered together in the context of broad social, cultural, and political changes. His administration began to address the general questions of poverty in its proposals for amending the Social Security Act in 1962. This act carries, along with its fundamental charge of providing funds for old-age pensions, the authorization of most social welfare programs and their associated implementing structures. The 1962 amendments provided for significant expansion in support for schools of social work and for programs designed to train large numbers of social workers.[7] Kennedy's staff had adopted the view that poverty's effects could be softened through the efforts of "helping" professionals who could shepherd poor individuals into employment training programs, adult literacy programs, family counseling, and the like. The goal, as it emerged, was one of integrating poor individuals into a predominantly affluent and productive economy.

Social-cultural movements and political movements share an inability to be precise. Once set in motion, events develop independent momentum, and demands grow apace. Frequently, there is an overshooting of the mark far greater than any participant could have anticipated. It is certainly the case that the civil rights movement, which came to national prominence with the Montgomery bus boycott in 1963, was extremely influential in setting the tone for national domestic policies in the mid-1960s. Television news focused on the marches, demonstrations, and violent clashes between southern police and black "militants." Scenes of police using dogs and high-pressure fire hoses on unarmed and passive, nonviolent demonstrators were carried into homes across the United States in the evening broadcasts of the networks, and, for the first time, widespread attention was fixed on the reinforcing unfairness of racial discrimination and poverty. There is little doubt that these events, and television's new facility for presenting and interpreting them, contributed to demonstrations in hundreds of cities that expressed the frustrations many felt, both directly and vicariously, as a result of racism and poverty. Marches, demonstrations, and dramatic acts of petition directed both to the public officials and to the nation's conscience broke down many barriers and inhibitions. Frustrations and reduced inhibitions combined to produce social unrest and rioting.

President Kennedy's assassination brought into office Lyndon B. Johnson, an effective manipulator of Congress and a former U.S. Senate Majority Leader well-schooled in Democratic domestic policymaking. The protests of early 1964 stimulated President Johnson to act more directly and to move more quickly than Kennedy had done.

Of all the actions taken in the year following President Johnson's assumption of the presidency, two—the Voting Rights Act of 1964 and the Economic Opportunity Act (EOA) of 1964—most directly altered the scope and politics of local use of federal money. The Voting Rights Act initiated enforcement procedures and sanctions that served to channel black political frustrations toward elections in southern cities and towns. The "War on Poverty," as the EOA was called, introduced a new style of interaction between Washington and local governments that was partially responsible for heightening tensions and raising expectations among poor blacks in urban areas—at the same time that the Voting Rights Act was supposed to channel into formal indirect electoral confrontations the frustrations of southern blacks.

The EOA's response to social unrest redefined the official conception of poverty. Rather than interpreting the task as one of facilitating the integration of poor individuals into the economic mainstream through the assistance of social workers, the new view of the problem of poverty stressed the systemic, structural nature of poverty and prejudice. Participation—direct, confrontational, and indigenously led—became the generally accepted view of what was required, at least among the Johnson Administration's so-called "poverty warriors." Significantly, to implement the programs funded by the War on Poverty, the Johnson Administration designed a system that largely bypassed the traditional institutions of local government. The administration put implementing authority in the hands of new structures, community action agencies (CAAs), which intended to operate with the "maximum feasible participation" of the poor themselves. This bypassing of the existing local governments was designed to undercut racist mayors and governors in the south and to introduce a new configuration of power in nonsouthern cities.[8] In the beginning, roughly half of the funds distributed were to be used to operate programs designed in Washington, whereas the remainder were to be distributed in response to proposals submitted by local CAAs to Washington.[9]

With the money and the authority to act, local CAAs became new factions to be reckoned with in many local political systems. Although most elected officials recognized the War on Poverty as a reaction to the urgency of social unrest, they deeply resented being bypassed. They also found the style of politics based on direct participation of the poor extremely frustrating. Compromise could not be reached, in this context, by means of the usual quiet, behind-the-scenes bargaining long familiar to local officials.

Previously, local politicos had always had the upper hand. Demonstrations did occasionally take place, but, except for a few church-related workers among the poor, most demonstrators had no means of support that would enable them to spend days, weeks, or months in political activity. Mayors and members of council had merely to wait until their adversaries drifted away. But, now, television coverage was giving new leverage to leaders among the poor and black populations, and federal money was making possible the prospect of sustained confrontational politics.

As the salary source of community organizers, War on Poverty money stimulated and sustained a new style of politics. Graduates of the newly enlarged Graduate Schools of Social Work, where community organization was a popular course of study, were prominent among the organizers of the poor in central cities. The unpredicted convergence of these events changed the substance of national programs from the physical (Bricks and Mortar) orientation to the social, to programs designed to support people and to enrich the opportunities of the poor.

The reaction of national government to urban rioting was to spend money as rapidly as possible and to do so through the available mechanisms—namely, the War on Poverty program and categorical grants-in-aid. Estimates vary, but the number of different urban-relevant categorical grant programs grew from approximately 100 in 1962 to about 600 in 1968.[10] The rate of growth was thus quite substantial, reflecting not only the public reaction to urban unrest but also the effects of the 1964 national elections. When the country rejected Barry Goldwater, it also voted out of office many conservative members of Congress. The 89th Congress, which took office in January 1965, was an unusually liberal Congress faced with unusually dramatic and pointed domestic problems. As violence in the name of civil rights and economic justice shook city after city, and brutality against civil rights workers in the deep South seemed to threaten the very fabric of society, Congress

funded, and the federal bureaucracy developed, social programs designed
to redress political and economic inequities.

As the discomfort of local elected officials faced with War on
Poverty "warriors" increased, these officials brought pressure on Congress
to move away from direct funding of programs and organizing of
schemes developed and operated by representatives of the poor. The
three changes made by federal officials produced a more predictable
and "managed" style of poverty programming.

First, funding within the War on Poverty was shifted away from
the "local initiative" programs and directed instead to the "national
emphasis" programs. As a result, fewer dollars were spent on community
organizing and demonstrations, with more being funneled to such
programs as Head Start, Meals on Wheels, and the Job Corps. Second,
discussion began openly in Congress about changes to be made in the
War on Poverty program when it came up for reauthorization in 1967.
Prominent among the changes suggested (and later actually made) was
the "Bosses and Boll Weevils" amendment. Introduced by Representative
Edith Green of Oregon, this amendment enabled city governments to
take control of their local War on Poverty agencies, the formerly
independent CAAs. It was called the "Bosses and Boll Weevils" amendment by opponents because it pleased northern big city machine bosses
and southern sheriffs equally; both groups regained power and were
freed from having to deal with direct participation by angry citizens.
Finally, the Johnson Administration sought to cool down the intensity
of political conflict in urban areas by moving toward a more managed
style of federal aid for local governments. The vehicle for this shift
away from the politics of confrontation and redistribution was the
"Model Cities" program.

Model Cities programming was a return to the comfortable and
predictable state of affairs that characterized the Bricks and Mortar
period in national-local relations. Although a part of its funding was
directed to social programs, its most important emphasis was directed
to capital projects, namely, physical construction. As the War on Poverty
program was allowed to dwindle, and as its funding was systematically
reduced, the more successful programs were spun off to be housed
under Model Cities auspices.

The Model Cities program represented an attempt to show that
well-coordinated projects, planned and implemented by formal, existing
local government institutions, could meet the needs of the poor for
both social programs and rehabilitation of physical infrastructure—
housing, schools, commercial districts, and so on. Citizen participation
was to take the form of election of neighborhood representatives to a
Model Cities board, which in turn would negotiate with government

and private actors over projects that might be sponsored. Model Cities neighborhood elections were notoriously low in turnout, often attracting only 3 to 7 percent of the eligible voters. From the perspective of the local politicos, this was seen as evidence that the large demonstrations and direct participation of 1964–1965 had been a temporary aberration.

The Social Unrest–Social Change period ended with the election of 1968. In roughly six years, big cities had gone from limited dependence on federal funding to a situation in which they were, if not quite dependent on federal money, at least experienced with and eager to utilize it. The emphasis had changed from use of federal money on capital (physical infrastructure) projects to social programming of all sorts. Even those physical projects associated with the Model Cities program tended to reflect the new social orientation—community mental-health centers, neighborhood health centers, recreation centers, and subsidized housing for the poor were built.

The channels of interaction between these centers and the local governments returned to what they had been before the period of "Social Unrest and Social Change": Categorical grants required local officials to apply, approval was granted at the discretion of federal managers, and implementation at the local level was subject to federal supervision. To an important degree, the funds available were distributed on a competitive basis, and some cities became more adept than others at what came to be known as "grantsmanship." Competition thus conducted meant that some cities and smaller local governments were underserved; moreover, their representatives were, understandably, resentful. (It is argued in Chapter 8 that an important factor contributing to successful grantsmanship was the inclusion of a congressional representative on the relevant committee in the House of Representatives.)

During the Social Unrest–Social Change era, the combined occurrence of instant information via television news, well-documented and graphic instances of economic and racial unfairness, and a receptive national government produced a domestic policy system that was centered around the presidency and the federal bureaucracy. Experts, intellectuals, and spokespersons for functionally specific interests lobbied for additions or changes to programs. Although the term "city" was used frequently, and the whole array of functional problems was called "the urban crisis," it was the power of television that enabled a national liberal elite to focus public attention on the problems of poverty. Cities, with their high densities of population, became the focal point of concern, but the pressures for change and the ideas and proposals for programs were centralized in Washington. Those who sought change could concentrate their efforts in one place, and coordination of tactics was facilitated. As a result, national policy was significantly altered toward redistribution of benefits and opportunities.

In response to their loss of power, city officeholders pushed for the "Green Amendment" to the 1967 reauthorization of the EOA.[11] The amendment put CAAs back under the control of city hall, thus effectively squelching the more raucous sorts of direct-participation demonstrations and bringing the administrators of the several social programs under the purview of elected officeholders. Along with the shift to a national emphasis on the Model Cities style of citizen participation (i.e., formal elections for quasi-governmental boards) and to the Green Amendment, several lobbying agencies who acted in the name of formal city officeholders redoubled their efforts. The National Association of County Officials, National League of Cities, U.S. Conference of Mayors, and International City Managers Association grew rapidly in importance as elected officials sought to regain control over the spending of federal dollars.[12] Although the main lobbying efforts—which defined the nature and extent of public policies adopted in Congress—remained centralized in Washington, the renewed presence of city officeholders as parties to the debate about public policy encouraged the democratic spreading of benefits across more local jurisdictions. The concern with economic redistribution (as a function of the War on Poverty) and the targeting that accompanied it were deemphasized. Intellectuals and social reformers were out; elected officials and bureaucrats were in.

The rapid growth of intergovernmental grants-in-aid to local governments produced some overlap of function and a good bit of confusion concerning roles, authority relations, and so forth. In 1968 Congress passed the Intergovernmental Cooperation Act in an attempt to bring better management to bear on aid to local governments. This act changed the manner in which funds were distributed to states and local governments, and it introduced comprehensive planning and coordinating procedures in an attempt to avoid frustrating delays and duplication and overlap of function.[13] The emphasis on management—on procedures, accounting details, bank deposit rules, and the like—showed how far federal funding of local programming was being institutionalized. The question was no longer whether such funding would or could occur, but how best to carry out the distribution of funds. Fine-tuning of administrative links in the intergovernmental system characterized this joint venture. Managers at both levels, national and local, were bringing their methods into congruence.

New Federalism

The transition to the third period of intergovernmental funding can be traced to the election of 1968. Richard Nixon entered the White House with a plan for ending the Vietnam War and with a commitment to decentralize power from the national domestic cabinet departments to the states; moreover, as he said over and over to the consternation of liberals everywhere, he meant to give "power to the people." The management emphasis of the Intergovernmental Cooperation Act of 1968 was built upon by Nixon's staff in several ways. Most importantly, the "New Federalism" strengthened the capability of the executive branch to oversee and evaluate federal expenditures by converting the Bureau of the Budget into the Office of Management and Budget, thus considerably widening the analytic capacity of the office. True to form for managerialism, the intergovernmental programs later supported by the Nixon Administration tended to reflect the need for certainty and predictability and to remove the uncertainty and discontinuities of political procedures.

The two characteristic themes of the New Federalism were the distribution of benefits by formula (as opposed to distribution by annual or triennial deliberation) and the shifting of debates over program substance away from Washington to the states and local governments. The shift to distribution of funds by formula occurred in three different programs, for different reasons in each case but each with similar effect. The State and Local Fiscal Assistance Act of 1972, commonly referred to as General Revenue Sharing (GRS), implemented an idea that had been pushed by some intellectual reformers, management-oriented government analysts, and big city mayors. Because the federal income tax collection system tends to be so much more efficient and elastic than the local tax collection systems, principles of sound management could be served by simply turning back to the states and local governments a portion of the revenues collected at the national level. To the extent that the federal tax system is truly progressive, a modest amount of redistribution could take place, but the heavy burden of administrative rules and regulations was to be eliminated. This was money with no strings attached. Resistance to the idea of letting cities enjoy spending money that they did not have to take responsibility for raising led to a definition of the formula (by which distribution took place) that included elements of local tax effort as well as the population factor. Congress attempted to penalize local officials who substituted GRS funds for taxes they "should" have raised. Most observers conclude that it is not possible to measure the extent to which substitution took place, but that it would be a pretty poor politician who could not make use of the increased flexibility provided by the quarterly GRS allotments.

The debate over the terms of the formula replaced the two-stage process previously associated with grants-in-aid. Grant programs required congressional approval (initially and at intervals of one to three years thereafter) and were subject to bureaucratic approval and supervision throughout the period of program use. Formula distribution of funds simplified the political and administrative work required to get things done. Mayors enjoyed having funds that they had not had to raise taxes to get, and efficiency-minded analysts liked the simplicity and predictability of the formula. How the funds were spent became a function of local and state political processes rather than that of national debate and Washington lobbying.

An additional managerial development took place in terms of certain decisions concerning the Social Security Act amendments of 1972. Although the payment of retirement benefits under the Social Security program is not directly relevant to the local politics of spending federal money, it is linked to the shifts toward "managerial predictability" that characterized the New Federalism period. Until 1972 changes in benefit levels occurred only through congressional action, and congressional willingness to vote increases in benefits tended to find voice every other year, well in time for members to take credit for them while campaigning for reelection. In a move designed to deprive the Democratic congressional majority of this boon and to make the actuarial management of the Social Security system more precise and predictable, the Nixon Administration pushed through a change that linked the rate of increase in benefits to the rate of increase in prices, or cost of living.[14] This "indexing" of program benefit levels to some standard, objective measure of the economy was a major step toward automating the decision process and removing benefit increases from the political arena. Of course, unprecedented increases in the inflation of price levels since 1973 made this move a fiscally damaging one, but that is apparent only in retrospect. At the time, it was of a piece with the swing away from politicized decisionmaking at the center and toward management-oriented program administration.

From the perspective of local politics, the central element of New Federalism was the Housing and Community Development Act (HCDA) of 1974. As the sole survivor of Nixon's planned Special Revenue Sharing package (the other elements having failed to materialize as Nixon became preoccupied with Watergate problems), the HCDA was an attempt to combine quasi-automatic distribution of funds with decentralization of political debate about the substance of programs. As the turbulence of the 1960s had shown, when debate was effectively centered in Washington and sophisticated lobbying techniques were harnessed to highly publicized appeals to economic and racial fairness, extensive and expensive programs of redistribution followed. The more Republican way of doing things called for dividing up the debates over substance among the fifty states and the 30,000 or so municipal and township governments. In this way, liberal coalition-building and manipulation of publicity were circumvented. No matter how heated or intense the debate might become at the local or state level, even in the largest cities, it was unlikely that the nation could be swept along toward what were seen to be unduly redistributive policies. Thus, national political ends—those of the conservatives of both parties— were served by the decentralization of political debate over program substance. To the extent that the block grant programs envisioned under the Special Revenue Sharing approach followed the no-strings approach pioneered by GRS, no national administration would risk being embarrassed during campaign periods by having to defend itself against charges of wasting money on redistributive programs. "No strings" also meant "no targeting."

The Housing and Community Development Act of 1974 did not provide for block grants in pure form. It lumped together seven categorical grant programs—urban renewal, model cities, water and sewer facilities, open space, neighborhood facilities, rehabilitation loans, and public facilities loans—and distributed funds by formula, but it limited the kinds of uses to which funds could be put as well as stating certain national objectives.[15] Grants of money to cities under the Housing and Community Development Act were called "Community Development Block Grants" and came to be known as "CDBG funds." The HCDA itself is usually referred to as the "CDBG program." The formula by which money was divided up among communities was based on population, condition of housing, and poverty levels (weighted twice). In addition, "hold harmless" provisions protected those cities whose grantsmanship had gained them grant support far beyond that specified by the formula. For a transition period of four years, the competitive "winners" were gradually reduced to a level of support determined by the formula. The success of the HCDA in spreading funds is shown by the fact that whereas in 1974, prior to consolidation, the seven urban renewal and other grant programs were being distributed to 975 communities, by 1979 there were 3,305 approved Community Development Block Grant (CDBG) communities.[16] As early as 1975, over 3,200 local governments were receiving HCDA funds.[17]

Limiting Participation through Hearings. Under the new block grant approach, the locus of decisionmaking for policies and projects in the local community was shifted away from the vertical system of functional specialists who had come to dominate the grant-in-aid system to local political systems across the country that differed widely in structure, style, and stage of development. Along with this shift to local-level policymaking, the HCDA of 1974 formally called for citizen participation in the process of choosing how the funds were to be spent. To qualify for entitlement funds under the formula, a community had to supply a Housing Assistance Plan and to keep citizens informed through notices and hearings. Many communities opted for citizen participation limited to an annual series of public hearings. Traditionally used as a means of consultation with citizens, the public hearings reduced the effective leverage of the citizen to the lowest level acceptable in democratic systems. In this sense, the idea of citizen participation had come full cycle from the heady days of the War on Poverty and the boardroom style of citizen leverage. Even the Model Cities program, with its system of specially elected boards of overseers drawn from the citizenry, carried a sense of the legitimacy of the vote. But public hearings as a general mode of citizen involvement took citizen participation back to the style of the 1950s.

It was indeed the case that breaking away from the vertical structures of grantsmen and Washington bureaucrats eliminated much of the intercity competition and a good bit of the red tape associated with grant-in-aid supported projects. The local political systems that were now charged with deciding how to spend HCDA money were not, however, overly concerned with, nor particularly knowledgeable about, problems of poverty. In most large city political systems, "development" now means physical development and "projects" mean buildings. As with the role that citizen participation played in the New Federalism, the substance of the HCDA program reverted to the style of the 1950s.

The period of New Federalism did not really end; rather, it went into a state of suspended animation as President Nixon became engulfed in his Watergate problems. President Ford was overwhelmed by the initial shocks of the OPEC-induced crisis in 1974 and preoccupied with the resultant inflation as well as the need to campaign for reelection. Nixon's unfinished ploy to move most federal intergovernmental aid to the block grant form under the Special Revenue Sharing idea was set aside to wait for a better time.

Post–New Federalism

The Carter Administration did not produce a major change in intergovernmental funding arrangements, but the centralized lobbying activities of liberal, social program–oriented groups found a more receptive audience in Washington. The reauthorization of the Housing and Community Development Act in 1977 became an opportunity for members of Congress, liberal interest groups, and federal administrators to participate in what has been called the "creeping categorization" of the block grant.[18] The "categorization" of a block grant refers to the tendency of special interests to add strings, or conditions, to the use of funds, thus reducing the flexibility of recipients.

Many federal executives in the Carter Administration recognized the tendency of local and state political officials to prefer distributive policies over redistributive policies. Distributive policies are those that provide new benefits to participants already in the game, rather than to new participants. As a concrete example, developers seeking use of HCDA funds for construction of office buildings were more likely to get a sympathetic hearing from mayors than were groups of "welfare mothers" seeking funding for a day-care center. Many of the 1977 amendments to the HCDA reflected the liberals' desire to target benefits to the needy, as opposed to the natural tendency of state and local politicians to favor the well-connected.

The most significant amendment was a change in the formula itself. Under the original legislation, three factors—population, over-crowded housing, and poverty (counted twice)—formed the basis for fund allocation among cities. The decline of population in the North and the surge of growth in the Sunbelt resulted in a sharp reduction of funds for older northern cities. The 1977 amendments included two formulas and communities were allowed to opt for whichever formula most benefited them. The added formula introduced the idea of counting "population growth lag" (which clearly benefited the Northeast) along with poverty and age of housing. Other changes in the HCDA came through new regulations issued by the Department of Housing and Urban Development (HUD) in March of 1978. HUD Secretary Patricia Roberts Harris reflected the Democratic concern for targeting federal funds by requesting that 75 percent of the CDBG grant "principally benefit" lower-income persons. In addition, citizen participation was emphasized by requiring communities to submit a formal Citizen Participation Plan, and concentration of program activities in coordinated revitalization projects (rather than for widespread improvements in roads and the like) was encouraged.

The reintroduction of "strings" via regulations reflected the Democrats' desire to ensure that the main thrust of the New Federalism be blunted. Suspicion that local governments would tend to find new convention centers, shopping malls, and office buildings more attractive than housing for the poor and service centers for the aged motivated the attempt to impose the 75 percent requirement. Similarly, the dual formula was an attempt to underscore the Democratic belief that federal purpose should include softening the blows of regional economic decline at least as much as it includes underwriting boom town infrastructures. These attempts to overlay the new block grant program with rules and regulations produced some impediments to the hell-bent determination of certain local developers. But municipal experiences with GRS and HCDA had by now produced a dependence on such funding arrangements, as well as a degree of institutionalization at the local level that made turning back impossible.

TABLE 7.2
Total Professional Planners Employed Per 1,000 Residents and
Percent Change 1972-1978 for Selected Cities

	1972	1978	% Change
Philadelphia	.020	.026	+ 30%
Rochester, N.Y.	.051	.064	+ 25%
Houston	.009	.014	+ 56%
Los Angeles	.040	.047	+ 18%
Baltimore	.045	.102	+127%
Pittsburgh	.048	.050	+ 4%
St. Louis	.023	.064	+178%
El Paso	.058	.065	+ 12%

Source: "Expenditures, Staff and Salaries of Planning Agencies,"
Planning Advisory Service, American Society for Planning Officials,
Report No. 278, March 1972, pp. 20-21; Report No. 334, July 1978,
pp. 26-27.

The New Federalism put tremendous pressure on local governments to develop administrative systems and procedures to deal with their new responsibilities. At the risk of oversimplification, we can point to two developments at the local level that seem to reflect that impact: the growth in the use of planners (indicating a growth in the relative importance of planning departments) and the adoption of multiyear planning.

Many local governments reacted to their new responsibilities by assigning administrative functions to the planning department. Indicated in Table 7.2 is the growth in employment of professional planners for some selected cities. Although the numbers for St. Louis may disproportionately reflect population loss as well as growth in planner employment, on the whole the figures represent accurately the real growth in bureaucracy at the local level. Standardized for population growth, the increases are real and reflect the greater technical responsibilities of local governments. When coupled with an aggressive redevelopment program, as in Baltimore, the rate of growth becomes impressive indeed. Even Pittsburgh, where Mayor Pete Flaherty reduced the city payroll by 30 percent in the early 1970s, shows the effects of devolved responsibility for technical decisionmaking.

Along with bureaucratic growth at the local level has come a more subtle shift to longer-term, or multiyear, planning. The HUD regulations of March 1978 recognized this need, partly in reaction to the start-up difficulties experienced by many local governments in the first two years of the program. Criticism centered on the inability of cities to spend their funds in the year in which they were allocated. To some extent, these delays were caused by lack of capability, although in some cases politics certainly played a part.[19] With the increased autonomy of spending decisions came increased vulnerability to demands for expenditures. One way of insulating against such demands is to have a long-range plan that absorbs most of the CDBG funds over a period of years, leaving only a small portion for use in responding to ad hoc proposals that may arise in the course of public hearings. This institutionalization of procedures, and the growth of bureaucracies to oversee and operate them, characterized the style of the Post–New Federalism period.

The Carter Administration came to an end with the election of Ronald Reagan and with a shift to the right most notably represented by the election of a Republican Senate and a conservative, though majority Democratic, House of Representatives. It is clear that the Reagan Administration is committed to extending the block grant idea to include human services as well as housing and community development. Republican plans appear to call for the devolution of decisionmaking power to the state level rather than the local level. One can reasonably predict a rapid growth of bureaucracy at the state level and a concomitant growth in the importance of lobbying activity at the state level.

Indeed, the Reagan Administration seeks to shift the unpredictable messiness of lobbying and politics over federal programs to the states and cities. If successful, it will retain a "professional" management role for the federal government in which funds are allocated by formula, almost automatically, from Washington to the states and cities. Lobbyists and political groups seeking changes will be forced to divide their efforts among fifty states and thousands of cities. The potential for any group to focus the attention of the nation on its cause will be severely reduced from the peak level achieved in the 1960s. The more conservative cast of state and local political systems and the ability of states and cities to institutionalize their decisionmaking procedures against ad hoc disruptions are both likely to reinforce a managed, predictable, less socially oriented system of intergovernmental relations.

Impact of the "Managed" State on Politics

As this brief history of the political aspects of federal funding of local activities shows, broad political goals can be implemented by altering the form and substance of programs dependent on federal money. Democratic concerns with redistribution and equity were manifest in the rapid proliferation of functionally precise, locally targeted, nationally controlled grant-in-aid programs of the "Social Unrest–Social Change" period. Similarly, the broad political goals of the Republicans— minimum expenditures for redistribution, conservative policies through decentralized decisionmaking, and local expenditures centered on buildings—were enhanced by breaking the connection between intellectually based national movements and the policies bought by federal money. The movement toward institutionalization of local dependence on federal funds into idiosyncratic local bureaucratic systems was only temporarily delayed by the 1977 amendments to the HCDA and the 1978 regulations issued by HUD.

Several large-scale studies have attempted to analyze the impact of CDBG in terms of general categories of expenditures.[20] The findings of these studies are complex, but in general the experience with CDBG has been seen to be an adaptive one for both national and local officials. By 1979, 85 percent of CDBG funds were being spent on three of the eight categories of "national objectives": Elimination of slums and blight (37 percent), conservation of the housing stock (31 percent), and more rational use of land (17 percent) absorbed the bulk of the expenditures.[21] Although conservation of housing stock is very likely to be redistributive in effect, "slum clearance" and "more rational use of land" could mean anything. The 1977 amendments added economic development as a national objective. In 1978 this objective absorbed 8 percent of CDBG expenditures; in 1979, 16 percent.[22] The most rapidly growing part of the program nationally, economic development exemplifies a trend toward local projects that combine several types of funding (e.g., UDAG and CDBG) from the federal government and "leverage" these funds with private investment in new buildings and infrastructure designed for commercial use. Many observers view this as a positive development, but its long-run impact on local economies remains to be seen. Clearly local bureaucracies have matured to the point that regular relationships with business interests, banks, and developers now constitute a city-level version of the "iron triangle" of policymaking: elected officials, bureaucrats, and special interests. Just as citizen participation has been relegated to the low level of public hearings, so it appears that economic development is returning to the style of the 1950s.

Conclusions

The modern history of intergovernmental funding arrangements reflects quite pointedly the tensions between management and politics. The principal theme has been one of increased institutionalization of apolitical procedures and more or less automatic distribution of funds by formula. But political shifts have occurred that have two important effects. First, the devolution of decisionmaking to local governments has undercut the ability of reformers to manipulate national attention and national policy. Second, the growth of local professional bureaucracies required to handle CDBG programming, coupled with the reduced status of citizen participation, has brought back to prominence the alliance between project-oriented planners and private business interests that characterized the Brick and Mortar period of the 1950s. The management perspective, in general, and the CDBG system, in particular, seem clearly to enhance the local preference for distributive, as opposed to redistributive, policies.

Notes

1. It is a theme of this chapter that these goals are in tension with one another. It seems appropriate that the second Brookings Institution monitoring report on the implementation of the 1974 Housing and Community Development Act, covering the Ford Administration's last two years, was entitled *Decentralizing Community Development*, whereas the third report, whose time period straddled the Carter Administration's 1977 amendments of the act, was entitled *Targeting Community Development*. See Paul R. Dommel, Richard P. Nathan, Sarah F. Liebschutz, Margaret T. Wrightson and Associates, *Decentralizing Community Development, Department of Housing and Urban Development* (Washington, D.C.: Government Printing Office, June 1978), and Paul R. Dommel, Victor E. Bach, Sarah F. Liebschutz, Leonard S. Rubinowitz and Associates, *Targeting Community Development*, Department of Housing and Urban Development (Washington, D.C.: Government Printing Office, April 1981).

2. See John F. Kain, "The Distribution and Movement of Jobs and Industry," in *The Metropolitan Enigma*, ed. James Q. Wilson (Washington, D.C.: Chamber of Commerce of the United States, 1967), pp. 1–31.

3. A good early work that pointed up the political aspects of urban renewal is Scott Greer, *Urban Renewal and American Cities* (Indianapolis: The Bobbs-Merrill Company, Inc., 1965).

4. See Herbert J. Gans, *The Urban Villagers* (New York: The Free Press, 1962), and Marc Fried, "Grieving for a Lost Home: Psychological Costs of Relocation, in *Urban Renewal: The Record and the Controversy*, ed. James Q. Wilson (Cambridge: M.I.T. Press, 1966), pp. 359–379.

5. See Richard A. Cloward and Lloyd E. Ohlin, *Delinquency and Opportunity* (New York: The Free Press, 1960).

6. See, especially, Deil S. Wright, *Understanding Intergovernmental Relations* (North Scituate, Mass.: Duxbury Press, 1978), Chapter 3.

7. Gilbert Y. Steiner, *Social Insecurity: The Politics of Welfare* (Chicago: Rand, McNally and Company, 1966), Chapter 7 and pp. 257–260.

8. This was an uncharted course and one that produced disruptions and bitterness. Two different perspectives are to be found in Sar A. Levitan, *The Great Society's Poor Law* (Baltimore: The Johns Hopkins Press, 1969), and Daniel P. Moynihan, *Maximum Feasible Misunderstanding* (New York: The Free Press, 1969).

9. Sar A. Levitan, *The Great Society's Poor Law*.

10. Deil S. Wright, *Understanding Intergovernmental Relations,* pp. 54–55; John J. Harrigan, *Politics and Policy in States and Communities* (Boston: Little, Brown and Company, 1980), p. 44.

11. Sar A. Levitan, *The Great Society's Poor Law,* pp. 66–67, 103.

12. Suzanne Farkas, *Urban Lobbying* (New York: New York University Press, 1971).

13. Raymond A. Shapek, *Managing Federalism* (Charlottesville, Va.: Community Collaborators, 1981), especially Chapters 1 and 2.

14. Martha Derthick, *Policymaking for Social Security* (Washington, D.C.: The Brookings Institution, 1979), Chapter 17.

15. Raymond A. Shapek, *Managing Federalism,* pp. 195–201.

16. Mary K. Nenno, "Community Development Block Grants: An Overview of the First Five Years," *Journal of Housing* 37 (August–September 1980), p. 436.

17. Ibid.

18. U.S. Congress, Advisory Commission on Intergovernmental Relations, *Block Grants: A Comparative Analysis,* report A-60 (Washington, D.C.: Government Printing Office, 1977).

19. An excellent source for getting a sense of the "politics" of managing the CDBG program is the transcript of a conference among the research associates involved with the large Brookings study: U.S., Department of Housing and Urban Development, *CDBG Execution: Problems and Prospects* (Washington, D.C.: HUD, Office of Policy Development and Research, March 1979).

20. Paul R. Dommel et al., *Decentralizing Community Development.*

21. U.S., Department of Housing and Urban Development, *Fifth Annual Report, The Community Development Grant Program,* June 1980, Table II–2, p. II-6.

22. Ibid.

8

Congressional Politics, Federal Grants, and Local Needs: Who Gets What and Why?

Roger Friedland
Herbert Wong

Do cities get federal aid because of what they need or because of who represents them in Congress? If the latter, does it make a difference whether a city is represented by Democrats or Republicans? Are senators better than members of the House of Representatives at getting money for cities? Is membership on particular committees helpful in getting funds? These questons are important in trying to understand the politics of federal grant distribution and in analyzing the politics of urban renewal. But they are also difficult to answer.

As indicated in previous chapters, cities have been losing their financial independence for some time while Congress has become increasingly involved in local finance. Localities have come to depend heavily on revenues that are raised centrally and on programs of expenditure that are legislated nationally. This trend has political consequences. National politicians have more control over how much money local politicians have to spend and what they use it for. Local politicians cannot use the local purse to make policy by themselves.

Relations between the federal government and local governments therefore involve more politics than they previously did, and it has consequently come to matter more what a city's "partisan face" is like in Washington. The representatives of national parties that control Congress or the presidency want to shape the distribution of federal funds as a way of bolstering their own and their party's electoral support, and they thus attempt to develop programs that will benefit those constituencies most likely to provide that support.

The relationship between the national Democratic party and urban blacks exemplifies this process. Between 1940 and 1960, three million blacks migrated from the South, the vast majority moving into the industrial cities of the most populous northern states. Their allegiance to the national Democratic party became of extraordinarily strategic significance to the party's ability to maintain power nationally.[1] In the 1960 contest between Kennedy and Nixon, for example, black northern Democratic votes allowed Kennedy to carry key states. Not surprisingly, the War on Poverty, adopted in 1964, was a federal program designed by Democrats to provide benefits to urban blacks. Because they were concentrated in the old industrial cities, traditionally centers of support for the Democratic Party in any case, those cities benefited from the numerous programs associated with President Johnson's efforts to eradicate poverty.

As state and local governments grew increasingly dependent on federal aid, their budgets became correspondingly sensitive to those shifts in the balance of national political power that affected the intercity distribution of federal monies. Certain cities were helped by a Democratic president, whereas others benefited from a Republican: The types of grants favored by Democratic presidents disproportionately helped the big declining cities of the industrial Northeast and Midwest, and the grants developed by the Republicans channeled funds to many cities that had not received much federal largesse under the Democrats.

Categorical Versus Block Grants: The Democratic Versus the Republican Presidency

In the 1960s federal aid was given largely in the form of categorical grants that specified the purpose for which the city could use federal funds and that subjected the recipient city to numerous and detailed regulations. Many categorical aid programs were directed to the central cities of the Northeast, a traditional bastion of Democratic support. In particular, project grants were used to shape local policy. Project grants are a kind of categorical grant: Not only do they specify a purpose for which the city must use federal funds, but they also require the city to apply for each project it wants to fund and the federal agency that administers the program to approve each project before monies are allocated to the city. The urban renewal program, which provided federal funds for the clearance and resale of urban land, was an example of a program dispensing project grants.

The project grant gives a large amount of power to the federal bureaucracy to approve and disapprove local applications for funds and to ensure that localities use federal funds for the purposes they have been authorized to serve. It is a very intrusive form of federal intervention in urban policymaking. On the one hand, it allows the federal bureaucracy to decide which cities will receive funds. On the other, it requires that funds be spent for precise purposes, thus allowing the federal government to target particular groups (such as low-income populations) within cities as beneficiaries of the program.

Even though categorical grants remained the most important form of federal aid under the Republican presidencies of Nixon and Ford, a gradual shift occurred away from them to block grants. Block grants differ in important ways from categorical grants: They specify a broad rather than a precise purpose for which federal funds must be used, do not require cities to apply for funds on a project-by-project basis, and distribute funds to cities on the basis of a formula decided upon by Congress rather than at the discretion of the executive agency. Block grants, primarily due to the use of formulas, allocated money to a greater number of cities than did categorical grants. In particular, they benefited wealthier suburbs, smaller cities, and towns—which tended to support the Republican party.

As Owen has argued in the previous chapter, the Nixon Administration's shift to block grants had a strong impact on the categorical aid programs in the area of community development. Both the urban renewal and Model Cities programs were consolidated in 1974 into the Community Development Block Grant Program (CDBG). CDBG's program objectives were broad and ambiguous: to benefit low- and moderate-income families and to prevent and/or eliminate slums or blight, emphasizing physical as opposed to social development. Localities were given much more autonomy in the spending of federal monies. Urban renewal provided substantial power to a separate special-purpose re-development agency, which developed strong links to the Department of Housing and Urban Development (HUD) in order to secure its approval for its program. CDBG, by contrast, put the power over community development back into the hands of elected officials and mayors in particular. Accordingly, HUD was given much less discretion over who was funded or how the money was spent. Although application procedures were retained, they were largely nominal compared to the old categorical aid programs. The big political issue was the composition of the formula that determined the allocation of CDBG funds.

The CDBG program *entitled* all central cities, large suburban cities, and some counties to funds, totaling about 640 jurisdictions in 1978.[2] The formula by which 75 percent of all CDBG funds were distributed used three elements: population, overcrowded housing, and poverty. Poverty was twice as important in the allocation as either the size of population or the extent of overcrowded housing. The use of this formula and entitlement procedure redirected the flow of federal money. Of the 640 jurisdictions that received entitlement funds, 309 received little or no funding under those programs (the urban renewal and Model Cities programs in particular), which were discontinued and folded into the CDBG program.[3]

The initial CDBG formula provided the central cities with 42 percent of all program funds, whereas under the old project grant system, central cities had received some 72 percent of all funds.[4] Similarly, the northeast had previously received some 56 percent of all funds. Under the initial CDBG formula, it received only 46 percent. Representatives of those districts favored by the old programs succeeded in inserting a "hold harmless" provision under which no jurisdiction would receive less money than it had obtained, on average, during the previous five years.[5] Although this provision allowed these districts to maintain their *level* of funding, it did not prevent them from receiving a declining *share* of the funds.

Defenders of the formula argued that it measured real need. The formula, however, tended to reward only those local governments that were growing rapidly, those that were, according to critics of the formula, better able to rely on the market to replace slums. The formula also gave much weight to poverty, a consideration that favored southern cities, which had higher levels of poverty than their northern counterparts. Representatives of the northeast objected to the construction of the formula. In 1977 they proposed additional elements to be included— such as the rate of growth or decline in population size and city age— so as to funnel more funds into those cities that were losing their resource bases and thus having the greatest need for replacement of their aged infrastructures. In the House, members from the northeast were almost unanimously in favor of the formula change, whereas those from the south and west were almost unanimously opposed.[6] The former succeeded in their objective, and the new formula shifted the share of funds back toward the older central cities of the northeast.

By the time of Carter's election in 1976, CDBG, because of its wide distribution of funds and its relative lack of federal strings, had developed support from a wider constituency than the old urban renewal program ever had. Carter therefore kept CDBG as a major program in the community development area. He had received overwhelming support from the cities' blacks, for which reason HUD introduced regulations that would expressly target 75 percent of CDBG funds to low-income communities and low-cost housing in particular. But in 1978 the regulation was overridden by a Democratic Congress the constituencies of which were more diverse and which thus wanted to keep the benefits of CDBG widely spread.

In sum, then, Presidents Johnson and Carter proposed grant programs that tended to favor the older central cities from which they, and the Democratic party generally, derived much of their electoral support. Presidents Nixon and Ford used the power of the presidency to shape federal grants to the benefit of newer cities and suburbs from which the Republicans obtained much of their support.

Congressional Politics and
The Distribution of Federal Funds

Presidents are not the only ones who consider how various programs will affect their constituencies. Members of Congress, too, have an important stake in how their electoral districts fare in the allocation of funds. Data on the distribution of federal funds are routinely collected by congressional districts, and members of the House of Representatives monitor these data to see how much their constituents are benefiting. These politics of distribution play a large role in the passage of new intergovernmental legislation, whether it involves categorical aid or block grants. The politics vary, however, according to which type of aid is involved. In the case of categorical grants, the distribution of federal funds is affected by specifying the purpose for which the funds may be used and by attempting to influence the discretionary choices of the federal bureaucracies. In the case of block grants, the distribution of federal monies can be changed by modifying the formula.

There are several reasons for which the nature of a city's congressional delegation might affect its ability to obtain funds. First, federal agencies such as HUD are executive agencies: Their top personnel are appointed by the president. Cities whose representatives in Congress are of the same party as the president have privileged access to such agencies. Second, federal agencies are monitored and protected by specific House and Senate committees. It is through these committees that legislation affecting the funding and operation of the agency must pass. It is these committees upon which the agency must rely to define its organizational and programmatic interests on the floor of the House and Senate. Third, certain committees and certain leaders within them— committee chairpersons in particular—are power brokers within the House and Senate. Maintenance of their political support can be absolutely crucial for securing the legislative authority to continue a program or for fighting successfully for increased authorization of funds. Preferential allocation of agency funds is one way to get that support.

There is substantial evidence that HUD's allocation of project grants was indeed influenced by Congress. One of the better studies investigating the politics of HUD grants was carried out by Theodore Anagnoson. By studying the distribution of HUD water and sewer projects to counties between 1968 and 1970, Anagnoson found that even when counties were equally eligible, equally interested in obtaining the funds, and equally needful of such federal assistance, they were not always equally successful with HUD. Those counties whose representatives sat on the congressional committees with oversight responsibility for HUD were likely to have more projects authorized than those that did not.[7] The allocation of urban renewal grants most likely reveals similar patterns of congressional influence.

In the case of urban renewal, in fact, national politics impinged upon the ability of localities to obtain urban renewal funds in two ways. The purposes for which those funds could be used and the ability of the federal government to deny funds to those who did not use them in that way favored those cities who *could* use them in that way. Because central cities had the severest slum problems and the greatest interest in using public authority and funds to eliminate them physically, or at least to move them elsewhere, they received the vast bulk of urban renewal funds.

But central cities nonetheless had to compete for limited urban renewal funds, monies distributed at the discretion of HUD. And it is in this arena that the congressional representatives of a city would make themselves heard. In the next section of this chapter, we shall measure the extent to which congressional representation mattered in the distribution of urban renewal funds among central cities in the period between 1961 and 1968. Using urban renewal as our case, we shall try to answer the questions we asked at the beginning of the chapter.

Toward this end, we shall specify the extent of political influence in the allocation procedures of a major categorical grant. In spite of the growth of block grants, categorical grants are still important in the federal aid system. And project grants have not disappeared, either. In 1975, according to the Advisory Commission on Intergovernmental Relations, two-thirds of all categorical grants were awarded on a project-by-project basis. The following analysis, then, provides an insight into the politics and dynamics of our federal grant system.

The Distribution of Federal Project Grants: A Model

An adequate model of the intercity distribution of discretionary federal grants must distinguish between local interests in securing federal funds and federal interests in allocating them. Access to federal monies thus involves local application and federal approval. Localities that receive few funds may simply be applying less frequently, or they may have been discriminated against in the federal distribution process. A local government's pursuit of federal funds is a function of its local interest in obtaining such funds, the information it has about program opportunities, its administrative capacities to make an application, and its anticipated influence in the grant distribution process. The success of the locality in actually obtaining funds is a function of the volume of its efforts to obtain funds, the extent to which local conditions are consistent with the programmatic objectives of the federal program, the agency's assessment of the locality's ability to implement the plan, and the influence of the locality's national representatives with respect to the federal program. The same factors that explain local application also potentially explain federal distribution, although the two are conceptually different.

Local governments do not pursue funds from all federal programs, nor do they pursue all with equal intensity. For example, in the 145 communities that make up the Southeastern Wisconsin Regional Planning Commission, 73 failed to apply for even one of the ten federal grants for which they were eligible.[8] Cities have been unequally interested in federal pollution control grants, Law Enforcement Assistance Agency funds, urban renewal and War on Poverty monies, to name but a few. Local interest reflects the extent to which local governments perceive federal programs as meeting local needs and/or the extent of their aversion to federal intrusions on local policy autonomy. Houston, for example, did not participate in urban renewal due to both its aversion to federal intervention as well as the success of private redevelopment. Similarly, federal agencies' distribution of their scarce resources reflects their assessment of the extent to which federal policies will meet local needs and bolster support for program expansion. Wasted funds, all else being equal, can become a political liability.

Application for many federal programs often involves complex patterns of interagency coordination, the devotion of large numbers of personnel to grant application, and the building of local support. In the case of urban renewal, federal procedures for project approval were complex and lengthy. The average renewal application was two and one-half inches thick and weighed fifty-three pounds.[9] A HUD management study indicated that there were 4,000 discrete steps in the process of completing an urban renewal project.

Given the risk that funding will not be forthcoming, cities must decide how to use limited administrative resources in approaching the federal government for funds. Application for federal funds can be costly in terms of personnel. City employees who are used to apply for one federal grant cannot be used for other purposes, including application for other grants that the city may be more likely to obtain. Cities with greater administrative capacities not only have the resources necessary to prepare applications, but they can probably also achieve economies of scale in doing so, thus realistically implementing larger and more complex projects. Research indicates that those communities that have greater planning capacities tend to apply more often for federal grants.[10]

Reciprocally, federal agencies make evaluations of the local agency's capacity to implement federal programs. If a city has the bureaucratic infrastructure necessary to make a federal program a success, the federal agency will have fewer responsibilities for securing compliance with federal objectives and, ultimately, a greater payoff in terms of electoral support for continuation of its program.

Finally, local governments have difficulty in obtaining adequate information on federal program opportunities, the legislative and administrative guidelines of which are continually changing. In 1968, Representative Roth noted that ". . . only the largest cities and states have the necessary money and staff required just to keep abreast of the programs from which they might benefit."[11] Members of Congress are a vital link between the cities and the federal government, for they represent an important source of information about federal program opportunities. Because the members of Congress are interested in obtaining federal resources for their constituents, they are likely to keep the constituents abreast of those programs that would benefit them. Similarly, those members who are influential in the grant distribution process tend to communicate their influence to their constituents. They use their ability to secure benefits for their constituents to maintain local visibility and support.[12]

Conversely, federal agencies will be receptive to the promptings of those representatives who hold potential influence over the agencies' prospects for favorable authorization and legislation. And, finally, executives may use the agencies' distribution of funds to build support for their political party, at both the congressional and presidential levels (see Table 8.1).

Because the distribution of federal funds is ultimately contingent upon a local government's pursuit of those funds, both application and distribution need to be included in a formal model. Local attributes— needs, administrative capacity, and political power—affect both local application and federal distribution. Their effects on both application and distribution need to be estimated simultaneously.

TABLE 8.1
Locality Attributes as Explanations for
Local Application and Federal Allocation

Variables	Explanation for	
	Local Application	Federal Distribution
Local socioeconomic conditions	Local interests in program	Congruence with programmatic objectives
Local administrative capacity	Local capacities for application	Local capacities for implementation
Local representation in national government	Program information; anticipated influence.	Local influence in national distribution; local constituencies for national political elites

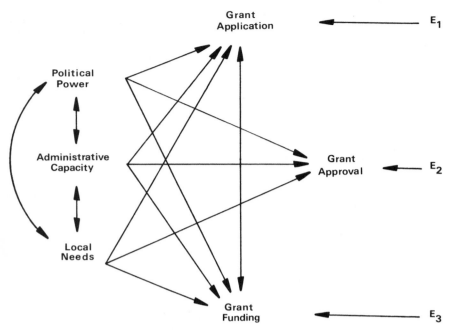

FIGURE 8.1   A Model óf Political Power, Local Needs, and the Distribution of Federal Urban Renewal Grants.

Methodology

In an attempt to determine how these local attributes affect the distribution of federal urban renewal funds, we shall use a structural equation model (represented in Figure 8.1) consisting of three inter-dependent equations: the determinants of city application for federal funds, of federal approval of that application, and of the level of federal funding authorized.

The structural equation model allows us to measure the *relative* impact of different local attributes on city application for, and receipt of, federal funds. First, the regression coefficients allow us to estimate the effects of congressional representation, holding all other factors constant. Thus, given two cities with representatives who are unequally powerful and with different needs for redevelopment, we can use the statistical procedure to measure the effects of each factor independently of the other factors. The standardized coefficients allow us to compare the relative impacts of different factors, thus indicating which factors are the most important in explaining why some cities received more federal funds than others.

Second, the structural equation model allows us to determine the relative impact of local characteristics on the demand for federal funds as opposed to the supply of federal funds.[13] Certain cities may receive more funds because they have a greater need for a given program and therefore apply more frequently. Other cities with even greater needs may not apply as often but may instead be favorably treated by HUD in its decisions about allocation of funds.

The first equation examines the relative impact of a city's needs, administrative capacity, and national political power on its demands for federal funds (i.e., the number of applications it makes for such funds). The second equation looks at the impact of these city characteristics on the number of projects authorized by the federal government, controlling for the question of whether a given city has submitted a greater or smaller number of applications relative to other cities. The third equation analyzes the impact of city characteristics on the total amount of renewal funds received by a city, in this case controlling for the number of applications the city has made, as well as the number of those applications that were approved.

Urban Renewal

As indicated in the previous chapter, the federal urban renewal program, initiated by the 1949 Housing Act and modified by subsequent amendments, was a major innovation in federal urban policy. City governments were empowered, if they so chose, to purchase central city land through eminent domain powers in accordance with a federally approved plan. Federal approval had to be secured on a project-by-project basis. The local agency would then clear the land, provide public infrastructure, and resell it to private developers or construct public buildings on it. The federal government would pay for up to two-thirds of the difference between the costs to the city of land acquisition and preparation and the revenues the city received when it resold the land to private developers.

The program initially attempted to ensure city construction of low-rent housing, by specifying that a project had to be in a predominantly residential area. However, it did not require the cleared land to be redeveloped for housing. Further, the residential emphasis of the program was gradually weakened. Over the years, increasingly large percentages of the federal capital grant were allowed for non-residential purposes (1954: 10 percent; 1959: 30 percent; 1965: 35 percent). Renewal sites no longer needed to be in the severest slum areas. Urban renewal could be used to expand universities, hospitals, and cultural centers.

In terms of actual private construction, urban renewal was not used predominantly for residential reconstruction. In the large central cities studied here, about 19 percent of all cleared acreage went to residential construction. Nor was urban renewal a program devoted to construction of low-income housing. Indeed, some 90 percent of the low-income housing stock it destroyed was not replaced in the form of low-income housing.[14] Nevertheless, as the residential and low-income emphasis of the program weakened, central city urban renewal accelerated.

Urban renewal was used to change land-use patterns that would have been more costly to change through the market. As the central city's office economy grew, central city land uses also changed. In the world of urban economics, most of the upward and outward movement of the new downtown economy takes place quietly through the market. Firms and households weigh the benefits of downtown accessibility against their demands for space. Those who expect to benefit most from accessibility and who can make most intensive use of the relatively small downtown locations will tend to outbid others for the privilege of a central location. This power to command central locations is largely granted by the market—an outcome of one's income and of the relative benefits of accessibility versus space.

But urban land is not allocated by the market alone. In the economic transformation of the central city, those firms that economic theory suggested would bid highest did not rely entirely on the market to secure their downtown locations. They frequently used the powers of government to facilitate land use changes, changes often difficult to achieve through costly haggling over patchwork assembly. The firms also used the powers of government to construct the complementary public infrastructure that made their investments profitable. Of all the urban programs that put public authority at the service of private investment, urban renewal was the most visible and the most controversial.

The growth of the downtown office economy, then, required new land—land that was difficult to acquire due to fragmented ownership, large-scale deterioration, and the persistence of small proprietors who survived on family labor and a loyal neighborhood clientele. Urban renewal helped push a bulldozer through all these obstacles. Interviews with developers indicated that powers of eminent domain were the program's most important features. Those powers provided the legal means to force small businesses out. The predominant form of enterprise displaced by urban renewal was the small merchant with a localized, often ethnically distinct, clientele and a small production shop. By 1959, over 100,000 businesses had already been displaced from 650 urban renewal sites.[15] Unable to move back to the renewed area, unable to replace their clientele, unable to absorb the costs of moving, the dislocated firms either folded or saw their sales decline in new locations, often outside the central city altogether.[16] Some small proprietors did not go without a fight, however; they held out for high prices or refused to sell altogether. Thus, public renewal was time-consuming. Private renewal of downtown sites *without* the powers of eminent domain often took even longer.[17]

Urban renewal not only encouraged private investment, but it also stimulated the complementary public capital spending necessary for private investment to proceed.[18] Indeed, it stimulated new municipal expenditures beyond those required by statute.[19] By 1971 local governments had invested $3.9 billion in public construction related to urban renewal (roads, parking structures, public transit, sewerage, and other public works), or 21 percent of the total public and private investment on renewal sites.[20]

Urban renewal did stimulate private investment. Although the actual economic impact of urban renewal has been inadequately studied, most evaluation studies of this program assume that the private investment associated with it would not have taken place in its absence.[21] New tax revenues were generated, but those revenues were usually allocated, often by law, to finance the related public construction.

In order to change land-use patterns, however, cities first had to obtain the necessary monies from the urban renewal program. In order to acquire such funds, cities had to apply to Washington for approval of each project they wished to fund. Completion of each project involved three distinct stages: planning, execution, and implementation. During the planning stage, cities developed a plan for which they secured the explicit approval of their elected officials and the implicit approval of potential developers and investors. During the execution stage, cities negotiated with HUD to secure its approval and funding authorization. Implementation occurred once a project began execution of city land purchase, clearance, and resale to private developers.

Congressional Power

As already noted, one of the most important external linkages a city has to the federal government is its congressional representation. The city's congressional representatives are both a source of information about changing federal program opportunities and a source of influence affecting the allocation of federal funds. A city's congressional power has three distinct components: membership on congressional committees with oversight authority for HUD, partisanship with respect to that of the executive branch, and general influence within congress.

One important source of city congressional power is determined by whether or not the city has representatives on the committees and subcommittees with oversight responsibility for the department that allocates urban renewal funds. In the case of urban renewal, the Senate and House Banking and Currency committees had general oversight responsibility for HUD, and the housing subcommittees had specific responsibility for urban renewal. The committee members were in a position both to know about changes in urban renewal program guidelines and to influence the behavior of the agency for which they had legislative responsibility. They also constituted a critical support group with respect to HUD's requests for budgetary allocations and legislative changes and, consequently, had privileged access to HUD on behalf of their constituencies. Although Banking and Currency's orientation is alleged to be more policy oriented than constituency oriented,[22] according to an executive official in HUD, "special pains are made to fill their needs."[23]

A second source of city congressional power is the partisanship of its delegation. A city's congressional representatives are likely to have more influence over the allocative decisions of HUD—an executive agency—when they are of the same party as the president. Top HUD officials are appointed by the president, and HUD tends to provide a city's congressional representatives with privileged access if they are of the same party.[24]

A third dimension of city congressional power is its general influence within Congress. Federal agencies depend upon the support of influential members of Congress to secure appropriations and supportive legislation. Such members may therefore have more impact than others on HUD decisionmaking. General congressional influence has two associated sources: seniority and committee membership. The more continuously a city's congressional delegation has remained in office, the more skill, information, and strategic influence that delegation is likely to have.[25] Seniority also translates into membership on more powerful committees and into occupation of committee and subcommittee chair positions within them. "Exclusive" committees, such as Appropriations or Ways and Means, have generalized influence over the inner workings of Congress. Composed of the most powerful representatives in the House, such committees are particularly sought out for their ability to obtain benefits for a constituency.[26]

Administrative Capacity

The ability of a city to complete technically complex application processes and to coordinate the myriad tasks and constituencies that project implementation requires is likely to be determined by its own internal administrative capacities. One indication of the quality of personnel and the diversity of skills available to execute a city's complex program is the city's functional scope (the range of services for which the city is responsible). Urban renewal execution requires diverse municipal skills: site acquisition, land-use planning, infrastructure development, commercial sales, tax assessments, and so forth. If city governments already contain a complex division of labor, their administrative capacities are likely to be greater. Research indicates that cities with greater overall functional scope have higher levels of fiscal performance for those single functions for which they are responsible.[27] In addition, they are more likely to develop urban renewal programs independently of their socioeconomic environment.[28] Finally, cities with greater functional scope have higher "capacities for mobilization"—as indicated by analysis of total municipal expenditures, War on Poverty funding, and urban renewal spending.[29]

Local Needs

A variety of local needs stimulated local interest in urban renewal. Urban renewal offered a means to enhance local economic growth, particularly downtown-oriented retail and office activity, and, in fact, downtown retail and office interests were key local proponents of local urban renewal.[30] The rise of the office economy, in particular, required major land-use changes.

Elimination of deteriorated local housing was one of the major legislative intentions of urban renewal. Central cities, however, were more responsive to residential deterioration around the downtown area than to such deterioration in other parts of the city. Although land was relatively cheap on the periphery of the downtown area due to poor housing, it was likely to remain a poor investment unless many invested simultaneously.[31] Downtown economies that were surrounded by poor residential districts therefore had difficulty expanding. As earlier discussed, urban renewal offered a means to clear large areas and to plan simultaneous private investments. But because changing land use is both more difficult and more costly where land is highly built-up and densely used, urban renewal would likely be a more costly program in cities with high density than in those with lower density.[32] Finally, cities tend to vary in territorial size. Cities with large land areas have greater territories that, all else being equal, can potentially be renewed.

Operationalization and Procedures

In this section, we shall analyze the intercity distribution of federal urban renewal funds in the 130 central cities with populations of 100,000 or more as of 1960. These cities constituted the primary target for the federal renewal program and thus received the vast bulk of all federal renewal monies. The analysis will be confined to the distribution of federal funds between 1961 and 1968, a period of continuous Democratic control of both the presidency and congress.

Urban Renewal

A city's involvement in the federal urban renewal program will be operationally defined in terms of the total number of projects planned between 1961 and 1966, the total number of projects that received authorization between 1961 and 1968, and the total number of federal grants authorized for all projects executed between 1961 and 1968. These data were obtained from HUD's study, *Urban Renewal Project Characteristics*, published in 1966. Most of these projects were clearance projects. We used the number of projects planned between 1961 and 1966 so as to allow sufficient time for a project to secure federal approval. Projects planned in 1967 were not likely to obtain approval by 1968, given that the average time between local planning and federal government authorization was over two years.

Congressional Power

A city's congressional power will be operationally defined in terms of a city's congressional delegation. A given city delegation consists of all those representatives from districts that overlap the territorial boundaries of the city. Partisan power in the House of Representatives is measured in terms of the total number of Democratic or Republican members of Congress representing the city as of 1966.[33] In the Senate, it is measured in terms of the total number of Democrats (0,1,2) from the state in which the city is located. The oversight power of a city's congressional delegation is measured in terms of the total number of years in which members of the delegation sat on the House and Senate Banking and Currency Committee between 1960 and 1968. The general power of a city's congressional delegation is measured in terms of the average seniority of its representatives and on the basis of the number of representatives who sat on "exclusive" committees in 1966. These two measures were collected for the House only.

Administrative Capacity

A city's administrative capacity will be measured on the basis of its functional scope—that is, the total number of functions for which the city exceeded a minimum threshold of fiscal responsibility in 1962.[34] The functions considered were federally aided welfare, general assistance, education, hospitals, health, sanitation, parks, sewers, and the judiciary.

Local Needs

Population density is measured as the number of thousands of persons per square mile in 1960.[35] Land area is the total number of square miles in 1960.[36] Housing deterioration is measured in terms of the percentage of all dwelling units that were dilapidated—so defined if lacking hot water, private toilets, or baths.[37]

Tax burden is measured on the basis of property tax dollars per capita in 1960.[38] Housing decline in and around the Central Business District is measured in terms of the percentage of core families having an annual income below $4,000 as of 1960. The core is defined as all census tracts either in or contiguous to the Central Business District.[39] Retail activity is measured on the basis of per capita retail sales in the central city as of 1963.[40] Finally, office activity is measured by the per capita total number of corporation headquarters of the top 1000 industrial firms in 1963.

Regional Capacity

Southern Democrats have voted more like Republicans than like northern Democrats on urban issues.[41] Given the idiosyncratic nature of Southern political culture, a regional control was included in the analysis below. States from the deep South (Louisiana, Alabama, Mississippi, Florida, Georgia, and North Carolina) were coded 1. All others were coded 0.[42]

Empirical Findings

Application for Funds

In the equation explaining intercity variation in the number of urban renewal applications between 1961 and 1966, two political variables have significant effects. The regression coefficient for the variable of Democratic representatives indicates that for every additional Democratic representative from the city an additional .59 applications are

TABLE 8.2
Means and Standard Deviations of Critical Variables (n=130)

	X̄	SD
Application	4.29	4.70
Authorization	3.13	3.48
Funding	5778.56	5605.08
House Banking	.61	1.29
Senate Banking	1.40	1.57
Democratic Reps.	1.23	1.84
Republican Reps.	.48	.75
Democratic Senators	5.24	2.52
House Seniority	56.88	6.79
House Committee	.45	.73
Population Density	5.99	4.25
Land Area	73201.04	82911.69
Core Poverty	.45	.15
Housing Dilapidation	.07	.05
Tax Burden	52.20	38.61
Office Activity	.11	.10
Retail Activity	5.24	2.52
Functional Scope	4.80	1.81
South (= 1)	.13	.34

made. The regression coefficient for Republican representatives is .71; cities with an additional Republican representative in Congress would thus have more urban renewal applications. It follows that the more representatives a city has in the House, the more likely it is to apply for urban renewal funds.

None of the other political variables are statistically significant, indicating that cities with greater representation on the Senate and House Banking and Currency Committee, which has oversight responsibility for HUD, did not make a greater number of applications. Similarly,

TABLE 8.3
The Determinants of Urban Renewal Application, Authorization,
and Funding, 1961-1968

	Unstandardized Regression Coefficient (Standardized Regression Coefficient)		
	Application	Authorization	Funding
House Banking	- .12 (-.06)	.62*** (.24)	4804*** (.18)
Senate Banking	- .08 (-.05)	- .03 (-.01)	- 1814 (-.08)
Democratic Reps.	.59*** (.41)	.29** (.16)	5454*** (.28)
Republican Reps.	.71** (.21)	- .45 (-.10)	- 624 (-.01)
Democratic Senators	.05 (.05)	.01 (.01)	- 1753** (-.13)
House Seniority	- .00 (-.01)	.00 (.00)	55 (.01)
House Committee Power	- .02 (-.00)	- .18 (-.04)	3090 (.06)
Population Density	- .01 (-.01)	.12** (.14)	1435** (.16)
Land Area	- .0970** (-.32)	+180 (-.05)	597300 (.01)
Core Poverty	4.69** (.27)	2.27 (.10)	-16308 (-.07)
Housing Dilapidation	2.88 (.06)	- 6.78 (-.10)	62587 (.09)
Tax Burden	.02** (.32)	.00 (.04)	8.54 (.01)
Office Activity	16167 (.07)	28762 (.09)	80390811 (.02)
Retail Activity	-958.8 (-.14)	-1006** (-.11)	3590621 (.04)
Functional Scope	- .11 (-.07)	- .03 (-.02)	3015** (.15)
South (= 1)	- .44 (-.06)	.02 (.00)	3195 (.03)
Application	-- --	.71 (.53)	- 425 (.03)
Authorization	-- --	-- --	4203*** (.41)
Intercept	.92	1.54	- 22902
r^2	.34***	.80***	.84***
n	107	107	107

**Significant at the .05 level   ***Significant at the .01 level

cities with more Democratic senators and with more senior and powerful committee representation did not make more renewal applications. Although the size of a city's congressional delegation in the House affects its rate of applications, neither the nature of its representation in the Senate nor its representation on the House oversight committee affects that rate.

Local economic conditions, however, do have a significant effect on central city application for urban renewal funds. Among the economic variables, the two statistically significant ones are core poverty and tax burden. The variable of core poverty is measured in terms of the core families (area around the Central Business District, abbreviated CBD) having an annual income below $4,000 as of 1960. The mean of this variable is .45, indicating that, on average, 45 percent of the core families fall below the poverty level. The regression coefficient for core poverty in this equation is 4.69, which can be interpreted to mean that one unit (equal to 100 percent) increase in poor families in the CBD would lead to 4.69 more applications for urban renewal. By extension, a city with 10 percent more poor families in the CBD would have .469 more applications. The regression coefficient for the variable tax burden is .02, indicating that an increase of $1 per capita of property taxes would lead to an increase of .02 in applications. Therefore, a city with $50 more per capita property taxes will have one more application for urban renewal.

Finally, a city's land area also proved to have a significant effect on the number of applications. The regression coefficient for land area is $-.097$, indicating that a city with 100 square miles more land area made about 9 fewer urban renewal applications. Thus, cities with larger land areas made significantly fewer applications. Cities with more dilapidated housing, with weaker retail or corporate office activity, and with greater functional scope did not make more renewal applications.

Approval of Urban Renewal Projects

The second equation explains intercity variation in the total number of urban renewal projects approved for execution between 1961 and 1968. Two aspects of a city's congressional representation have significant effects. Representation (whether by Democrats or Republicans) on the House Banking and Currency Committee and the number of Democratic representatives in the House both proved to have a positive effect on a city's ability to gain project authorization. The regression coefficient for the variable of House Banking is .62, indicating that every additional year of membership on the House Banking and Currency Committee will lead to .62 more authorizations for city urban renewal projects. The regression coefficient for the number of Democratic representatives is .29, indicating that for each addition of one Democratic representative in Congress, the city is expected to have .29 more urban renewal project authorizations. Thus, cities with greater representation on the House Banking and Currency Committee and cities with a large number of Democratic members of Congress had a significantly greater number of projects authorized by HUD.

Not all political variables, however, contributed to a city's ability to secure urban renewal project authorization. Cities with greater representation on the *Senate* Banking and Currency Committee were not able to secure more urban renewal projects. Similarly, such cities were not favored in the distribution of urban renewal projects even if their congressional representatives were very senior or sat on the powerful "exclusive" house committees. Finally, cities with greater Republican House representation and cities located in states with strong Democratic representation in the Senate also were not favored in the grant distribution.

Population density, on the other hand, did prove to have a significant positive effect on the number of authorizations. The regression coefficient for population density is .12, indicating that for each addition of 1,000 persons per square mile in the city there is a corresponding .12 increase in authorization of renewal projects. By contrast, retail activity had a negative effect on the level of authorization. The coefficient for retail activity is −1,006, which can be interpreted to mean that one unit ($1,000) increase in per capita retail sales in the central city would lead to a corresponding 1,006 fewer authorizations. Given that average per capita retail sale is .0017 (i.e., $1.7), the coefficient indicates that cities with $1 more per capita in retail sales are expected to have one fewer authorization. This equation controls for the number of applications for urban renewal projects. As expected, cities with greater numbers of applications are expected to have more projects authorized. Land area, core poverty, corporate office activity, housing conditions, tax burden, functional scope, and region have no significant impact on the intercity distribution of urban renewal authorizations.[43]

Total Funds Allocated Per City

The third equation reveals the intercity variation in total federal grant monies approved for urban renewal projects executed between 1961 and 1968. The political variables have the same effect as that revealed in the second equation. In this third equation, the regression coefficient indicates that each 2 years of membership (whether for a Democrat or a Republican) on the House Banking and Currency Committee is worth $4,804,000 more in federal monies for urban renewal projects. Correspondingly, the regression coefficient for Democratic representatives is 5,454, indicating that for each addition of one Democratic representative in the Congress, the city is expected to receive $5,454,000 more in federal renewal monies. In short, cities with strong representation on the House Banking and Currency Committee and with a larger Democratic congressional contingent receive significantly more federal monies, independent of the number of projects approved. Again, as in the second equation, the other political variables—namely, seniority, committee power, membership in the Senate Banking and Currency Committee, and Republican representation—do not have any significant effects on the distribution of federal grants.

Here, too, population density has a significant positive impact on federal grant levels. The regression coefficient for population density in the third equation is 1,435, indicating that for each addition of 1000 persons per square mile in the city there is a corresponding $1,435,000 increase in federal monies. A city's administrative capacity also has a significant positive effect on the total level of grant funding. The regression coefficient for functional scope is 3,015, indicating that cities with one more functional responsibility obtain $3,015,000 more in federal monies. None of the other local economic characteristics affected renewal grant levels. Finally, controlling for the number of projects authorized, the number of projects planned by the city has no significant effect on the level of funding received by the city. However, the level of renewal funding is strongly affected by the number of projects that have been authorized during the period. The regression coefficient for authorization is 4,203, indicating that each addition of one project authorized will lead to $4,203,000 more in urban renewal monies.

Discussion

Overall, the findings indicate that congressional power affects the distribution of federal urban renewal projects; local needs, however, primarily affect the distribution by their impact on whether or not a city applies for federal project funds. Not all forms of congressional representation matter equally, nor are all stages of policymaking equally accessible to the impact of local needs and congressional influence.

A city's representation in the House of Representatives also affects the distribution of federal renewal grants. Cities with a large contingent of Democratic members of Congress and with representation on the oversight committee for HUD—Banking and Currency—were more likely to have their proposals approved at a higher level of federal funding; further, those with larger congressional delegations applied more frequently for renewal grants. Local representation in the Senate, however, did not enhance a city's ability to obtain federal renewal funding. Thus, the impact of partisan and oversight committee representation is contingent upon its location in either the House or Senate.

That a city's House representation is important in terms of its ability to obtain federal funding, whereas its Senate representation is not, reflects differences in the calculus of reelection in the two bodies. House representatives not only face more immediate reelection, but they are closely tied to specific urban constituencies. They are less able to build a public image by authorizing legislation. They sit on fewer committees than Senators, who tend to be spread rather thinly across many committees and subcommittees. As a result, House members are more likely to make increased use of the committee powers they do have and to spend more time and energy in distributive favors for their constituencies. Finally, the process of coalition building in the House requires that winning coalitions comprise a substantial proportion of urban representatives. In the Senate, it is not only possible for individual senators to act without regard to a particular urban constituency, but winning coalitions can also be more easily constructed without regard to urban constituencies in general.

Cities with more representatives in the House, of whatever party, submitted more applications for funds than did cities with fewer representatives. This suggests that members of Congress of both parties acted as conduits of information. Cities with a large number of representatives, *of whatever party*, were more likely to be aware of changing program opportunities. However, although cities with a higher number of Democratic representatives obtained more funding than did cities with fewer Democratic representatives, those cities with a higher number of Republican representatives did not receive more money than those with fewer Republican representatives. Thus, only those cities represented by Democrats, the dominant party (and, by the same token, strategically placed with regard to HUD), were able to obtain any advantages in the distribution of renewal funds.

Furthermore, although cities with representation on the strategic House oversight committee for HUD—the Banking and Currency Committee—do not apply more, they *are* more likely to have their proposals approved and at higher funding levels.[44] Therefore, cities that submit the same number of applications and are represented by *either* Republicans or Democrats on the oversight committee get preferential treatment. Representation on the committee, consequently, was particularly helpful for those cities represented by Republicans.

One pertinent issue to be assessed by means of the structural equation model is the *relative* importance of partisan and oversight committee representation in obtaining authorization and funding. What is the relative value to a city of having strong Democratic representation

TABLE 8.4
Breakdown of Political Influence on Urban Renewal Funding*

| | Project Authorization | | | Funding | | |
	Direct	Indirect	Total	Direct	Indirect	Total
House Banking	.24	-.03	.21	.18	.08	.26
	(114%)			(69%)		
Democratic Reps.	.15	.23	.38	.28	.14	.42
	(41%)			(69%)		

*Entries refer to standardized partial regression coefficients, for the structural and reduced forms.

in the House, as opposed to representation on the House oversight committee, in terms of the city's ability to obtain large amounts of urban renewal funds? The answer is found in Table 8.4, which provides a breakdown of the total effect of a city's Democratic and House Banking and Currency representation on the number of projects authorized and on the level of renewal funding authorized.

The number of authorized projects is contingent, in part, upon the number of projects for which a city has applied. The amount of funding authorized is also contingent upon the number of projects authorized and upon the number of projects for which a city has applied. The *direct effect* of Democratic or House Banking and Currency Committee representation on authorization indicates the impact of such representation, controlling for the number of applications made by the city. The direct effect of Democratic or House Banking and Currency Committee representation on *funding* indicates their impact, controlling not only for the number of applications but also for the number of authorizations. The *total effect*, on the other hand, indicates both their direct effect on authorization (and funding) as well as their indirect effect (by stimulating more applications and/or authorizations).

The results in Table 8.4 indicate that the strength of a city's partisan representation in the House has a greater *total* impact on the likelihood that its projects will be authorized and on the level of funding received than does a city's position on the House oversight committee. Being on the oversight committee does not affect rate of application, but having a larger number of representatives increases this rate. Application, in turn, has a fundamental impact on the funds that a city is likely to receive. If the rate of application is held constant, we find that representation on the House Banking and Currency Committee has a more powerful effect than does partisan representation. However, the rate of

TABLE 8.5
The Total Value of Congressional Representation

	Applications (Number)	Authorization (Number)	Funding ($1,000)
Democratic Representatives	.59	.71	8177
Republican Representatives	.71	.05	-725
House Banking and Currency Representatives	-.12	.54	7199

application varies among cities, and this variation is important in relation to their ability to get urban renewal funds. Because of the importance of representation for application and, in turn, of application for authorization, the strength of a city's Democratic representation in the House has a greater effect on authorizations received than does membership on the oversight committee. Thus, although cities with representatives on that committee are more successful in obtaining authorization for their projects than those cities with greater Democratic representation (B=.24 versus .15), more authorizations are given to cities with stronger Democratic representation because they apply more frequently. If we turn to the total level of funding authorized, we again find that Democratic cities obtain more funding than cities with representatives on the oversight committee—again, because they apply more frequently.

It follows that cities with strong Democratic congressional delegations receive more money both because they apply more often and because their projects are more likely to be approved. Such cities are also likely to get more money for each project approved. Whether this is because they apply for more costly projects or whether they are more likely to get what they ask for cannot be determined here.

Table 8.5 indicates the actual value of congressional representation in terms of the number of projects planned and authorized as well as the level of funding received. The coefficients displayed are the total metric coefficients in the reduced form specification. For each additional Democratic representative, controlling for other factors, cities obtained $8.17 million more in urban renewal funds. For each additional four years on the House Banking and Currency Committee, cities obtained authorization for another renewal project.

Although local needs were clearly important in compelling cities to *apply* for urban renewal funds, not all needs were equally important. Fiscal strain and constraints on downtown expansion appear to be important factors favoring city interest in the renewal program. Local economic conditions such as office and retail activity did not generate local application. Poor housing, which was one of the program's initial legitimations, had absolutely no effect on a city's interest in application. Cities were eager to use urban renewal to restructure downtown land use, to stimulate more fiscally productive activities, and to augment the city's expenditure capacities in the face of high fiscal burdens.

Although local needs stimulated city application for renewal funds, they had no effect as direct determinants of federal authorization and funding. The federal bureaucracy was not directly responsive to local needs in its allocational decisions. The direct effect of such local needs— core poverty and tax burden—on both authorization and funding levels, controlling for application level, was insignificant.[45] The effect of local needs on a city's renewal authorization and funding levels depended primarily upon its stimulation of local applications, not upon its influence on federal allocation decisions.[46] Local needs, as defined in this study, were taken into account by HUD officials only to the extent that needier cities applied more and that the rate of application was related to project approval. The linkage between need and urban renewal funds was an indirect one, to say the least. By contrast, being represented by Democrats had a direct effect on a city's ability to get funds. Needy cities represented by Republicans applied as often as those represented by Democrats, but their success rate was much lower. Thus, *a city's congressional linkage clearly matters much more than its local needs in terms of its ability to obtain renewal funds.*

Finally, a city's administrative capacity, as measured by its functional scope, does not have any effect on either the volume of applications its makes or the number of authorizations it receives. However, cities with greater administrative capacity are more likely to receive higher levels of renewal funding. Whether this indicates an ability to plan larger projects, an ability to negotiate more effectively with HUD, or a higher evaluation of local capacities on the part of HUD cannot be determined here.

Conclusions

Federal grant programs are ostensibly designed such that those cities with the greatest need for federal aid will be able to receive the most funds. The present study indicates that recognition of the needs specified in federal legislation may induce cities to apply for those federal funds for which they are eligible, but federal agencies may be singularly ineffective in determining how federal bureaucracies allocate project funds. Given their political vulnerability, federal agencies are likely to allocate their discretionary funds to those constituencies whose representatives have the most power over their future funding and legislative authorization. These constituencies are not necessarily those with the greatest need as specified in the objectives of federal legislation.

The kind of political representation a city has in Congress thus makes a difference with respect to its ability to get funds from the federal bureaucracy. Because House representatives represent smaller constituencies and have less visibility in general policymaking, they are more eager to obtain funds for their districts than are senators, who represent whole states and are more visible in the Senate policy making process. Therefore, the nature of a city's representation in the House of Representatives is more important to its finances than is its representation in the Senate. Because federal grants are under the direction of specialized committees, the ability of a city to obtain funds from a particular federal grant will also be affected by membership of its representatives on the relevant House committee. Finally, the party affiliation of cities' representatives is very important. In this study, cities represented by Democrats in the House were far more successful in obtaining urban renewal funds than were those represented by Republicans.

During the period examined, only one party—the Democratic party—controlled the presidency, the Senate, and the House. This study therefore cannot tell us what the "politics of project categoricals" might have been under the control of *different* parties in the legislative and executive branches; yet it does give us an insight into the effect upon cities of having a dominant national party. When such dominance does pertain, local finance seems to be strongly affected by the party affiliation of the representatives for the city. Those representatives a city's voters choose to represent them in the House, then, are of significance to local as well as national elites.

The finding that local needs per se have not directly affected the allocation of urban renewal project grants has important implications, albeit very tentative ones at this point, concerning the debate about the form that federal aid should take. If many categoricals are replaced by block grants, as President Reagan wishes, it is not necessarily the case that local need will always be considered less than it was under categoricals. After all, local need was certainly not the primary criterion by which urban renewal project funds were allocated. Thus, at least theoretically, states may take local need into greater account than have federal agencies.

Such a possibility runs counter to the position taken by many Congressional Democrats—that states will ignore local needs, whereas Congress does not. Certainly the Democrats, who were so influential in allocating the project grants studied here, have a political interest in keeping their power by retaining categoricals, but it is not clear that all needy cities have the same absolute interest in such retention. Although this study is speculative, it does pose the need for further research on the relative importance of local need and "politics" in the allocation of federal monies.

Above all, this study suggests that even if President Reagan does succeed in replacing some categoricals with block grants, Republican control of the Senate is unlikely to affect significantly the distribution of the remaining project grants. Only if the Republicans manage to gain control of the House are they likely to have a substantial impact on the distribution of such grants. The House is clearly the locus of political conflict over the allocation of project grants, and the party that controls the House, as opposed to the Senate, will also determine who benefits from that type of federal aid to cities.

Notes

We would like to thank John Mollenkopf and Theodore Anagnoson for their suggestions and criticism. Alberta Sbragia has been a source of unrelenting support and an incisive editor throughout.

1. Frances Fox Piven and Richard Cloward, *Regulating the Poor: The Functions of Public Welfare* (New York: Vintage, 1971).

2. Paul R. Dommel, "Block Grants for Community Development: Decentralized Decision-making," in *Fiscal Crisis in American Cities: The Federal Response*, ed. L. Kenneth Hubbell (Cambridge: Ballinger, 1979), p. 235.

3. Ibid.

4. Ibid., p. 237.

5. Carl E. Van Horn, *Policy Implementation in the Federal System: National Goals and Local Implementation* (Lexington, Mass.: Lexington Books, 1979).

6. Dommel, "Block Grants," p. 239.

7. J. Theodore Anagnoson, "The Politics of Federal Grant Distribution: HUD's Water and Sewer Program," paper presented at the 1979 Meeting of the Western Social Science Association, Nevada, California.

8. Robert M. Stein, "Federal Categorical Aid: Equalization and the Application Process," *Western Political Quarterly* 32 (December 1979):396–408.

9. Richard T. LeGates, "Can the Federal Welfare Bureaucracies Control Their Programs: The Case of HUD and Urban Renewal," Working Paper No. 172, Institute of Urban and Regional Development, University of California, Berkeley, 1972.

10. Stein, "Federal Categorical Aid."

11. Selma Mushkin and John F. Cotton, *Sharing Federal Funds for State and Local Needs: Grants-in-Aid and PPB Systems* (New York: Praeger, 1969), p. 17.

12. Bruce E. Cain, John A. Ferejohn, and Morris P. Fiorina, "The Roots of Legislator Popularity in Great Britain and the United States," Center for the Study of American Business, St. Louis, Missouri, 1979.

13. See also Stein, "F- leral Categorical Aid."

14. Joseph Fried, *Hou...ing Crisis U.S.A.* (New York: Praeger, 1971), pp. 88–89; U.S., Congress, Senate, Committee on Banking, Housing and Urban Affairs, *The Central City Problem and Urban Renewal Policy, A Study Prepared by Congressional Research Service, Library of Congress, for the Subcommittee on Housing and Urban Affairs*, 93rd Cong., 1st sess., 1973.

15. Martin Anderson, *The Federal Bulldozer: A Critical Analysis of Urban Renewal, 1949–1962* (Cambridge: M.I.T. Press, 1964), p. 68.

16. Roger Friedland, *Silent Powers* (London: Macmillan, forthcoming 1982).

17. Leo Adde, *Nine Cities: The Anatomy of Downtown Renewal* (Washington, D.C.: The Urban Land Institute, 1969).

18. Alan Walter Steiss, *Local Government Finance: Capital Facilities Planning and Debt Administration* (Lexington, Mass.: Lexington Books, 1975); Gerald Manners, "The Office in Metropolis: An Opportunity for Shaping Metropolitan America," *Economic Geography* 50 (April 1974):93–110; Thomas Muller, *Impacts of Land Development* (Washington, D.C.: The Urban Institute, 1975).

19. Edward M. Gramlich and Harvey Galper, "State and Local Fiscal Behavior and Federal Grant Policy," *Brookings Papers on Economic Activity* (Washington, D.C.: The Brookings Institution, 1973):15–58; Richard D. Bingham, *Public Housing and Urban Renewal: An Analysis of Federal-Local Relations* (New York: Praeger, 1975); U.S., Senate, *The Central City Problem and Urban Renewal Policy*.

20. U.S., Senate, *The Central City Problem and Urban Renewal Policy*.

21. John C. Weicher, "The Fiscal Profitability of Urban Renewal Under Matching Grants and Revenue Sharing," *Journal of Urban Economics* 3 (July 1976):193–208; William L. Slayton, "The Operation and Achievements of the Urban Renewal Program," in *Urban Renewal: The Record and Controversy*, ed. James Q. Wilson (Cambridge: M.I.T., 1966); Anderson, *The Federal Bulldozer*.

22. Richard Fenno, "The Internal Distribution of Power: The House," in *The Congress and the American Future*, 2nd ed., ed. David Truman (Englewood Cliffs, N.J.: Prentice-Hall, 1973); Richard F. Fenno, *Congressmen in Committees* (Boston: Little, Brown and Co., 1973).

23. Interview carried out in 1973.

24. Interview with HUD official, 1973.

25. David R. Mayhew, *Congress: The Electoral Connection* (New Haven: Yale, 1974); Fenno, *Congressmen in Committees*.

26. David W. Rhodes and Kenneth A. Shepsle, "Democratic Committee Assignments in the House of Representatives: Strategic Aspects of a Social Choice Process," *American Political Science Review* 67 (September 1973):889–905.

27. Susan A. MacManus, "The Impact of Functional Responsibility and State Legal Constraints on the 'Revenue-Debt' Packages of U.S. Central Cities," paper presented at the World Congress of Sociology, International Sociological Association, Uppsala, Sweden, August 1978; Roland Liebert, "Municipal Func-

tions, Structure and Expenditures: A Reanalysis of Recent Research," *Social Science Quarterly* 54 (March 1974):765–784.

28. Roland J. Liebert, *Disintegration and Political Action: The Changing Functions of City Governments in America* (New York: Academic Press, 1976).

29. James Lincoln, "Power and Mobilization in the Urban Community: Reconsidering the Ecological Approach," *American Sociological Review* 41 (February 1976):1–15.

30. Edward C. Banfield and James Q. Wilson, *City Politics* (Cambridge: Harvard, 1963); John Mollenkopf, "The Post-War Politics of Urban Development," *Politics and Society* 5 (1975):247–295.

31. Maurice Yeates and Barry J. Garner, *The North American City* (New York: Harper & Row, 1971).

32. Bingham, *Public Housing and Urban Renewal*.

33. These data were taken from the *Congressional District Data Book, Congressional Staff Directory, Congressional Directory*.

34. Liebert, *Disintegration and Political Action*.

35. These data were taken from the *County and City Data Book, 1962*.

36. It would be impossible to include population size in the same model, given its perfect functional relationship with area and population density. The model could not be estimated, given the perfect collinearity.

37. These data were taken from the *Census of Population and Housing, 1960*.

38. These data were taken from the *County and City Data Book, 1962*.

39. These data were taken from the *Census of Population and Housing, 1960*.

40. These data were taken from the *Census of Business, 1963*.

41. Demetrios Caraley, "Congressional Politics and Urban Aid," *Political Science Quarterly* 91 (Spring 1976):19–45.

42. The four-equations model we posed is essentially a hierarchical non-recursive model. The residuals of the first equation (application) might be correlated with the residuals of the second equation (number of authorizations), which might be correlated with the residuals of the third equation (total federal grants). In this case, for all the equations the coefficients would be inefficient, and the standard errors of the estimates would be biased or inconsistent. For the second and third equations, the coefficients would also be biased and inconsistent. The only way to adjust for this problem of correlated residual across equation is through the use of instrumental variables with seemingly unrelated regression. However, in this model we cannot identify the correlated residual with an instrumental variable, because all the independent variables are included in all three equations. In order to examine the effect of the correlated residual, we dropped the variable of application in the second equation and the variables of application and authorization in the third equation to see whether there is a definite difference between the reduced form and the structural form. The reduced form coefficients did not change our substantive findings as compared with the structural form, and we can therefore conclude that the

correlated residuals across equations do not have any significant effect on the findings.

43. Neither the exclusion of projects planned in both equations nor the elimination of all cities that have not applied since 1949 changed the results.

44. An alternative theory can be specified that would account equally well for the observed relationship between representation on the House Banking and Currency Committee and contemporary levels of urban renewal authorization. Namely, members of Congress from cities that already receive a disproportionate number of authorizations for urban renewal would seek membership on the Banking and Currency Committee in order to maintain the flow of funds into their cities and to claim credit for it. Such a model would not be inconsistent with the results. It would only suggest that the policy effects of contemporary representation on the oversight committee are spurious. The covariance between committee representation and urban renewal activity would derive from a common direct cause—namely, previous urban renewal activity. In order to examine this argument, we included in the model, as a control variable, the total number of urban renewal projects authorized for the city between 1949 and 1961. If urban members of Congress get themselves onto those oversight committees that have previously provided their constituents with disproportionate funding, there should be no relationship between contemporary committee representation and contemporary urban renewal activity—having controlled for previous urban renewal activity. In fact, such a control for previous urban renewal activity did not change the impact of House Banking and Currency membership on urban renewal authorization and funding. Furthermore, the determinants of current representation on the House Banking and Currency Committee were analyzed. Cities that had previously obtained a large number of renewal project approvals did not have greater contemporary representation on the House Banking and Currency Committee.

Finally, it might be argued that federal agencies operate based on an incrementalistic logic, such that a city's current allocation becomes a function of its past allocation. If this is the case, previous urban renewal authorization will be a strong predictor of contemporary authorization. However, previous levels of authorization do not have a direct effect on current levels of authorization or funding. Rather, their effect is mediated through a higher number of urban renewal applications from the city to HUD. Thus, a city's previous success in obtaining HUD monies conditions its current willingness and ability to seek further funds.

45. The following is a breakdown of the direct and indirect effects of local needs on urban renewal authorization and funding:

	Project Authorization			Funding		
	Direct	Indirect	Total	Direct	Indirect	Total
Core Poverty	.10	.14	.24	−.07	.09	.02
Tax Burden	.04	.17	.21	+.01	.07	.08

46. In the second and third equations, which indicate the number of authorizations and total federal grant monies, we have run a different model selected for only those cities that had applied for urban renewal funds between 1961 and 1966. The coefficients for this alternative model did not alter any of our main findings. Therefore, we can conclude that selection biases for application do not have a significant effect on the findings.

Index